Images of Truth

Images of Truth

REMEMBRANCES AND CRITICISM

BY

GLENWAY WESCOTT

Everything that is possible to be
believed is an image of the truth

WILLIAM BLAKE

Essay Index Reprint Series

BOOKS FOR LIBRARIES PRESS
FREEPORT, NEW YORK

Portions of this book were first published in Atlantic Monthly, Harper's
Magazine, Southern Review, Town and Country, *and* Vogue. *"An Intro-
duction to Colette" is from* The Short Novels of Colette, Dial Press, 1951.
"Break of Day" appeared as the introduction to Break of Day *by Colette,
Farrar, Straus & Cudahy, Inc., 1960.*

Library of Congress Cataloging in Publication Data

Wescott, Glenway, 1901–
Images of truth; remembrances and criticism.

(Essay index reprint series)
CONTENTS: Fiction writing in a time of troubles.
--Katherine Anne Porter personally.--Somerset Maugham
and posterity. [etc.]
    1. Fiction--20th century--Addresses, essays,
lectures. 2. Authors--Correspondence, reminiscences,
etc. I. Title.
PN3503.W4 1972   809.3   77-167436
ISBN 0-8369-2730-3

PRINTED IN THE UNITED STATES OF AMERICA
BY
NEW WORLD BOOK MANUFACTURING CO., INC.
HALLANDALE, FLORIDA 33009

TO MONROE WHEELER,

LIFELONG.

Contents

Images of Truth

Chapter One

Fiction Writing in a Time of Troubles

Grief is a species of idleness.
—SAMUEL JOHNSON

This volume consists of informal portraiture of two or three fellow writers near and dear to me, and of certain blessed elders and betters, with loving commentary on their production of stories and novels.

While happily working away, in marginal relationship to the work, I have been led to try to define and profess my own faith in the narrative art, with particular beliefs about it that have stayed unchanged in my mind for many years, regardless of my personal ability or inability. For which purpose let me take a text, as religious writers and preachers do, but a pre-Christian secular text: the beginning of the eleventh book of the *Odyssey*. Do you recall the tale it tells?

Odysseus, coming back from Troy to Ithaca, lost his way; and his mistress, Circe, advised him to consult the ghost of Tiresias about it. As you may recall, this ancient soothsayer had been cursed and stricken with hermaphroditism as a result of having come upon a pair of serpents (perhaps the demigod and demigoddess, Cadmus and Harmonia, in their serpent phase) and watched them entwining in intercourse. Long afterward, an argument having arisen between the supreme god and goddess, Zeus and Hera, as to which sex, male or female, enjoyed intercourse more keenly, they asked Tiresias to settle it, and he said female. Whereupon Hera caused him to go blind; but Zeus decreed that he should live seven lifetimes and keep his wisdom always. This wisdom Odysseus desperately needed, to plot a course for himself and his fellow mariners back to their native land.

They were then in the Cimmerian country, a place somewhere between the ocean and the underworld; a miserable shadowy coast inhabited by only a few pirates in caves. There on the beach Odysseus dug a hole about eighteen inches square and eighteen inches deep; and he moistened the sand all around it with milk and honey and wine and water; he said prayers; and he sacrificed a couple of sheep in such a way as to fill the hole with their blood; and with this as a lure he invoked a great company of ghosts, among them the proud seven-lived Theban seer, by whom he was given the necessary information for his homeward journey; and afterward he talked the night away with other thrilling phantoms.

For many a year the few dozen lines in which this is narrated by Homer have charmed and uplifted and exercised my mind. I reread them yesterday, in translation, not in Greek. For I am, roughly speaking, an autodidact; the University of Chicago at which I did spend one school year and a half was under the sway of the elective theory of education at the time. I own only four translations: Pope's, and Ezra Pound's, which is a paraphrase from the Latin of a humanist named Divus, and Lawrence of Arabia's, and the quite recent prize version by Robert Fitzgerald.

In a personal way I have always associated the passage with an old popular song, the burden of which is losing one's way and wanting to get back home. I remember the first time I heard it, when I was a small boy in a small town in Wisconsin, long before I had read any ancient literature. Another boy, the first friend for whom I ever felt great affection, the first friend who ever felt great affection for me, sang it. It was in the evening. We had had a picnic supper of sandwiches and apples, with a bottle of beer, upon the brow of a hill over a small lake on the outskirts of the town, and we had stayed to see the sunset. As I did not like beer, my friend had imbibed all the bottleful and was just slightly drunk. As it happened I had never before seen anyone under the influence in a happy way. (All my family abstained, except my grandfather in the long decline of his life when he had a Civil War-induced stomach ailment and, under doctor's orders, took a little Marsala, or perhaps Madeira, in a tablespoon. The family farm was ringed round with German immigrants of peasant stock; but they all drank unhappily, whipping their horses and chasing their children.)

On our way home my friend strode on ahead, down the hill and into town and along the narrow, uneven sidewalk, toward the mansion of his parents and my grandparents' small house. As it was between day and night, in back yards and on various lanes children were still in swings, and lovers already in hammocks. A little unknown dog attached itself to us, wagging its tail. None of this apparently meant anything to my friend, absorbed in his mysterious selfish alcoholic condition. He was no longer paying any attention to me; I tagged along after him. I was twelve years old; he was fourteen or fifteen, and his voice had changed not long before that. As loudly as he was able, in the tones of his half-manhood somewhat unmanageable, unaccustomed, he sang the Odyssean refrain, inebriation and fatigue, uncertainty and homesickness, which no doubt he had heard older boys and grown men sing when they were befuddled.

In the years that have elapsed since then I have seen a great deal of drunkenness; in one way and another it has been important to me. In convivial circumstances of all kinds I like those around me to be intoxicated, short of sickness, short of violent melancholy and ugly temper. Two friends of mine have been true alcoholics, roistering and hypochondriacal, anguished and unable to stop. For my own part I never really cared whether I drank or not; nevertheless, a decade ago, for reasons of health, I had to stop. In a nouvelle entitled *The Pilgrim Hawk*, I painted a little portrait of a drunkard; and recently in a brilliant brief treatise on the history and the problem of drinking I was cited as an authority, of which I am proud.

I mention all this to make a point that, to my mind, is of the utmost importance in general morality; and that, furthermore, is a matter of principle and preference in literature and the other arts.—Moderation is a good thing in itself. Think how many of the decisive factors in our lives are neither good nor evil: i.e., love and intellect and industriousness and patriotism and sport and other exercises of the body. The principle of restraint and limitation works both ways, works indeed in every way. A small family is praiseworthier than any heedless passionate proliferation. Pleasant intoxication upon occasion is preferable to absolute sobriety. In the matter of overpopulation, and in cases of compulsive alcoholism, ruinous gambling, sickening excesses of drug addiction, or mass production of pornographic reading matter, the objection is not to children, or to the beverage or the game or the chemical or the eroticism; it is to the exorbitance, the exaggeratedness. For one can destroy oneself as handily with medicine as with poison (though perhaps not so fast); sicken oneself not only with pot but with bread and milk and cream; ruin oneself with philanthropy as with horse racing; exhaust oneself in the marriage bed exactly as in the brothel or the Turkish bath.

In literature and the arts, I think, this same rule applies, especially as to the length and breadth and inclusiveness of the work, and as to the degree of its unconventionalities of style and structure. Originality, that is to say, individuality—that mere uniqueness which distinguishes one face from every other face, one life history from every other (likewise any given sunset and leaf and bird and bug from all the sunsets and leaves and birds and bugs that are almost identical, but not quite)—is of greater importance than any extreme innovation, or one-man revolutionizing effect, or disturbance of the art for disturbance's sake. It often happens, indeed, that the work of followers of the famous innovators gives greater pleasure and means more to the public and to posterity than the revolutionary work which led the way.

The essentials in literature (perhaps more demonstrably than in music or painting) are enjoyment and communication; not the given creative man's outburst of skill and ego, not the mere stupefaction or submissiveness of the reading public. In cases of extreme and difficult writing what the public often does is to express admiration while just pretending to read. Pleasure and understanding from the reader's standpoint depend largely on the more lasting aspects of the language and on logicalities of grammar and syntax. Allowances always have to be made for him, as to his fatigue and bewilderment and error. Just as mere physical stature more than anything else determines the length of a bed, and the conformation of one's buttocks, the design of a chair, reader psychology keeps influencing literature, in the way of a stubborn rejection of the inordinate and the elaborate, an irresistible veering away from the riddlesome. There are limits to innovation; strong creative personalities constantly break through them and go beyond them, but they re-establish themselves, with an impressive similarity, down through the ages.

My conclusion is that brilliancy of ego, headstrong and headlong display of intellect, powers of elaboration, poetical afflatus, and that frenzied and exalted artistry which is like drunkenness, play an important part in literature; but as regularly as clockwork, most of the time, everything of that sort has to give way to a prosaic simplicity, to brevity and explicitness, and to traditional themes and immemorial symbols and images.

In Greece (in Delphi, if my memory is correct) there is a famous meaningful bas-relief known as "The Truce of the Two Great Gods." Long ago Eva Palmer Sikelianos, the American lady who, having married a Greek poet, spent her fortune putting on performances of Sophocles and Euripides in modern Greek, showed me a photograph of it. Once a year Apollo, the god of reason and light and music and medicine and prophecy, journeyed to the North for a holiday among the Hyperboreans, his remotest worshipers, and during that absence would always lend or sublet his temple to Dionysus, the god of unreason and madness, of ecstasy and drunkenness. In the bas-relief their antithetical and complementary hands touch, as the one departs from the temple and the other enters. To my way of thinking these are two most salutary and crucial factors in literature and the arts (as in morals and in life in general): reason and unreason touching hands; and the limitation of the occupancy af the drunken unreasonable god to just the vacation time, once a year.

One night when I was not a small boy in Wisconsin, but an expatriate in the south of France, and an enthusiast about the religious thinking and the collective storytelling of the Greeks, I heard another more recent American drinking song. I was looking down from a balcony of the Hotel Welcome over the white stone quay and the beautifully formed small harbor of Villefranche (of mythical Greek origin), with the arm of Cap Ferrat shadowy around it. An old American battleship lay at anchor, vague and asleep, twinkling over the water. The bar on the ground floor of the hotel had just closed, and there were four of our sailors arguing about something in melancholy, monotonous voices under my balcony. One of them suddenly cheered up and strode off by himself, and gracefully, conceitedly, went and tiptoed upon the very edge of the quay, as if it were a tightrope; and balancing there, he sang the more recent song, Odyssean also: "Show Me the Way to Go Home." Drunk as he was, I suppose the fun of singing made him drunker. He fell into the sea. His friends having pulled him out, he tried to fight one of them; but the other two made peace. Then they threw their arms over one another's shoulders and all began to sing, and went up the steep street toward Nice, singing.

This triad of things haunts me: the question of Odysseus on the Cimmerian shore, the tipsiness of the friend of my boyhood singing one common drinking song, the immersion of the sailor in the harbor of Villefranche singing another. It is a principal question in the very nature of mankind: the way home, wherever the wayfaring has been, and whatever the homeless feeling refers to or amounts to. In our time, history has posed it perhaps more solemnly than it has ever been posed before, in song or story, in epic or in tragic drama.

In the first quarter of this century we were all so happy at home in the several fortunate democracies, and so made ourselves at home abroad also in blessed places of expatriation, the counties of England, the hill towns of Italy, the south of France, that we took happiness for granted; which played us false in due course. Wherever we happened to be corporeally, in space and place, around us we had a favorable ambience, and up ahead there were vistas somewhat open and luminous and extensive; we felt fortunate; a general felicity was the habitation of our hearts, the seat and basis of our talent. In the state of our minds, at least, peace seemed permanent.

World War I, which was hideously destructive in reality—it slaughtered a generation, shook the foundations of the world, loosed the whirlwind, weakened important governments, brought on revolutions—did not change things in the spirit and in creative and philosophical orientation as much as you might think. If you reread the literature of the twenties and reconsider any number of the lives that were most typical of that time, you will be impressed by its optimistic, progressive mentality, above all. Even with respect to politics, until the League of Nations demonstrated its weakness, until the National Socialist Party came to power in Germany, we had hopes, high hopes, high enough!

Then as now, in cold warfare and hot warfare alike, silly people and easily discouraged people would ask one another: what are we fighting for? As a rule, naturally, we fight simply to regain what we had before the fighting began; we fight for another opportunity to remedy the faults and inequities of the general way of life that we have idly or ignorantly put off doing anything about when we had the time and the wherewithal. Certainly not Utopia, perhaps not even giant strides ahead; but a prospect of improvement, a chance to progress. In many respects life on this earth is irremediable, we know that. But even the natural and absolute earthly tragedies (of which death is incomparably the greatest) are easier to bear if they come upon us in circumstances of some stability, in a familiar and domestic context, with some notion of everything's eventually getting better, for one's offspring and other beloved youngsters, if not for ourselves; with some feeling of immortality, by means of continuing and self-renewing traditions and the enduring structures of art and literature, if not in the old religious way.

I have not forgotten my theme; it is not arms and the man—it is the fountain pen and the typewriter, and men, women, and children, as the literary art, and especially narrative art, is concerned with them. But in this modern time it is difficult if not impossible to consider any one aspect of our existence, or of reality at large, separately from any other aspect; perhaps it isn't even desirable to do so. For evidently everything is connected and involved in fact. We learn to think almost entirely in contrasts and juxtapositions, in the famous antinomies: good and evil, land and sea, day and dark, art and ignorance. It probably is the right way to think. If our fathers and grandfathers at the beginning of the century had borne war in mind as well as peace, we might have kept the balance in our favor.

Be that as it may: those contrasts and antitheses are basic to literary art. What we call the creative spirit really does not create anything. It evokes and recollects and relates. It is a mere inclination of our good nature and our good will, stooping and bending close to evil in order to understand it. It is a flashing of our small individual light, as best we know how, into the general darkness.

Some men (for whatever reason) have an especially acute sense that mankind is in the dark, in innocence or ignorance; that something is lost, either the meaning of the experiences behind us or the difficulty or the heart's desire confronting us next, on the way to the future. They are most apt and able to become literary artists, and in that capacity to investigate the situation in some respect, to reveal things a little.

It is legendary that in the Crimean War, when the allied expeditionary force about to invade that southernmost part of Russia found itself extremely short of maps, a certain commanding officer, in despair, trying to figure out his geographical situation and to solve his tactical and logistical problem, made use of a Ouija board.

Now, certainly all our allies, and at least one of the powerful nations confronting us, with dangerously mingled feelings of hostility and fear and envy, have maps enough, including some absolute marvels made by electronic cameras in unmanned space vehicles automatically whirring in circles in the stratosphere, televising their findings back to headquarters. But still our governing classes and chiefs of state seem not to have much sense of direction, either literally or figuratively; the best they can do is to feel their way along in terrible obscurity and trepidation, perhaps on a collision course. Naturally a writer is inclined to suggest that, in lieu of Ouija boards, they read more books, beginning with the *Iliad* and the *Odyssey*.

Obviously enough, in wartime, whenever or wherever it may be, the whole world is an *Iliad;* cruel and compulsive and convulsive. It is even more noteworthy that in our present peacetime (we call it peace) the whole world is an *Odyssey;* which is a clear and instructive analogy, not farfetched. Think how many men there must be at any given moment, day after day, night and day, erring hither and thither across the sea, not just sailors but wretched land-lubber-types as well, such as scientists and engineers and journalists and secret agents, seasick half the time, in boats often as rudimentary as Odysseus'; not just on the mere Mediterranean but on the entire extreme ocean all around the earth, which no longer seems to have a center; not just on the briny deep but in the sky as well, beyond the sound barrier, beyond the atmosphere. We have extended our world a little but with no absolute or basic change; it is not unlike Odysseus'. The elements still overlap and intermingle, the dark and the daylight, the fire and the ice, the quick and the dead; and our recent space excursions have been by water as much as by air.

For every Icarus there are a hundred thousand Odysseuses still; for every one who goes weightless, a hundred thousand are seasick in the rudimentary boats, and a hundred thousand heartsick, on beaches every bit as dark as those of the Cimmerian country, with hardly any idea where they are, certainly not the remotest notion how to get where they hope they are going. Have the seven lives of Tiresias run out? What about some sheep's blood for him? Has his thirst abated, has his wisdom also turned to mere idealism and optimism and fear and propaganda in the modern way, our foolish way?

Certainly the misery and bravery of humanity now, the subject matter available to us, for any and every sort of world-wide, heroic, exalted, and visionary literature, is as great as, perhaps greater than, anything vouchsafed the ancient Greeks or any of the other literature-loving peoples in history. But there is not the least likelihood of our producing anything epical or universal or commensurate with present reality.

Even those of us who stay comfortably and sedentarily at home in fact, elderly men, disabled men, women of genius, on farms or in idyllic small towns or in retirement in places like Florida and California, are kept closely in touch, by means of the mass media, with others' seafaring and airfaring and with the general darkness and lostness, the blood soaking into the sand; and no answer from Tiresias yet. The literary inspiration also is dispersed all over the place, the heart in morsels, the mind divided.

In imagination everyone (everyone who has any imagination) is now expeditionary to some extent, and in some sense a refugee, and revolutionary in a way. Some of us have wondrous genius, many of us have considerable serviceable abilities, but not for the too haunting, too vast, too challenging subject matter, the whirlwind that we too are whirling in. Neither Odysseus nor any man along with him wrote the *Odyssey;* that came centuries later. Which we regard as a sufficient excuse for our not managing to write the various minor things of which we certainly are capable.

I remember an exchange of letters about this with Thornton Wilder in the spring of 1948. I had written to him in one of my melancholy fits, though with nothing really to complain of: my bodily health holding up well; my family angelic around me, guardian-angelic; the work I had in hand of intense interest to me (only somewhat beyond the range of my talent).

For various reasons I had been longing to travel abroad again for a year or two, and lacked the courage to do so. At that time of my life, I thought, any new and important writable experience or theme was apt to make me abort the piece of work that I had in progress, or perhaps I should say, in process. For as a matter of fact nothing was progressing for me very well. Certainly in Western and Central Europe (then as now) there were fearful themes: the recurrence of the everlasting and characteristic animus of European mankind in which a great part of civilization in the past was forged and fused, hammer on anvil, hot metal in cold water, for which there is not room on that mere peninsula of Eurasia any longer; the intellect of France infected with German philosophy, existentialism, etc.; and other symptomatic matters painful to my mind.

Just after this letter of mine, as it happened, Wilder delivered an address at the annual Ceremonial of the American Academy and National Institute of Arts and Letters. He entitled it "A Time of Troubles," and in great part it seemed intended for me. He did not declare in it that all periods of human history have been equally and constantly troubled. He did not deny the possibility of various future utopias based on this or that revolutionary daydream. He admitted, indeed, that in our time little old ladies who have hitherto led sheltered lives are to be seen crawling over the refuse heaps at the edge of town looking for something to eat, while other nations, particularly this nation, ostentatiously hoard or dump or destroy mountains of good food, thus making themselves targets for future vengeance. He did allude to the worse and worse murderousness of our more and more scientific wars.

But, he pointed out sternly, the periods of peace and security and benevolence in the past have been but interludes: "brief, circumscribed, parochial, well-fenced and exceptional." Let us never, never, regard them as a norm. Every age has to be its own norm.

Upon rereading Homer, Goethe remarked that "the *Iliad* teaches us that it is our task here on earth to enact Hell daily"; with which grim statement Matthew Arnold concurred. On that pleasant afternoon at the Institute, Wilder quoted all three of these authorities on the human situation; and Kierkegaard to boot.

Finally, he declared to us that the creative man is under no obligation to supply final answers to the great tragic questions or "to balance the books of good and evil." In so far as he is called upon to go through hell in his life, all he has to do about it creatively is to depict that life, to paint a portrait of himself experiencing it, and to express his various emotional responses. To most writers of consequence, he concluded, "Ages of Security and Ages of Anxiety look much alike."

Just emerging from my fit of sadness, I was touched to the quick by this discourse. Wilder is an inspiring, admonishing, cautionary, exemplary man, though not goody-goody (the example he sets us is not always good).

I learned later that he had had no thought of admonishing me particularly that afternoon. My sad letter had gone to New Haven, and he was elsewhere; so that it did not reach him until some time after the Ceremonial; and presently he replied to it, still upon a challenging and reproachful note. Somehow he had not altogether enjoyed giving the Blashfield address but it was worth giving, he wrote, if in any way it suggested to me that "writers can be doubly lively under lowering skies, like porpoises."

Furthermore, he had been teaching somewhere that spring, and the university youngsters as of that date, he had found, were of a fine porpoise-like liveliness, self-inspiring and undaunted. Evidently it was people between forty-five and fifty-five, he noted, who took fright at world-wide disturbance and historic danger. It seemed to distract them from the painfulness of having to say good-by to their youth. As he well knew, I was forty-seven at the time.

In point of fact, the diminution of my youthfulness, the onset of my middle age, was not really frightening to me. But Wilder's error about me in this respect alerted me to an error of my own. It was not the heartbreak and seeming delirium and black incomprehensible state of the world at large, the Cimmerian situation, Odysseus lost, and Tiresias absent or silent, which had stricken me; it was the mere fact that my work had not been going well.

I am one of those blessed-accursed writers whom feelings of undeserved good fortune, perceptions or illusions of overabundant subject matter, enthusiasms of all sort, somewhat overwhelm and embarrass, and, as to the range and sufficiency of my talent, dwarf. I had been struggling with a kind of novel that did not suit me and did not fit the themes and remembrances and visions that I had to work with.

How I wish that the several early teachers and inspirers of my youth, and kind reviewers of my early published work, instead of calling constantly for maximum inspiration in the way of the full-length, realistic, naturalistic novel, had started me where fiction itself started, with the anecdote and the episode and the fable and the allegory and the fairy tale, and followed along with the reminiscence and the cautionary tale and the short story, letting the great novel form develop integrally, as an assemblage of materials requiring in each instance a particular handling for a particular expressive purpose, not an imposition of arbitrary pattern, not an adornment of vain style; as a mechanism of the writer's imagination directed at the reader's imagination, with sound and previously exercised component parts. But, in fact, professors of creative writing and indeed literary critics have their own problems; surely it is a folly to expect them to know things that it takes many a creative writer half a lifetime to find out.

It is one of the magical and fantastic things about art, perhaps especially literary art: there is a kind of health and ill-health about it, right and wrong, perdition and salvation. When it goes wrong, when talent breaks down or dries up or withers away or grows painful, as a rule it is a matter of misunderstanding or of not mastering form. And, as a rule, the way to save it, the way it saves itself —and the way it may save its poor practitioner from his cramp and inhibition and impotence and shame—is by means of some reorientation of aesthetics, often some return to simpler concepts and structures of the literature of the past.

Almost any subject matter that comes forcefully to the writer's mind, or that he has his heart set on, will serve, will work, if his form is right. In this eclectic, vainly philosophizing era, in the midst of a century half maddened by disorders more ominous and onerous than those that particularly plague writers, there has been a great deal of obscuration and distortion of literary theory, especially with respect to fiction. The modernism of poets seems a simpler enterprise than any corresponding notion or concept of the narrative art; but poets have had a complicating influence, as so many of them make a profession or an avocation of reviewing books, and lay down the law to the rest of us.

I myself began as a poet, which is a not altogether advantageous background for a life of fiction writing. The art of poetry is word by word, in very close connections like lace, juxtapositions like mosaic. Whereas to tell a story as it should be told, especially a long story or a novel, we must cast an easier spell, looser and farther flung, inclusive of some imperfection; so that the reader can take it in his own way, as experience rather than as artistry, and if he pleases, retell some of it to himself in his own words, relive some of it. The novel writer does not want the novel reader to pause much, in the actual reading, in particular admiration of a given sentence or paragraph or page. The thing is to keep his mind on the move, credulous and emotionally responsive until the whole, greater than the sum of the parts, has been made clear to him. The prose of the verse-trained writer is apt to be too arresting, too conspicuously pictorial, too densely compressed, too euphonious, with effects of the music of the language.

We have to work that much harder, to make easy reading, but not too easy, lest we lull the reader to sleep. We learn, and we relearn; and always in any art there are good techniques to be developed even against the grain of the medium. There are important forms of fiction to which a slow or difficult style is not a handicap. By added artistry, the too artistic effect can be avoided or covered up. If we have energy enough, pluck enough, in the painstaking way, finally we break through our self-consciousness and we find some simple solution.

For weeks at a time I read nothing but poetry, though I never regret having ceased to write it. Once over the hump into middle age, the pleasure of exercising the talent that one has, sufficiently consoles one for the mere fancied genius of one's youth. But I often feel a kind of homesickness of mind; I steal back to the poetical standpoint; I retrace my poor, faltering, and divagating steps from the way I first undertook literature to the way it seems to be for me now; and I find myself tempted by very grand, arbitrary, and over-artful notions of narrative structure and craftsmanship. Generally speaking, I think that the inspirations of poets have been unbeneficial to the art of fiction, as they naturally incline to mere oddities and novelties of construction and style (to what I call triangular armchairs and procrustean beds, three-legged trousers, and three-fingered gloves).

Now let me remind you once more of my ancient text, beloved passage of epic Greek literature, prototypical of narrative art in general—"naked Ulysses clad in eternal fiction," to borrow the glamorous phrase which is in the foreword to Chapman's *Homer*. The scene of Odysseus on the Cimmerian shore is a good allegory or image of the more tried and true old notions of fictitious form; the three perennial types of novel that we may need to go back to, or at least to think back about.—

First, narrative of instruction and revelation; for example, to name some obvious contemporary volumes, Forster's *A Passage to India*, Maugham's *Christmas Holiday*, Richard Hughes's *The Fox in the Attic,* and (bringing my own work into the picture self-indulgently) *Apartment in Athens.*

Second, narrative of reminiscence and sentiment; for example, Willa Cather's *My Ántonia,* and my family chronicle, *The Grandmothers.*

Third, narrative of recreation and daydream, luring and exercising the reader's imagination this way and that, at liberty and at ease; for example, Isak Dinesen's "The Deluge at Norderney" or "The Monkey."

(There are also composite or intermediate forms, and one or two specialized categories, such as the historical novel, verging on scholarly truthfulness, and the philosophical novel, incorporating disquisitional and argumentative prose in some quantity.)

The greatest or the gravest of the functions of fiction is the first mentioned, the questioning of Tiresias. Indeed, we fiction writers question everyone and make what we can of the answers. We rouse up our own memories, experience scarcely worth remembering, time that has gone to waste all our lives; but it is not because we love the past; it is because we fear the future. It is not in self-love but to save ourselves, and others as well, if we are good at it. We raise the dead and we make them speak; but for those of us who are true novelists it is not as a means of expressing our particular opinion. We ask the dead questions and pass the information on. We do not simply utter our experience through them. They are not puppets, they have voices of their own; and the heart of every matter as we

see it seems to come to us from their knowledge, as it were independent of our knowledge, prior to our experience.

On the Cimmerian shore, by the trench or hole full of sacrificial
sheep's blood, Odysseus sat and waited, knowing that the spirits of
the dead are forever thirsty and would come at last. Which they
did, like a herd of shadowy cattle crowding each other around a
watering trough. Among them he saw the ghost of his own old
mother, Anticlea, and she whimpered for a sip of blood, but with
his sword drawn before him over the warm puddle, he refused her
pitilessly, refused them all, until at last Tiresias, the wise ghost,
appeared, and had the first drink, and told him how to get back
home to Ithaca. This is a prefiguration of the literature of revelation and guidance.

Then he let the other ghosts come forward—"thin, airy, shoals
of visionary ghosts," as Pope describes them—and take their sips of
blood, beginning with his mother. She told him what, for sentiment's sake, he wanted to hear; that his wife, Penelope, longed for
him so faithfully that she had insomnia; that his young son, Tele-
machus, had grown up to be a man and was well thought of, invited everywhere; that his aged father or stepfather, Laertes, had
fallen into second childhood, refused to sleep in his bed, stubbornly
went outdoors, even on chilly nights in the fall, and lay in the autumn leaves; and that the cause of her own death had been loneliness. Loneliness for whom? For Odysseus himself, her dear son, her
questioner. Touched by this, Odysseus tried to give her a hug and a
kiss. But, as she was a ghost, his arms clasped nothing; upon which
she explained to him something about death: it is an untying of
the nerves, so that the flesh and the bones and the psyche disperse,
dissociate. This beautifully exemplifies in miniature our fiction of
remembrance and reawakened, recalled emotion.

Odysseus stayed there on the haunted sands for hours that night,
to see what other extraordinary figures would come to his trough
of blood, a rush of female ghosts to start with, whom he lined up
in single file, so as to hear their cries and their confidences: Tyro,
to whom the god of the ocean made love in a little bower of water-
spouts, and who bore him twins; and Leda, the sweetheart of the

swan; and Ariadne "passioning," to use Shakespeare's participle for her; and horrid Eriphyle, who, for a fee or a bribe, betrayed her husband into military service; and a dozen others—thrilling creations of the collective narrative genius of ancient Greece, greater than that of any other people in history—whom the gloomy goddess, Persephone, presently drove away helter-skelter.

There also came, thirstily, Hercules, with various eddying spirits who were inferior to him but able to anger him with the noise of their wings; he kept glaring and drawing his bow and arrow. There came Tantalus, the personifier of insatiable desire; and Sisyphus, the personification of futility and existentialism; and Oedipus, the "pompous wretch." There came several great recent casualties of the Trojan War; notably Agamemnon, Odysseus' commanding officer, who sobbingly narrated how his wife had murdered him and not even respected his corpse afterward, leaving the eyelids open and the jaw unbound. Odysseus reminded him of the fact that in his family, the Atrides, none of the men had much luck with women; had not his sister-in-law, Helen, caused the Trojan War in the first place? There came Ajax, still in his battle array and battle anger, with a host of the "grisly forms" of those who fell by his truncheon, "shooting o'er the lawns of Hell," to quote another of Pope's magical passages.

When he got back home Odysseus narrated all these apparitions to the King and Queen of the Phaeacians and to their court, to amuse them and to beguile the time at a long banquet; singing for his supper, that is, yarning for his supper. In all this the *Odyssey* is the prototype of recreational storytelling and story writing. Often it is a renarration of tales already told over and over by everyone, and here and there it may seem to us modern readers meaningless and without a moral.

I believe that there is a more precise, potent truth in story than in philosophy. In a truthful account of something which has happened, our minds discover, almost without thinking, a kind of knowledge of the world which lies deeper and is less subject to perversion and change than all the rules of ethics cut and dried. The emotion of a story has a more pacifying, fortifying effect on our wild hearts than any amount of preaching and teaching. And in spite of our modern sophistication, our pride of economics and politics and science, wildness of the heart is still one of the most problematical and important things in the world. Sometimes it is our downfall and sometimes, if we understand it aright, our salvation. It may be good or it may be evil; it may be energy or only a fast fever.

As I have said, a great part of fiction is a diagnosis; and once in a while, when some class or profession or family of mankind has been spiritually sick, novels have prescribed something to relieve or cure the sickness. In great salutary works of this kind there may not be as much beauty or kindness or fun as we should like. The novelist has sat like Odysseus with his drawn sword and kept ordinary sentiments of humanity back a bit; refraining in his own person, as well as in the work, from a large part of what makes life pleasant and interesting.

Story reading or novel reading is a good pastime. For perhaps the majority of the reading public today it is no more than that. For my part personally, when I want literary recreation, relief from immediacy, release of tension, daydream at second hand, I infinitely prefer *The Thousand and One Nights* or Hans Christian Andersen, or Isak Dinesen, to any sort of romancing or fantasy-making about modern life. Of the ordinary, current, carelessly written, prosaic kind of novel you need a new one every few days, as it were a clean pack of cards for solitaire. Naturally, the proud hard-working writer is not content to have his work played with awhile, like a pack of cards, and then scrapped. But this happens; pastimes change month by month or year by year. Even those parts of the *Odyssey* intended to amuse banquets, those catalogues of armament and enumerations of princes and compendia of legends which were a riddle and a charm for the general public in olden time, now have gone out of date. We have to keep looking things up in Bulfinch or in Lemprière. Whereas the questioning of Tiresias and the pathetic report of Odysseus' mother have meant more and more to us as the centuries have passed.

In order to last a novel must be functional. To be sure, it must entertain, and it must convince, and it must thrill somehow; but it must also help. It must be adaptable to, and serviceable in, people's lives as they privately lead them day in and day out. Speaking for myself, once more, I find the present world so enthralling and alarming that I scarcely care to read fiction at all unless it gives me some theme worth thinking about after the reading is done; unless it alleviates and sweetens the experience I am involved in; unless as I go about my business and my pleasure I can feel in myself some increase of clarity and ability thanks to it. "The only end of writing is to enable readers better to enjoy life, or better to endure it," said Dr. Johnson.

It need not have what you would call noble subject matter. In my opinion one of the best short works of fiction ever written, one of the likeliest to last, is *Adolphe* by Benjamin Constant, a harsh little love story, a case of adultery and satiety and vanity. Think when it was written: Benjamin Constant was reading it aloud to the Queen of Holland when the news of the Battle of Waterloo was brought to the palace, which interrupted them.

But whatever the rulers and the chiefs of state and ministers of state and the party secretaries and the dictators and various rabble-rousers and the generals and admirals and the scientists, physicists and electronic engineers and biochemists and geneticists and various brain-washers, have in store for us, we presumably shall always have some private life, domestic and social relationships and solitary private psychology, to cope with in ourselves and in others. If you are badly afflicted by your private heartache, whatever it may happen to be, and distracted by accidents of your previous experience, half realized, misunderstood or half forgotten; if you go wincing through life, baffled by yourself, stung by anxiety, bothered by conscience, falling in and out of love for example, uncontrollably —as it might be, in the worst weather in the world, a stumble and a slip on a slushy sidewalk into an unclean gutter—the chances are that you will make a botch of whatever you have to do.

Almost a hundred and fifty years have elapsed since Benjamin Constant wrote *Adolphe*. It is still important, interesting, and enlightening. To this day, a man I know who is wise and kind and apt to worry, when a love relationship starts in the circle of his friends, presents the lovers with a copy of it, as one might give quinine to travelers departing to the tropics. This is the kind of thing that works of fiction are good for.

The last book read by Maupassant before he went mad, that is to say, while he was going mad, was Tolstoi's *The Death of Ivan Ilyitch.* (Someone in Paris informed Tatiana Tolstoi of this, and she recorded it in her journal.) This is another of the purposes and functions of narrative literature: a sort of secular extreme unction; spiritual sedation, with some vision of a potential better life.

Its techniques and various spellbinding effects on readers' minds go back to ancient illiterate times, before the concept of romantic love took hold of us, indeed prior to the Christian sense of mental health and salvation.

Many years ago in the spring I visited Marrakech, the chief southern city of Morocco, and I remember its novelists, if they may be called that: storytellers seated on the ground in the market place, uttering the serial installments of their art to a public which for the most part was unable to read, probably still is unable. There were sorcerers and snake charmers there as well, whose public disdainfully stood around or walked around, looking down on what was done for them. The story lovers, for the most part, sat crosslegged, as the storyteller himself did; with others who had not found room to sit, pressed close around, in order not to miss anything: a ring of men of many complexions and various casts of countenance, with differing reactions to the given tale; some grinning or brooding with a pout or with a frown, some breathing hard in childish suspense. They came and went, according to their other interests and pressures of the day, or according to the intrinsic interest of the subject matter and the more or less spellbinding effect of the telling in different parts of the tale; but I noticed three or four who stayed spellbound for an hour or more at a stretch, as the afternoon wore on.

There were two such narrators when I was there. The one I liked best narrated very loud and never laughed at his own jokes or put on airs of virtuosity or vanity, but scowled a great deal, flashing his eyes, then shutting them tight, and sitting in silence for a while, to consider the next development of his plot. He made me think of blind Homer, and reminded me of the fact that, for a storyteller, a sort of blindness to everything except the story is a good thing.

The sobriety of the Moorish storyteller notwithstanding, evidently part of what he told was funny. The ring of shoulders shook with laughter, and one or another of the darker-skinned among them would make a characteristically African gesture of hugging himself; but all soundlessly, lest they miss a sentence. Their amused faces soon quieted down; all their eyes refixed on the narrator, to assist their ears. When their expressions intensified and hardened, I guessed, it reflected something pathetic in the plot, or something sensual. They never gave one another a glance, perhaps from moment to moment were scarcely aware of the collectivity around them; each separately rapt away by the art of the yarn, keeping it to himself, or between himself and the yarn-spinner, as though the enjoyment of it were a kind of love.

How I wanted to understand what the story was about! The narrator's exalted, hard-working face and the ring of the other faces, credulous and uneasy but pleased, piqued and confused my imagination. When I was a child in Wisconsin my Chicago uncle and aunt gave me a volume of tales from *The Thousand and One Nights,* illustrated in color. Presumably the subject matter of those afternoons in Marrakech derived in some measure from that masterpiece of the Near East, as it had been inherited and altered by successive tellers and gradually exported westward as centuries passed. But the inspiration and the techniques of the two Moors or Berbers cross-legged there in the market place, telling and retelling, with improvisations and changes and reinterpretations to suit each successive occasion and faraway place, dated much farther back than Scheherazade and her lord and master, to classical antiquity and indeed prehistory.

The tales in that beloved volume almost everyone on earth must have in mind, however vaguely; but I remember the illustrations better than the text: immense scenes of burning stone with caverns in them, weird gardens and prisonlike walled cities crowning the horizon far off, and Aladdin, and Sinbad, and one of the genii, bright-eyed, sunburned, and nude, except for a white loincloth which the wind whipped out after him, like tail feathers of a vast loose bird. I think that must have been the first representation of the human body unclothed (almost unclothed) that I ever saw. Certainly it was the first pictorial art to excite my puerile admiration; the work of Maxfield Parrish, a painter famous in those days who painted somewhat in the style of Salvador Dali.

I wonder whether anyone who knew Arabic—or was it Berber? —ever sat down here in the market place in Marrakech and made note of its tales. Our energetic but culturally somewhat idle, irresponsible civilization neglects things of greater consequence than this: great chances missed, good works put off, good stories not told, or told perhaps and not written, in one ear and out the other. The happy prolixity at the foot of the bell tower, the Koutubia by name, left me vaguely disheartened and abashed, reflecting that half of one's individual life is wasted on one, half of the world goes to waste. A part of my indulgence in these characteristic, repetitious, melancholy notions was due to my not understanding what the voices of the market place said.

I often think that if I had never been bitten by the ambition to produce stories and novels and other works of what is called "original" literature—if I had not made solemn promises to three or four men and women whom I love and to whom I am indebted—I might have spent my life translating and translating; a blissful life.

The voices of the market went on and on until the landscape of the foothills of the Atlas was washed with volatile sunset color in the distance, then dulled by nightfall; and the prayer-master called from the bell tower.

Chapter Two

Katherine Anne Porter Personally

The only real voyage is not an approach to landscapes but a viewing of the universe with the eyes of a hundred other people.

—MARCEL PROUST

Having had the pleasure of lifelong friendship with Miss Porter, I find it irksome to call her "Miss Porter." It has been mainly a comradeship of the literary life, and on that account perhaps, in conversation and in correspondence, I often address her as "Porter." A host of her fellow writers and others speak of her and to her as "Katherine Anne," with or without a basis of intimacy. Somewhat like Jane Austen, or like Colette, she has an unassuming sort of celebrity that invites or at least inspires friendliness. Let me now also take the fond informal tone, to celebrate the publication of her novel *Ship of Fools*, twenty years in the making.

First, some facts: She was born on May 15, 1890, in Texas, in "soft blackland farming country, full of fruits and flowers and birds," on the banks of a branch of the Colorado River denominated Indian Creek, small and clear, unimportant but unforgettable. She went to a convent school, perhaps more than one, and was an uneven student: A in history and composition and other subjects having to do with literature, but, she admits, "D in everything else, including deportment, which sometimes went down to E and stopped there."

She spent an important part of her girlhood in New Orleans, and afterward lived in New York City and in Mexico City and in Paris and in Baton Rouge, Louisiana, and in more recent years, in upper New York State and in Southern California and in Connecticut and in Washington, D.C. Prior to *Ship of Fools,* she published five short novels or nouvelles, and approximately twenty short stories (my count), and several dozen essays and criticisms and historical studies; quality always instead of quantity. She is an incomparable letter writer, sparkling, poignant, and abundant, and a famous conversationalist.

Now let me try to describe her, as to her physical presence and personality. Like many women accustomed to being loved, she dreads and disapproves of photographers, although in fact usually she has lent herself well to their techniques, and they have been on her side. I remember one of her diatribes, some years ago, against a photographer and an interviewer sent by one of the news weeklies, who, she said, had caught her unawares and committed a misrepresentation of her. In the photograph in question when it appeared she looked (to me) like Marie Antoinette young, her hair perfectly coifed and powdered-looking, playing her typewriter as though it were a spinet. And it amazed me to note how skillfully she had been able to simplify the record of her life for the interviewer also.

She has in fact a lovely face, of the utmost distinction in the Southern way; moonflower-pale, never sunburned, perhaps not burnable. She is a small woman, with a fine figure still; sometimes very slender, sometimes not. Her eyes are large, dark, and lustrous, and they are apt to give one fond glances, or teasing merry looks, or occasionally great flashes of conviction or indignation. Her voice is sweet, a little velvety or husky. In recent years she has familiarized a great number of appreciative fellow Americans with it, by means of reading and speaking engagements, and phonograph recordings.

I remember hearing her read her finest nouvelle, "Noon Wine," one summer afternoon in 1940, at a time of cruel setbacks in her personal life, in a little auditorium on the campus of Olivet College planted with oak trees. It was hot and the windows stood open. The oak trees were full of bluejays, and they were trying to shout her down. Were they muses in bird form, I remember humorously asking myself, inspiring her to cease publicly performing old work, to start writing something new? (In fact it was later that year that she began *Ship of Fools*, then temporarily entitled *No Safe Harbor*.)

She must have had a bout of bronchitis that spring or summer; she almost whispered the great tale, breathing a little hollowly, with an uneasy frayed sound now and then. Certainly there were not as many decibels in her voice as in the outcry of the jays. Nevertheless, her every tone carried; her every syllable was full of meaning and easy to understand, just as it is in print.

Certainly not muses, she protested years later, when I had written her a reminiscent letter about our brief sojourn together on that campus: "Jays are the furies, never trust them, never be deceived by them."

They congregated on the hilltop in Connecticut where she then lived, "thieving and raiding and gluttonizing everything in sight," depriving even the squirrels of their peanuts, and of course driving away from the seed table "all the little sweet birds" that she especially wanted to feed and save.

Characteristically, she had in mind a certain hierarchy of the bird world, poetical but perhaps not just. One day she looked up and discovered hawks hovering over the wood-lot and the meadow, closer and closer, and it came over her with dismay that by drawing the small birds together she was simply facilitating matters for the predators. That was the underlying theme of *Flowering Judas*, the story that made her reputation in 1930, a theme of intense concern to her all her life: involuntary or at least unintentional betrayal.

But, she wrote, the songbirds of Connecticut "were skilled and quick, and we know that they can make common cause and chase a hawk away; we have seen that together, have we not? And in some way, I cannot hate a hawk; it is a noble kind of bird who has to hunt for living food in order to live; his risks and privations are great. But the jay! there is no excuse for his existence, there should be a bounty on every ugly hammerhead of that species!"

Throughout human history hawks have been thought godlike, or at least comparable to the greatest men of action, our heroes, our lords and masters. In this letter Katherine Anne seemed to make some identification of the small birds with men and women of letters and of the arts, a somewhat more modern fancy. In a later letter she referred once more to *Cyanocitta cristata*, the middle-sized hammerheaded ones, as emblematic of certain intrusive parasitic persons who devote themselves to writers, perhaps to her more than the average. "They are as rapacious and hard to fight off as the bluejays," but, she boasted, "I have developed a great severity of rejection that I did not know I was capable of. We were all brought up on the Christian and noble idea that we have no right to deny our lives and substance to anyone who seems to need either or both. Never was a fonder delusion." And then with characteristic love of justice, even in the midst of irritation, she reminded herself that, to some extent, life and substance had been contributed to her by certain persons in her day; how had those persons known that she was a songbird? Are there, for human beings also, what ornithologists call "field marks"?

One of her "field marks," I think, is a profound, inward, hidden way of working; not just thoughtfully, methodically, as perhaps prose writers ought to be able to work, as indeed in her case the finished product suggests that she may have done. "I spend my life thinking about technique, method, style," she once told me. "The only time I do not think of them at all is when I am writing."

◆

The years on the hilltop in Connecticut appear to have been the crucial period in the composition of *Ship of Fools*. In a letter dated April 26, 1958, she described her daily life there: "I need to keep submerged in the same mood and state of mind for *weeks* at a time, very hard to explain to people who need a change and recreation every day, and sometimes several times a day. Of course I do a little baking, and I water the plants, and walk in the meadow, and even read a little now and then, mostly poetry, but I have stopped listening to music. I must keep silence." (The bread that she bakes, I may tell you, people come miles to eat.)

Literary critics and historians have often remarked the mighty contributions of the female sex to literature, far and wide and always. For the most part those who have done the contributing have been spinsters, nuns, courtesans, invalids, a little exempt from the more distracting, exhausting aspects of womanhood as such. Katherine Anne, throughout her youth and middle age, led a maximum life, concomitantly with her perfect, even perfectionist story writing. As I have remarked, she seems to like to simplify a part of the record of her existence for any sort of questioner. In fact, except for essentially private matters of love and marriage and ill-health and economics, it really has been simple. And therefore I (and other friends), instead of concentrating on ascertaining all the realities, the dates and the names and the locations and so on, have always interested ourselves in what might be called story material about her, somehow more characteristic than her mere biography.

For example, when she was a girl somewhere in the South, she had to spend months and months in a sanitarium with a grave pulmonary illness, diagnosed as one of the baffling, uncommon forms of tuberculosis. She was too ill to have visitors. Letters also evidently were overstimulating and exhausting. Even books seemed not good for her; her reading had to be rationed, just a few pages at a time. Then it was discovered that the intense restlessness of her bright eyes gazing at the ceiling, examining and re-examining the furniture, staring at the solitude, gave her a temperature. Her doctor therefore prescribed that a restful green baize cloth be placed over her face for an hour or two every morning and every afternoon, as one covers the cage of a canary when one doesn't want it to sing. I feel convinced that if anything of the sort were done to me I should give up the ghost, on account of the autosuggestion and the discouragement. Not Katherine Anne! That was only the beginning of a lifetime of delicate health and indomitable strength.

All this balance of physiology in her case, strong constitution, poor health, has mystified those who care for her. Perhaps the physicians whom she happened on here and there—"the pulse-takers, the stethoscope-wielders, the order-givers," as she has called them— have been mystifiers in some measure. One of them, in upstate New York, told her that her trouble was all a matter of allergies, and when she inquired, "What allergies?" his answer was, "You're allergic to the air you breathe."

Another, in California, she wrote me, "set out to change my chemistry, which made him say tst, tst, after a very thorough going-over, and he aims to supply all my lacks and to suppress all my internal enemies. There is about the whole project something so blithely Californian that I cannot but fall in with it."

Still another, a young one in Connecticut, pleased her by practicing "real materia medica," and not saying anything at all about her state of mind or her nervous condition. She has always objected to having strangers, even specialists, fussing around in her psychology, comparing them to the most disrespectful, disrupting type of cleaning woman. "They mess the place up; they don't know where things belong, or what goes with what."

One year at Christmastime, when she had been felled for ten days by some form of influenza and had been taking one of the sulfa drugs, she got up out of bed, though in mortal weakness; took a look at herself: prettily dressed, with "her hair in a curl or two," with an expression on her face which she could not quite make out, "distinctly remote, disengaged, full of mental reservations"; and then in a longish letter undertook to make clear to me her whole view of life. But it was unclarifiable, inexplicable, she had to admit, even to herself as she was living it, "because its truth or falseness cannot be known until the end."

Therefore, instead, she concluded that letter with an account of the medicines she had been taking: "a fantastic row of apothecary's powders, pills, and potions, all of them in the most poisonously brilliant colors, amethyst and sapphire and emerald and purple, each with its own mission of soothing or elevating the spirits, calming the heart or stimulating it, loosening the phlegm and tightening the nerves, stopping the cough and lowering the fever.

"As for the sulfa, I have had to take a tablet every four hours for two nights and two days, and never once did my mind fail to wake me at the right hour, on the hour, like a little radio station. Once I slept stubbornly, and was waked finally by a sharp rapping

at my door. It was four in the morning; the whole house was asleep
and quiet. I sat up in bed, knowing Who had done it."

It is hard to read this slight incident rightly, with its capitalized
Who, suggestive of the commissioning of Mozart's never-finished
Requiem by Whoever that was, a being never seen again, and of
other such myths. But, stop and think, if that rapper at Katherine
Anne's door at four in the morning had been Death, He would
have stayed his hand and let her sleep and skip the sulfa. That was
in 1943; it is pleasant to think that the greater part of *Ship of Fools*
was written on time borrowed from Him.

No doubt about it, there are warring forces in Katherine
Anne. Is it that her physique wearies of having to house a spirit so
strenuous and emotional, and now and then tries to expel it or to
snuff it out? Or is it instinctive in her soul to keep punishing her
body for not being superhuman, for not being ideal, for not being
immortal? Neither has ever exactly prevailed over the other; both
have been invincible. Nothing has come of the great dichotomy; or,
to be exact, literature has come of it.

"Every force of instinct and every psychic evil in us," she once
wrote, "fight the mind as their mortal enemy; but in this as in everything else I have known from the beginning which side I am on,
and I am perfectly willing to abide by my first choice until death;
indeed I can't do otherwise. For death it must be in the end, so far
as the flesh is concerned; but what lives on afterward can be honorable." To wit, twenty-six works of fiction of different lengths, honorable and (I am sure) durable; and more to come.

She lived in Mexico for a good while when she was young, and a
number of the men who revolutionized that intense and artistic
though primitive nation were her friends. In 1922 she brought the
first exhibition of Mexican-Indian folk art north of the border, but
only as far north as Los Angeles. One of the revolutionaries wrote a
song about her, "La Norteña," which, I have heard tell, has become
a folk song; little companies of young singers, mariachis, like boy
scouts in a dream, sing it in the streets. I understand that another
lady also lays claim to it. Be that as it may; "Flowering Judas"

softly resounds with music of that kind, strummingly accompanied and perhaps mortally seductive.

Some years later in Paris she wrote another Mexican tale, a nouvelle in memoir form, "Hacienda." It is a rarity in her lifework in that it is all à clef; mainly a portrait of the great Russian film maker, Eisenstein, with others of note, helpers and hinderers of his work in Mexico, clustered around. It has a singularity of style also, somehow an outdoor style, leafy and tendrilous, seeming to weave itself into a fabric without her usual touch; soft breezy sentences, with a warmth and animation unlike her earlier writing.

Certainly it points toward *Ship of Fools*. For some mysterious reason, perhaps nothing but the timing in her life, her recollection of Mexico evidently has lapsed less for her, subsided less, than that of other places she has lived. "Flowering Judas" had an odd, almost painful dreaminess, with only present-tense verbs; and in the first twenty pages of *Ship of Fools*, when the passengers are assembling and waiting to sail, as in "a little purgatory between land and sea," the half-Indian world seems to reach out after them, overstimulatingly, and it haunts the entire volume, across the ocean, though its subject matter is mainly German and American.

In another way the latest of her nouvelles, "The Leaning Tower," must also have served as a study for the future greater undertaking: a tale of Berlin on the eve of the Nazi revolution, when in fact Katherine Anne spent a winter there, and saw the dangerousness of the Germans, and understood how risky it was to fear them or, on the other hand, to be too simply prejudiced against them. Doubtless also, while writing it, during World War II, she was aware of the aesthetic pitfall of propagandizing in any sense, with the excitement of the time. She holds her breath in it.

Now to turn to another area of the legendry of Katherine Anne's life, which she has not perpetuated in any of her fiction.—Someone, years ago, used to say that at an early age she had been in the movies as a Mack Sennett bathing girl, along with Gloria Swanson and Mabel Normand et al. Certainly she was as good-looking as they, whether or not she could have performed as funnily. For some reason I never quite like to question or cross-question her about things; but I once ventured to do so about this. It was a matter of journalism, she explained, not show business. Commissioned to write an article for some newspaper or magazine she pretended briefly to be a comedienne for the sake of the realistic detail and local color.

Not so long ago she had a try at earning her living by script writing. Her first Hollywood assignment was not so much to write as to be attached in an Egeria-like or muse-like capacity to a famous producer, now dead. For a while this amused her; at least she sent back to the Eastern seaboard amusing reports of it. "One or the other of us," she reported—he had another salaried writer also at his beck and call, perhaps more than one—"tosses a tiny shred of an idea at him. He seizes it out of the air and without stopping for breath constructs a whole scene. He then asks us what we think of it, and as we open our mouths to answer, he says, 'It's a wonderful scene. Now what else have you got in mind?' And the thing is repeated; sometimes we just sit there for two hours." What he had in mind, or perhaps I should say, in the works, was a film about Queen Elizabeth I.

Presently she began to feel like "a fox with his leg in a trap," gnawing away at it; and by the end of the thirteen-week stint contracted for in the first place she had persuaded her famous man that she was not the inspirer he needed. A part of their maladjustment, she sensed, was the fact that he was a Christian Scientist, whereas she had been brought up a Roman Catholic. During the thirteen weeks he had seemed deeply disapproving of the large salary that he or his studio had been paying her; but suddenly, she wrote, when she was on her way, he "began to worry about my future. What on earth was I going to do now? where was I going? did I have any money? I was happy to be able to tell him that I was relatively rich and wasn't going anywhere."

In fact she was relatively poor; apparently they had been paying her in Confederate money or fool's gold or something. Not seeing any other solution for her practical problems just then, she transferred her talents to another studio, where she was put to work on a film about Madame Sans-Gêne.

All her life Katherine Anne has been bewitched by the hope of ceasing to be homeless, of settling somewhere and getting her books and manuscripts and notebooks out of storage and within reach somehow, on shelves and in filing cabinets and in ring-binders. With the evanescent Western money she bought a small segment of mountain for a building site, but could not keep it. One day as she sat peacefully writing in a rented ranch cabin in the Mojave Desert a Western wind arose and tore out a window frame over her desk and slightly fractured her skull; once more, the Furies! But, never forget, the Furies sometimes are on the side of the angels. She did not properly belong out West, at least not then.

In subsequent years, a good deal of the time, at intervals, she has had to depend on the universities and colleges for her livelihood. As a rule, at the beginning of her various stints or bouts on campuses, she has been persuaded by the literature-loving educators who have arranged things, or she has persuaded herself, that not much actual pedagogy would be required of her. Usually, however, they seem to have got the harness on her in some way. I remember a letter from a very great university indeed, in the Middle West, specifying her teaching schedule: only five hours a week actually behind the microphone in the classroom (so specified in her contract) and only about eighty term papers to be read and graded. But she also had to examine the manuscripts of the more creative young persons on campus and to advise them in hour-long sessions; about fourteen of these a week. Also once a week she had to give a spontaneous hour-long lecture to some special class or group or club. It may be that no trained and experienced professional would find this schedule at all onerous or unfair. To Katherine Anne, as a mature woman of genius in delicate health, perhaps somewhat proud and euphoric, with so much creative work of her own not only in mind but partly on paper, and covered by publishers' contracts, it seemed hard; and all too often her university engagements were terminated by illness.

❖

As the quantity of my quotations will have suggested to you, I have been rereading my precious file of long letters from her, and another set addressed to Monroe Wheeler, about two hundred in all. She and I made friends in Paris in 1932 and began our correspondence upon my return to this country in the autumn of 1933, and it has been continuous ever since. Yes, yes, probably she should have repressed or restrained this long-distance friendliness somewhat, in order to produce more for publication. But as I peruse her letters, now that much of the circumstantial detail in them has ceased to be of interest, and therefore the main elements and outlines of her mind and her life appear more impressively, as it were a range of hills which the autumn has stripped of leaves, I am struck by something about them that may have conditioned her, even benefited her, in her art of fiction.

It is that they are extraordinarily, uniquely subjective: self-judging and explanatory and disciplinary, and self-defending, with matchless detail and finesse in all these mirrorings of the heart and the mind, shifting and shining, and, in a way, hypnotizing. Whereas in fiction she has been free from herself. In fiction she has maintained a maximum impersonality, a disengagement from any sort of autobiographical point of view, a distinctness between her own ego, her sensitivenesses and compulsions and illusions, and those of all the alter egos that she writes about, and an abstention from fantasy and lyricism and rhetoric, of which most novelists, indeed even many journalists and historians, are incapable.

It is almost startling to compare her with other famous twentieth-century women in this respect: Virginia Woolf! Colette! Even reticent and rather cold writers such as Maugham have made use of their shyness, exercised their self-consciousness, almost as a convention or a technique. As for the writing of our more extreme, compendious, sociological novelists, it is a sort of concavity, which almost teases one to deduce what they themselves are, convexly; rather like the shapes of ancient Pompeians in the awful layers of ashes from Vesuvius.

Katherine Anne is not like that at all. The objectivity of her narrative art, if I may apply to her Coleridge's famous formula (only Shakespeare really filled the bill, *he* thought), is a matter of sending herself out of herself; of thinking herself into "the thoughts and feelings of beings in circumstances wholly and strangely different" from her own: *hic labor, hoc opus.*

I believe that her vast self-expressive and confidential first-person communication to her friends, freshly inspired or provoked each time, swiftly produced on the typewriter, and not rewritten, scarcely reread, has served to purify her mind of a good deal of that pride and willfulness and narcissism and excitability by which the life-work of most modern fiction writers has often been beclouded, enfeebled, blemished. Of course her letter writing must have shortened her working days and used up incalculable energy, thus reducing the amount of her production of the more public forms of literature.

In the earliest of her nouvelles, "Old Mortality," a Northerner may mind the extremely regional feeling, the patriotism of the South, which is a group subjectivity. But even this is so much less soft and heady and spicy than the accounts that other fiction writers have given us of that important part of the world, its premises, its problems, that it seems almost bitter, like a medicine, like a lesson. At the end of it the protagonist, Miranda, realizes how much of her girlhood she has spent "peering in wonder" at other people's notions of the past, "like a child at a magic-lantern show," and resolves to close her mind stubbornly to all such secondhand remembrance, spiritual predigestion.

In "Pale Horse, Pale Rider," and in later stories featuring that same somewhat autobiographical Miranda—the best of which is perhaps "The Grave," an episode of almost mystical childhood, having to do with the closeness and connectedness of life and death, womb and tomb (as in medieval religious imagery)—all is self-possessed and responsible, thoughtful and indeed philosophical. What I call her impersonality applies even to the painting of her own portrait, when it is fictitious. And apparently the saving thoughtfulness, the mastery of her mind over every sort of old ideal and dark prejudice and grievance and self-flattery, takes place at the time that she stores things away in her memory, for future use; not just according to her formal intellect and her sense of story pattern when she begins to work. Again, we may see in this something of her classic practical womanly temperament, housewifeliness! Subject matter that she deems worth keeping she simply folds up a little, scales down a little, and deflates and dehydrates, with applications of sense of humor, sense of proportion, sense of justice, as it were against moth and worm and mildew and dust.

It pleases me to recall a conversation that I had with Katherine Anne while she was writing "Pale Horse, Pale Rider" and was having trouble with a passage in it toward the end in which Miranda, desperately ill, almost dead, was to see heaven. She told me that she herself, at the end of World War I, had experienced this part of what she had created this heroine to experience and to make manifest; and because, no doubt, it really was heaven, she found herself unable to re-see it with her lively, healthy eyes.

This conversation took place in a valley in New Jersey where I used to live, which has been turned into a water reservoir, gone forever! It was springtime; the sward or sod was moss green, strewn with little blue shadows under the trees half in leaf; the vistas upstream and downstream were dim, Bavarian-looking; and there were some soprano voices within earshot, I have forgotten whose voices. With characteristic, somewhat superficial helpfulness I proposed to my dear friend and rival, "Why not at that point just write a page about your inability to recede, your impotence to write? Eternal curtain, blinding effulgence! Let each one of your readers fill in the kind of heaven that his particular life has prepared him to go to, when his turn comes.

"What else is heaven, anyway?" I went on, where angels fear to tread. "What can it be, empirically, but the indescribable; the defeat of literature; the end of empiricism?"

To my amusement and perhaps regret, mingled with a little vanity, Katherine Anne did not take to this suggestion. She let "Pale Horse" go for another year, and turned to other work. She said au

revoir to her New York and New Jersey friends and went to live
for a while in Louisiana, perhaps waiting all that time to re-see
Miranda's heaven.

In due course, "Pale Horse, Pale Rider" appeared in book form,
in 1939, with the vision worth a year's waiting: "thinned to a fine
radiance, spread like a great fan, and curved out into a curved rain-
bow." What comes before this also is extraordinary: Miranda at
death's door with the influenza of 1918, afraid of her doctor just
because he is her doctor, in charge of her death, and because he is
a German doctor, and because it is 1918. Even in Denver, Colorado,
where that story is set, a world war does not let one even die at
peace. I think that, if the years to come winnow literary wheat
from chaff as the past has done, this story may be valued as a unique
record of that modern curse and ailment, horror of the German,
which lapsed during the twenties, then began again; also as a prelude to *Ship of Fools*.

Miranda's beginning to recover from influenza is another extraordinary page; just less and less bitterness of pus in the naturally
sweet flesh, up and up toward life, with a wink of consciousness
more and more often. The strangest return, the way of the solitary
ego, the opposite of the great legend—the Orpheus in Miranda
keeping the Eurydice in her alive not by looking away but precisely
by contemplating what was happening every instant.

Of the three nouvelles in that volume, indeed, of the five that
she has published thus far, "Noon Wine" is the one that I love best.
I may say, parenthetically, that Katherine Anne herself objects to
my use of the borrowed French word and its several cognates, also
European in origin, novella, novelle, and novelette. I see her point.
As to vocabulary, whatever the problem, she is a purist, and it is
vulgar to trick out one's writing about writing with this and that
imported feather (though Poe did so a good deal). Also, as the
author, to date, of only one large-scale work of fiction in an era
when "novel, novel," is the word to conjure with, and when most
of the praise as well as the pay goes to bulky productions, she must
be glad of any nuance of one's criticism which will remind the
reader that "Pale Horse, Pale Rider" and "Old Mortality" and

"Noon Wine" and "Hacienda" and "The Leaning Tower" are major works. They are, indeed; and doubtless it took more skill, more time, and more creative strength to keep them to the length that, as it seemed to her (and as it seems to me), inspiration and sub-ject matter in those five cases called for than it would have taken to amplify them, to swell them up with self-generating detail, to spin them out with extra passages of introductoriness and didacti-cism and suspense and consequences, as large-scale novelists ordi-narily do.

But, for my part, I cannot wean myself from the use of the term "nouvelle," because it designates not just a certain length, let us say, twenty or thirty thousand words, but a scope and particular inspiration fundamentally differing from the several types of short story and the several variations of the novel. The nouvelle is an account of a limited number of characters in close connection, or in consequential or interesting contrast; and of their situation as a whole and their state of being in some detail and in depth, not just an incident or episode in their lives. It is a mode of narration in which the narrated time serves as a window to illuminate a re-moter past and to reveal something of a foreseeable future; multum in parvo, but very multum and not too parvo. It often shows as many facets of meaning as a novel, but it does not apply to as many levels of experience and observation and significance. Along with Goethe's novelle which is called *Die Novelle* and Mann's *Death in Venice* and Benjamin Constant's *Adolphe* and Mérimée's *Carmen* and Colette's *Gigi* and Melville's *Billy Budd* and Forster's *The Eternal Moment*, Katherine Anne's "Noon Wine" is a model of the form, an example for the textbooks.

It has an epic quality despite its small scale and modern dress, with only two heroes, one heroine, and one significant villain, expressing themselves commonly, and in natural pitiful circum-stances. The epic that it makes me think of, I may say, humorously but not insincerely, is *Paradise Lost,* because it has Lucifer in it, a very modern and American Lucifer named Mr. Hatch. Hatch, not exactly fat, "more like a man who has been fat recently"; Hatch, who goes to and fro "telling other people what kind of tobacco to chew"; Hatch, with the discovery and roundup of "twenty-odd escaped loonatics" to his credit. His prey this time is Olaf Helton, whose brother years before took away his harmonica, who therefore stabbed said brother with a pitchfork. He escaped, and since then has been working for lazy Mr. Thompson and his dear sickly wife. He has somewhat lightened their burden and much restored their prosperity. They have got in the habit of hearing what you might call his theme song, a drinking song, rendered over and over on a series of new harmonicas.

When Hatch appears on the scene it all goes like a charm, like a curse. To save Helton, as he thinks, Thompson kills Hatch. He is tried and acquitted; but the breach of the great taboo is too much for him to forgive himself. The Eumenides are in him, nagging, arguing; soon his state of mind is such that he frightens even his beloved wife. Therefore he condemns himself to death and executes himself. There is a most touching page toward the close which is like a song or an aria: Mrs. Thompson weeping to have Helton back, saying a sort of prayer against the violence of menfolk, kneeling before her icebox as if it were an altar; the icebox Helton had helped her to buy. This perfectly womanly woman, eternal bystander and born widow; and the typical hired man, the type of wrongdoer whom even the Eumenides might spare because there was no idea or idealism behind his wrong, whom everyone except the Hatches of this world must forgive; and the Thompsons' fine little boys, by the evolution of whose characters we are subtly made to feel time passing and humanity incessant: all these are exemplary, human and arch-human, in the grandest manner. Grand also, the way in which the murder of Hatch is made to epitomize our lesser losses of temper also, even the wielding of the jackknife of wit and of the little hatchet of righteous criticism, by which the psyche of the stupid man may be somewhat murdered and the heart of the murderous-minded man himself broken. Also it is a reminder of how evil may come of resistance to evil, of which the worldly man in this half-Germanized world needs to be reminded.

There is no end to the kinds of evil which Hatch typifies. You belittle him unfairly and unwisely if you assume that he has gone hunting his twenty-odd madmen just for the cash compensation. It has been chiefly to satisfy his clear sense of right and wrong; and to exercise the power to which he is entitled as a democratic citizen. There is some repression of the ego in our comfortable country, and therefore some perversion of it, therefore cruelty. Hatch has the legal mind, particularly what you might call the blue-legal mind.

Behold in him also political genius, which is psychopathic unless it is psychiatric, and in either case more oratorical than honest. At the start he positively woos Thompson, like a candidate for public office: Hatch "For Law and Order." And you might think that this hell-bent bullying technique would not get one vote; but you learn that it gets millions. In him also may be seen some evils of journalism, and some evils of the police, so worrisome and intimidating that one scarcely cares to comment on them.

Look at him as you like: he signifies always a little more than you have seen and seems larger than life-size; and you think that he must have more lives than a cat; and with facets like a diamond he throws bright, instructive flashes, on one thing and another. Thus I feel justified in having used that moot, incongruous word "epic." He is not only a man hunter, he is mankind as man hunter, sempiternal. He is not only a busybody, he is the great American busybody; godlike as only a devil can be. Lucifer! No wonder that Thompson at first is reminded of someone he has seen before, somewhere. Katherine Anne just mentions this, without explanation. It is perhaps the only signal she gives that she meant Hatch to be a personification as well as a person. Thompson hates him long before there has been a peep out of him about his man hunt; and so does the reader, surely, upon instinct. Hatch-malevolence can often be felt previous to, and lies deeper than, Hatch-activity. It lies so deep indeed that one is half afraid to say simply that it is evil. I always particularly resent the fact that he has kept, as you might say, virtuous, in order to accumulate a good conscience, as one might pinch pennies half one's life to invest in a big business; and his air of friendliness without affection, curiosity without imagination, and the detached manner of his invasion of the others' privacy. Of course it is scarcely detachment to get chopped open by one's host's ax; but I feel that this is the least that could be expected to happen to him in the circumstances, an occupational hazard. I resent the fact that he manages—Katherine Anne lets him manage —not to deserve it.

A specific and unabashed (though somewhat mysterious) morality works through and through this whole tale, like a fat, like a yeast, like an antidote. Katherine Anne does not pity Hatch, but seemingly she would like to; she abstains from despising him. Perhaps suspicious of the very clarity of her hatred of hatchism, she compensates the individual Hatch for it by a kind of demi-deification and enlargement. She is as careful about him as if she were wearing his face as a mask for her face, and this were confession of a misdeed of hers. Do not forget that both Helton and Thompson commit murder; and the latter's plea of self-defense is specious or erroneous, if not dishonest. Hatch is not to blame for anything except his being, and his happening to be just there, in juxtaposition with these others. For many years he has been doing what he attempts that day; no one has ever objected before; what reason had he to suppose there was any law against it? The written law is a makeshift, and the unwritten law all double meaning. In entire civilization, every one of us is partly responsible for this darkness. Katherine Anne, mild even as she contemplates murder, assumes responsibility.

Let me say finally that it is a great factor in my admiration of this story that she has not pointed out any one of the significances I have seen in it and tried to list. There was no need to, I admiringly think. As critic, pro tem, it is my pleasure to point. The feeling of the good and evil in question doubtless accumulated in her heart in the abstract, for years; and the contrast of the two, no, three kinds of humanity, and eternal warfare of the two equally sincere schools of morality, must have come to her mind one day with such energy that there was no resisting the impulse to show them in action, in an ideal bout. Then, because of her humane and womanly humility, abstraction blushed; abstraction bowed to fate, the truest fate of all, that of circumstance and coincidence and dialogue; abstraction stooped to human nature, and dressed itself and embodied itself in this episode, whether fact or fancy or a mixture.

One could not ask for a more objective work of fiction than "Noon Wine." Everything that it tells is a question of its time and its place and its conjunction of characters, only four principals, with nothing of that darkling presence and involvement and purpose of the author behind the scenes, between the lines, which may be said to give a poetical quality or a fourth dimension to narrative. It is freestanding, with little or no pedestal, little or no matrix; and her important essay about the writing of it in the *Yale Review* in 1956 (twenty years after the fact), though richly reminiscent of the little experiences with which it began—the blast of a shotgun, a scream in death agony, "a fat bullying whining man," a poor wife perjuring herself, a curvetting horse, a doleful tune—made it seem an even more absolute creation or invention than I had supposed on first reading.

That essay begins with almost a formula: "By the time a writer has reached the end of a story, he has lived it at least three times over—first, in the series of actual events that, directly or indirectly, have combined to set up the commotion in his mind and senses that causes him to write the story; second, in memory; and third, in the re-creation of the chaotic stuff." And toward the close of it she arrives at a more profound statement: "I do know why I remembered them"—that is to say, the shot, the scream, the horse, the tune (as it were, spark, pollen, seed, yeast)—"and why in my memory they slowly took on their separate lives in a story. It is because there radiated from each of those glimpses of strangers some element, some quality that arrested my attention at a vital moment of my own growth, and caused me, a child, to stop short and look outward, away from myself; to look at another human being with that attention and wonder and speculation which ordinarily, and very naturally, I think, a child lavishes only on himself." To be noted for future textbooks, components and instrumentalities of creative writing—various accidental or incidental evidences of the senses, things the writer sees and hears and feels, and their timing and sequence in relation to the more general processes of his private and inner life; a childish or childlike mind, maturing by fits and starts in one way and another, peeping out of the hidey-hole of self, giving things a second look, thinking things over, and lavishing its curiosity and wonder.

Yeats said—did he not?—that certain of our nineteenth-century classics, notably Emerson's essays and *Leaves of Grass,* were somewhat vitiated by their not incorporating or reflecting any large and clear vision of evil. But certainly Hawthorne and Melville were not limited to optimism and fond ecstasy. "Noon Wine" is of that lineage, grandly and sorrowfully envisaging right and wrong, both on the personal level, where something can be done about it, and in the sense of the sublime, the insoluble. Let me call attention particularly to the power and the complexity of the characterization of the villain in it, Hatch, a veritable Lucifer; brilliantly signifying more, at every point, than the author actually tells us, faceted like a diamond, flashing instructively in many directions. "Noon Wine" would make a fine opera libretto for a composer able to write duets and trios and quartets, without which (I think) music drama never quite touches the heart.

It always pleases me to note how little continuousness, impingement, or repetition there is between one of Katherine Anne's stories and another. In the case of most specialists in short fiction, as in that of painters of easel pictures and composers of chamber music, one finds some new order of artistry every few years; and between, only variants of the same inspiration or the same method, efforts to perfect, or indeed a copying of themselves without much effort. Katherine Anne, when not hitting high spots, really has preferred not to hit anything at all, at least not anything fictitious. She just keeps turning the pages of her mind until she comes to one that is untouched, to which she then applies a new pen, silvery and needle-sharp. Line the stories up: "Flowering Judas," "He," "The Jilting of Granny Weatherall," "The Cracked Looking Glass"; each advances a separate proposition in morals or psychology, solves an unfamiliar problem of form.

No theme except the given theme, one feels, could develop itself properly or transpire effectively in that particular setting and those circumstances. And yet she never forces the connection and congruity between the scene and the event. There is a minimum of anthropomorphism in her landscapes and changes of weather. Shapes and inanimate objects in her portrayal of the world are never geometrical or surrealistic or modernistic. Things are what they are; and what people do results directly from what *they* are. Everything is for the portraiture, inner portraiture mainly, and for the philosophy, which is almost entirely unspoken, and for the tale, the tale!

❖

Her most recent collection of stories was published in 1944. Recently four admirable short narratives, not portions of *Ship of Fools*, have appeared in magazines; one of them, "St. Augustine and the Bullfight," is (I think) a masterpiece, in a strange new form, a hybrid of essay and tale, of which I expect her to make further use. Also occasionally she has produced valuable pieces of expository prose. In every type of short work she is a ready writer, given a green light, and a little removal from sociability, and certain facilities in the way of board and keep.

But never a ready novelist! All that time, a third of a lifetime, her struggle with *Ship of Fools* has been going on. With the everlasting problem of her delicate health, and the other difficulties and jeopardies that I have tried to describe without making a melodrama and a sentimentality of her life, certainly she has not worked at the novel uninterruptedly; but she has kept up her dedication of herself to it, only it, and staked her reputation and her self-respect on it. "Even when I was a little child," she once said to me, "I knew that youth was not for me"—a sentence wonderfully expressive of her particular lifelong uneasiness, responsiveness to her fate up ahead, and great patience from start to finish, knowing or sensing that she was going to grow old at the appointed, self-appointed task.

Troubles, jeopardies, hardships; note that I do not say misfortunes. The perils and disorders, even the wounds of a war scarcely seem deplorable to the home-coming soldier (or to his grateful countrymen), unless his battle has been lost; not even then, if he has shown heroism and if his story has been nobly reported. The fearsomeness of childbearing and the fatigues of parenthood are unhappy only if the children perish or turn out to be good for nothing. Likewise one cannot evaluate the experience of a literary genius unless and until one has perused all that has resulted from it. Obviously a great deal of heartbreak and travail has been Katherine Anne's lot. But, but, let us remind ourselves, no fortunate and facile youthful or even middle-aged person could have written *Ship of Fools*. It has required the better part of a lifetime of unshrinking participation in life and unshirking endeavor, of hardheadedness and heat of heart and almost fanaticism, and now we have the result; and surely it must seem to her, in her weariness and pride, cheap at the price.

So many writers of our generation brought forth novels in our twenties, immaturely. Often they were novels in name only, enlarged tales, family chronicles, disguised self-portraits. Some of us then hit upon a formula or worked out a method, so as to produce narrative reading matter wholesale; and some of us, on the other hand, simply got tired of the great form, or despaired of it. With lesser fish to fry, we let the white whale go. Not Katherine Anne! And when, twenty years ago, as a famed specialist in the short story, she let it be known that she had begun a novel, she meant precisely that: a large lifelike portrayal of a numerous and representative society, with contrasts of the classes and the masses and the generations and the ethnic groups, with causes and effects in the private psychology of one and all, and with their influences on one another —every man to some extent a part of every other man's fate—and all of this made manifest in behavior, action, plot! Despite destiny, unfavorable in some respects, despite passionate life and personal weakness and disadvantages in the day and age and in our present heterodox American culture, Katherine Anne would be a novelist, a novelist, or else! As the time passed, there arose in literary circles a murmur of skepticism or pessimism to which (I hope) she herself was deaf.

Let me confess that, at one point, when she had confided problems and despondencies to me, I began to write her a deplorable though well-meaning letter, advising her to give up the novel, as such; to salvage stories and sketches out of the incomplete manuscript; and to go on to whatever she had next on her agenda. Thank goodness, I was persuaded by my closest friend to consign this melancholy suggestion to the wastebasket, and presently I paid Katherine Anne a visit on her wooded hill in Connecticut, where, as she said, she lived "on guard and secretive and solitary as a woodchuck peeping out of its hidey-hole." And she read aloud several chapters that were new to me, and I suddenly caught sight of what was in her mind, the great novel structure; the whole so very much more than the sum of the parts. I came away repentant, exalted, and did not lose confidence in it or in her again.

Ship of Fools began with a sea voyage that she took in 1931, and specifically, she says, with an account of it in a letter to her friend and fellow writer, Caroline Gordon. Ten years later she began putting it in fiction form, and gradually, perhaps somewhat unintentionally, it ceased to be a reminiscence and a tale and became a true and full-length novel: The ship *Vera,* that is to say, Truth, but with no abstraction other than that, no symbolism, on its voyage from Veracruz in Mexico to Bremerhaven in Germany via four intermediate ports of call, a voyage only twenty-six days long in the narrated fact, but in the art of the telling, with reference to many of the passengers, lifelong, in that something of their past and something of their future is included in it all along, by means of great flashbacks and mirrorings of motive and fate, by means of a prophetic understanding of the patterns of their lives still to be lived; about three dozen of them clearly delineated and memorable, some unforgettable: a lot of Germans and a Swede and three Swiss and four Americans, and some Mexicans and Cubans and Spaniards (a vague pitiful collectivity of hundreds of the poorest Spaniards, deportees, in steerage); every age group; aristocrats and professional men and artists and various bourgeois and riffraff and merchant mariners (and that shadowy Spanish proletariat) diversely involved in love and lust and mortal illness and craziness and chauvinism and cruel intolerance and religiosity, actively involved, in brilliant incidents with hallucinating dialogue; all things motivating one another, all things illuminating one another.

What in the world made us so negative, Katherine Anne's friends and enemies, and all the literary gentry? With the long, solid, closely wrought, and polished work in hand, the grumpiness about it for so long seems strange. Occasionally, when publication had to be postponed again, and then again, did I not sometimes hear in certain voices, voices well-meaning enough as a rule, tones of what in psychoanalytical parlance used to be known as Schadenfreude, exhilaration-when-things-go-wrong? Have I ever been guilty of just that myself? I believe not. But who knows?

Though almost certainly she has had no notion of it, she has been enviable for years. Her fame has been out of proportion to the amount of her work, however highly one might think of it as to its excellence. At least in theory, a good many of us would willingly have experienced her sadnesses, shouldered her burdens, faced up to her disappointments, in order to have produced just those few volumes of her short fiction (even giving up hope of the legendary novel) and to have felt her satisfaction in consequence. How proudly she spoke of her vocation at times, almost as though she were a ruler or as though she were a saint! "I have tossed a good many things considered generally desirable over the windmill for that one intangible thing that money cannot buy, and I find to my joy that I was right. There is no describing what my life has been because of my one fixed desire: to be a good artist, responsible to the last comma for what I write." Most of the time, at least much of the time, even when things have been in no wise flourishing for her, she has seemed somehow exultant, heroic, heroine-like.

Furthermore, she has a formidable wit, which may have troubled some people. Vide, if you have not taken cognizance of this, her satirical portrait of Gertrude Stein in *The Days Before,* or her more recent minority opinion of *Lady Chatterley's Lover,* by which some Lawrence admirers felt deflated as it were with beak and claw. I have tried to think of some sample of her humor in its briefer and sometimes even fiercer form, à vive voix or by mail, that it might be feasible to tell, naming no names. But hers is a type of humor that cannot be appreciated if the target is veiled. Of course in a way one is proud to be chastised with intellect and virtuosity like hers; at any rate one prides oneself on taking it stoically; but it may leave sorenesses of scar tissue, reflexes of spite. No matter.

It occurs to me that there is a minimum of laughter of any kind in *Ship of Fools*. George Moore maintained that humorousness always has a bad effect in a novel, disruptive of the illusion in it, drawing attention away from the characters in it to the humorous disposition of the author. I have never heard Katherine Anne say anything about this, but evidently her instinct has been in accord with that of the influential, half-forgotten Irish writer. Humor is one of the subjectivities, along with pathos and anger, powerful in her letters, distilled out of her fiction, for fiction's sake.

◆

Ship of Fools is a phenomenal, rich, and delectable book. Though I had read a good many parts of it in typescript and in serial publication from time to time, its qualities as they appear in book form far exceed my expectations: the hallucinating specificity; the supreme and constant meaningfulness of everything; the bewitchment of the story as such, or, to be exact, the stories (plural) interwoven; and a continual sense of cause and effect, both in the mind and in external circumstances, amounting to suspense but at the same time inspiring confidence in the judgment and truthfulness of the novelist; the main generalizations of psychology and morality as plain and acceptable as the face of a clock, the minute hand seeming to cause the hours, the hour hand the days, and subsequently the weeks and months and years and indeed, in retrospect and prospect, entire lifetimes. A good many readers are going to regret having been given snatches of this novel in magazines. An analogy in terms of music occurs to me: the themes best suited to large-scale polyphonic compositions do not make the shapeliest sonatas or the most moving songs.

I think that reviewers may be tempted to describe *Ship of Fools* as a grand-hotel novel, making a customary and convenient use of the title of a best seller of some years back: a contrivance of heterogeneous humanity cheek by jowl, a matching and contrasting of little plots, with a measure of general involvement as it were by chance, ring around a rosy, all of which one does find in caravanseries and sometimes in great country houses and in hospitals and, as it is in this case, on board ship.

But in Katherine Anne's novel this is only the superficial aspect and the rough outline. Essentially it is a theme novel, with great themes. Shall I undertake to list them? Femaleness, and the basic coercive-submissive (not to say sado-masochistic) relations of males and females; middle age; neuroticism; and several predestining historic matters: the influential mentality of American expatriates, egocentric but sensitive; the pre-Nazi mentality of otherwise quite ordinary middle-class and lower middle-class Germans, with their wild conceit backed up by fanatic hard work and co-operativeness within the group; the cold and sickening ferment of ideas like anti-Semitism. What the twentieth century has had to read in the newspapers is often worse than what Calvin found in the Bible.

It seems to me that she now paints her vision of evil with a more mingled palette, although there is less pathos about it than when she was young. Now no one is entirely blameless—even one of the children on the S.A. Vera is hopeless, and the other two are fiends —but, on the other hand, she never disregards or belittles anyone. On the whole I should say that all the qualities that I have praised in her previous fiction—that grasp of lamentable evil predestination, and the dead seriousness in general, the objectivity, the knack of verisimilitudinous portraiture (often like Frans Hals, sometimes like Goya), the natural-seeming style, the manner always responsive to, adjusted to, the matter, and suspense throughout, well regulated but with no trickiness—all are still praiseworthy in *Ship of Fools*, unchanged except for the tremendous change of scale.

The central part of *Ship of Fools* is the story of the amorous entanglement of a willful and clever American girl painter with a young fellow artist, whom she perhaps loves but does not like (and is disliked by). Adjacent to this is the portrait of a lonely divorced American woman of a certain distinction, whose rather passive and self-centered psychology erupts at last in a strange disgraceful action. Rather in the background, as the historiis personae are placed and arranged, and a little more remote from anything the reader is apt to have encountered in his own walk of life, with obscurer motivations and great pathos and a more intense episodic interest, there is another love relationship, somewhat tenderer than that of the young Americans, between a middle-aged Spanish noblewoman, whose life really has become hopeless in every way and who has taken to drugs, and a saintly German doctor with a hopeless heart condition, who supplies her with drugs and otherwise befriends her and loves her desperately.

There is only one Jew on board the Vera, one named Julius Loewenthal, and we are under no great obligation to be sorry for him personally; no one actually mistreats him; he seems not sorry for himself personally, only for the collectivity of Jews. He is bigotedly religious, even superstitious, and rabidly anti-Gentile. The victim of the German insolence and silliness is a good Aryan German, an oil-man named Freytag, with a beloved Jewish wife (not on board). When his miscegenation gets bruited about he is removed from the captain's table and seated with Loewenthal, who also gives him a hard time, hating to hear of a Jewish girl's having stooped so low as to marry one of the goyim, even a good one.

How rich it is, in human interest, tribulation, and reading pleasure; God's plenty, and indeed the devil's plenty also! In the area of love and sexuality, for example, we get to know and understand two somewhat sustained love affairs, in addition to the two that I have just mentioned; and four middle-aged marriages, with a pair of young honeymooners in ideal euphoria and peak activity in the background; and the uncomfortable unilateral sexual needs of three single males—a violent Scandinavian, a tough Texan, and a maddened German teen-ager; and the feverishness of a sextet of Cuban medical students; and the routine venality and occasional animal passion of a Spanish song-and-dance troupe; to say nothing of the presumable sex life of the poor multitude in steerage. In the course of the twenty-six days, the human cargo there on the lower deck is increased by seven babies, boy-babies.

In reading *Ship of Fools* one is less aware of structure than of movement, as it might be the movement of one's eyes lighting first on one thing, then on another, or on this person or that. For example, in Veracruz on the day of sailing, first we see an Indian, then an appalling mutilated beggar; whereupon a pair of passengers, obese German passengers, with an obese white bulldog, leave behind them on a bench a reminder of sandwiches, which the beggar drags himself to and wolfs down; and after that a patrol of soldiers or policemen, with rifles at the ready, marches in and takes the Indian away, perhaps to shoot him. Meanwhile the principal personages begin to come into view, singly or in pairs or in trios, friendly or hostile or indifferent. The reader gradually circulates among them, stirred at first only by curiosity; and the writer, as to the order and the emphasis and the dimensions of her writing, seems actuated at first only by a readiness to respond to the reader's interest. She keeps answering the questions that she keeps inducing us to ask.

The title is a revival of that of a moral allegory very famous all over Europe at just about the time that Columbus discovered America: Sebastian Brant's *Das Narrenschiff*. Katherine Anne read it not long after that voyage to Europe with which this vast and gradual work of fiction started. "This simple, almost universal image of the ship of this world on its voyage to eternity," she says in an introductory note, "suits my purpose exactly. I am a passenger on that ship."

Structurally, *Ship of Fools* is in three parts: I. Embarcation; II. High Seas; III. The Harbors—subdivided in about a hundred and fifty brief untitled sections. There are three epigraphs: A line of Baudelaire, *"Quand partons-nous vers le bonheur?"* When shall we set out toward happiness? A phrase from a song by Brahms: *"Kein Haus, Keine Heimat,"* No house, no homeland. One of St Paul's somber metaphorical sayings: "For here we have no continuing city . . ."

In the first hour of my reading I noticed that in the case of some passengers Katherine Anne gives us, in a section each, profoundly though swiftly, the whole being and salient features of the entire life story. Whereas her introduction of certain other people is much more casual, our penetration into their nature and mentality shallower, or at any rate slower, the disclosure of the past less dramatic. This puzzled me. Presently I realized that her complete, profound likenesses are of the less important, less complex characters; those that she presents easy-goingly are the principals, who are to be given the lion's share of the hundreds of pages up ahead.

It is a vast portrait gallery, with portraits of all sizes, hung here and there on the wall, high and low; and some of the portrayed ones seem to dance down out of their frames, some tumble out, some fight their way out, with fearful vitality. I can think of only one possible reason for anyone's not liking this book: just at the start the characters are almost too strong; one shrinks from them a little. No, you may say, I do not wish to spend another page with this smug glutton, or this hypochondriacal drunkard, or this lachrymose widow; no, not another word out of that girl in the green dress! But presently, having read a certain number of pages, you feel a grudging sympathy with one and all, or a rueful empathy, or at least solidarity, as a fellow human being.

I told Katherine Anne this one day on the telephone, and she said, "I promised myself solemnly: in this book I will not load the dice. We all do it, even you have done it; and so have I in my day, as you well know. But this time, I resolved, everyone was to have his say. I would not take sides. I was on everyone's side."

At that point I had reached only about page 100, and I replied to her, "Yes, my dear, but it might also be said that you are on no one's side."

This evidently surprised her a bit but she took it kindly. I wanted to go on and turn it into a great compliment. For, truly, this is one of the magic effects of the art of fiction at its very best: when the reader, knowing nothing in the world about a set of characters except what the writer has written for him, suddenly says to himself, Oh, I understand these poor people better than this literary person seems to; he or she lacks compassion or profundity or sociology or political sense or something. Thus each and every character is given a separate life. The umbilical cord is cut; the matrix cleared away. But Katherine Anne talks as brilliantly on the phone as in person; she interrupted me and distracted me. Anyway, who am I to lecture this woman of genius about her techniques, her spells? She must always know what she is doing, I think; at least she knows what she *has* done.

Some of the passengers on the Vera really are hateful or at least horrifying. For example, the half-dead old German who believes that to compensate for his own extremity God has conferred on him a power of saving others' lives by touching them with his terrible hand. He has himself pushed about in a wheel chair by his blond young nephew who loathes him. Concha, the youngest and prettiest of the Spanish dancers, who is enamored of blondness, cannot give herself to the sex-starved boy unless he pays her; her pimp-partner, Tito, would beat her if she did. She therefore tries to persuade the boy to murder the old man.

Another pair of the Spanish dancers, Lola and Tito, have twin children named Ric and Rac; male and female, though we can scarcely tell which is which. They seem more demonic than human, "infant gorgons intent on turning each other to stone"; and when their parents torture them for unsuccessfully stealing the noblewoman's pearl necklace, what we feel is scarcely pity; it is fear, fear of the worse and worse evil that cruelty to them will engender. The only thing that *they* are afraid of is separation; the pulling apart of their identical soul, if any.

There is one physical monster, pitiful and harmless, an S-shaped hunchback named Herr Glocken, and a kind of unfunny clown, a fat bellowing red-shirted political agitator. But these grotesque personages are on the very outer edges of the book; a little closer to our humanity than the professor's wife's vomiting white bulldog, but not much. They make a frame around the more important, less anomalous portraits; a baroque or rococo frame. This also differentiates Katherine Anne's novel from other novels of the grand-hotel type. She is not mainly interested in the patchwork and variegation of human nature. What fires and polarizes her mind are the themes (as I have said), the elements, the universal character- istics: mutual unkindness of lovers, gluttony and alcoholism, snob- bery and conformism, and political power, even that inevitably wielded by the captain of a ship at sea, and bourgeoisie versus des- titution, and immaturity versus senility—with scarcely ever a word about any of these subjects in the abstract, not a bit of intellec- tuality per se; only intelligence, constantly arising afresh from ob- servation.

There are superb episodes and quick little inner crises of this passenger and that, for better or worse. To suggest to you the range of Katherine Anne's fictive power, let me refer summarily to some of them; my memory leaping from peak to peak.—

The reverie of little Hans, the redheaded greenish-pale child of the alcoholic lawyer, terribly minding the body odor of his par- ents, but finding his own body odor sweet; wondering why in the one case, why not in the other.

The love-making of Amparo, the most talented of the dancers, and of her pimp, Tito, whom she truly loves; admirable alley-cat passion.

The confiscation of every sort of weapon on board, ordered by the captain after a fight in steerage, including the knives of a wood carver named Echegaray, the means of his livelihood, instruments of his art; he sits weeping piteously.

Dog overboard! it is the vomiting bulldog, flung over the rail by the fiendish twins. Man overboard! it is the poor wood carver, suicidal perhaps, but in any case giving his life to save the dog's life.

And just as his body, artificial respiration not having been at- tempted in time, is being lowered back into the sea with due rites, the entrance of three whales in the midst of the distant seascape, fountaining along.

The girls of Tenerife, where everyone goes ashore for a day, racing along with heavy water cans on their heads, thrillingly beau- tiful and provocative but chaste, with the Texan in vain pursuit of one of them.

The sad neurotic divorcee, when she has had a little too much to drink, and when the Texan is helplessly drunk, beating him in the face with her shoe, although she scarcely knows him; avenging herself by proxy for all her bad luck with inferior men.

❖

Having delivered the entire final typescript of *Ship of Fools,* Katherine Anne confessed to her editor, Seymour Lawrence, that she had scarcely been able to read it as reading matter; it remained work in progress for her even at that point. "Has it a form, a shape, as a whole?" she wanted to know.

"Yes," he answered, "it is like a great wave."

And so it is. It rises rather slowly and coldly at first, with an effect of distance, of remoteness from the reader's mind, indeed of smallness of scale. Gradually one is impressed, gradually one is enthralled, then lifted higher and higher, and submerged deeper and deeper, almost drowned. The wave breaks, at the end of Part II, with (let us say) the burial at sea of Echegaray, the heroic and/or suicidal wood carver. But by that time our responsiveness, intentness, and ravishment are like a wide shelving shore, a flat and curving beach. And for almost two hundred pages after the breaking of the wave, up it comes still, in long breakers or combers, some with subsidiary crests of great brilliance and violence.

Yes, like a wave. Incidentally, I note this peculiarity of Katherine Anne's style: she rarely indulges in figures of speech. One evening in my family circle I read about thirty of these pages aloud, and only one simile caught my eye: little greenish-pale Hans has freckles "like spots of iodine." No one since Stendhal has written so plainly, so glass-clearly; and my author carries about three times as much evidence of the senses as the author of *Le Rouge et le Noir* ever did, and she is much less inclined to infatuation and spite and eccentric argument than he was.

For a while after I have been reading her, my own way of writing —with impulsive images, with effects of cadence and pace, harmoniousness and dissonance, based on my way of reading things aloud, with ideas that I sometimes let language itself provide, and with a certain impressionism due to my having a memory at once excitable and faulty, resuccumbing to emotions of the past when I should be just mustering up the details—puts me to shame.

Now, to give a recapitulation and a close to this rambling study of my friend's lifework, let me quote another of her letters, somber once more, but blended with some of her malicious spirit; showing also her great virtue of steadfastness. It was written in Liège, Belgium, where she had been given a Fulbright Fellowship to teach at the university. In a letter to her I had vexed her with a weak reference of some sort to *my* age, and she chose to take it personally and struck back with an expression of some pathos and acerbity.

"When you and others younger than I, by I forget how many years, but a good number, complain of getting old, I think with dismay: What must they be thinking of me?"

Truly, I had not been (in that letter) thinking of her at all.

"I have had such a struggle to survive," she wrote, "so many illnesses that nearly crippled me when I was young, so many intimations of mortality before my time; I felt more decrepit at twenty-four than I have since; and now I do not have a proper sense of time. It does not chop itself like stove wood into decades convenient for burning. It is a vast drift in which I float, eddying back and forth, spinning round now and then, moving always towards no fixed point; but one day it will dissolve and drop me into the abyss."

In any case, she went on to say, she could never trust other people's eyes or judgments in the matter. "When I was sixteen, a woman of middle age, when told *my* age, said 'Ha, she'll never see eighteen again!' And when I was twenty-eight, a man, not at all malicious, guessed my age to be forty. Oddly enough, when I was fifty, another man, who loved me, also thought me forty; and I told him about the other guess, and wondered if I was never to escape from that particular decade."

Why, she asked me, should she worry about her visible years when others were so happy to do that worrying for her? Though she did not blame *me* for my worrisomeness, this sentence struck home.

She then told me her favorite story about age. She was lunching in

c

Hollywood with Charles Brackett, the distinguished screen writer
(who is an old friend of hers and of mine) and two important film
directors; a few tables away sat the then famous child actress
Margaret O'Brien, with her mother, her governess, her director, and
someone else. "And the three men at my table looked her over as
though she were a pony they were thinking of buying, and one of
them said, 'How old is she now?' and another answered, 'Six years
old,' and there was a pause, and then Charlie said, 'She looks older
than that.' There was a kind of nod-around among them and the
moment passed."

The concluding paragraph of this letter is a kind of prose poem:

"It is five o'clock, I am in a dowdy furnished apartment where
the keys don't turn, the gas cocks stick, the bathroom gadgets work
half way, the neighborhood is *tout-petit bourgeois,* the furnishings
are from the Belgian branch of Sears Roebuck, the place is subur-
ban, the wild yellow leaves are flying in a high bitter wind under a
smoky sky, and I have come to world's end, and what was my errand
here? There is nothing I wish to say to anyone here; does anybody
want to listen? But it does look as if here again, with all the unlike-
liness, the place and the time had met for me to sit at this table
three and one half feet square, and write something more of my
own."

Amen to that, says her perennially grateful reader. She did not in
fact write much in Liège. The autumn weather in that part of the
world and the Fulbright schedule of lectures proved too much for
her respiratory tract, and she had to come home. But it was not long
afterward that she settled herself in Connecticut and began to see
daylight as to her novel writing.

In that same letter of the dark night of her soul in Belgium, or
to be precise, teatime of her soul in Belgium, she declared that the
only disturbing thing about the passage of time, for her, was the
fact that she had four books all clearly conceived and partly begun
and waiting to be finished. Now, three to go! And now perhaps not
so many of us will care to bet against her.

Chapter Three

Somerset Maugham and Posterity

A rule of criticism: *"Do not dictate to your author; try to become him."*
—VIRGINIA WOOLF

Two or three times I have undertaken to write something about the lifework of Somerset Maugham, with somewhat the same slight bewilderment and difficulty each time. For a while all went well, in my mind, making my plan, according to the number of pages assigned to me and their intended destination and use, entertaining all the ideas that might conceivably and properly be applied in such a text; profuse and various themes, derived from a pleasant, friendly relationship and from a beneficial and enjoyable reading and rereading. But a profusion is not ideal when one has to produce a small prose work, as (come to think of it) Maugham himself has taught me, along with other lessons.

He used to say that he preferred not to read commentaries on himself. But every now and then, having weighed a thought or constructed a sentence, I would foolishly ask myself how it might strike him, evoking over the page his remarkable face, in which various elements of his character and effects of his life are (as you might say) interestingly inscribed or jotted down, in delicate crisscross wrinkles: his kind though choleric mouth; his fine eyes, one almost round and the other sharply focused with a slant, which you may see in Bernard Perlin's beautiful silverpoint portrait. Along with the feathery sound of my fountain pen on the paper, or between fits and starts of my typewriter, I seemed to hear his soft but authoritative voice, making an appropriate but not always very tactful remark.

Henry James said, in I cannot think what connection, that when a work of creative literature is very formally presented, escorted into the reader's mind with too many arguments and considerations, it is like having a dinner guest brought to the house by policemen. (This is not exactly quoted; he put it more volubly and portentously, in his style.) Nevertheless, when he himself came to collect his lifework, he posted prefaces in every volume, an entire constabulary of prefaces, armed to the teeth with intellect and imposingly turned out, with gold braid, and with spit and polish.

Maugham has written a good many little forewords, models of informality, pertinence, and good humor. Young writers especially ought to look for them and to give them thought; likewise his essay, "On Style (After Reading Burke)," and the little piece upon his sixty-fifth birthday, and his brief address at the Library of Congress when he presented the manuscript of *Of Human Bondage* to this nation, and a meditation upon his seventieth birthday, which is at the end of the volume entitled *A Writer's Notebook*.

Never having had any conviction that he was a genius, all his life he has used his head about everything having to do with writing, which cannot be said of many writers. He modestly and consciously learned to write; therefore it is easier to learn from his remarks, however cursory or circumstantial, than from more expansive, exciting documents of the vocation of letters such as James's prefaces. Maugham characteristically, hints more than he expounds; which is just as well, if your interest is personal and serious. You can make what you wish of his helpfulness, to suit your case.

You must not be misled by his rather small and offhand manner in this confidential expository writing; the English gentleman's self-satisfying modesty. Remember also, when his attitude seems to be inflexible in some sense, or when he harps on his preferences and theories, that sometimes this is his way of criticizing fellow writers whose reputations appear to him undeserved or unsound. All his life he has had to share the literary scene with various genius-types, posturing and boasting. This has inclined him to a sort of extreme unpretentiousness. Others have made a glamour of their pure artistry and integrity, without producing much; all blow and no go. He, on the contrary, has set up as a principle, even a duty, that nonstop productivity which comes naturally to him, and which he certainly enjoys, and which has profited him. Now and then he has seemed to suggest that anyone not capable of producing a great deal, or not willing to do so, might as well give up literature. Others have talked, in season and out, of their inspiration and dedication, message and messianic feeling. All or almost all his remarks have been carefully couched in terms of the mere profession of writing, the career of writing, even the pursuit of fortune by that means.

No insincerity in any of this, mind you! But a man cannot live for half a century in a great constant limelight, sought after and indiscreetly questioned in society, and subject to the changeable and illogical standards of the literary journalism of the day, without developing some self-consciousness.

For a long time he was the dean of novelists writing in English. By which advertisement-like statement I mean that for more than a quarter of a century he was the one, the only one, who had the admiration of an elite of highly cultivated, sophisticated readers and of a sufficient number of good fellow writers, with increasing influence on the younger ones, and at the same time gave great pleasure to, made sense to, and affected the lives of, a million or more ordinary mortals. What else is deanship? It is never a matter of unanimity. In the condition of contemporary literary culture especially, a small superior group in agreement or in coalition with the multitude is apt to overrule or overwhelm any objection that may start up in medium intellectual circles. Evidently this is what happened about Maugham, leaving perhaps a vague resentment in the minds of some of those who might have been expected to mold (and indeed unmold) contemporary opinion, and who scarcely did so in his case, who carped in vain.

For about a decade after World War II he seemed the most controversial of literary figures as well as the most successful. As literary controversies go, this had a certain distinction, in that nothing of miscellaneous thought was at issue, neither politics nor morals nor any other ideology. It was all about the narrative art; whether or not he deserved to be called a great or even a fine narrative artist, or only an ordinary producer of magazine stories and books for the lending libraries; whether his career has been a true vocation, or simply a case of ambition and energetic endeavor crowned with odd success; whether the shelfful of his fiction is of a high category or just a present plaything for the mind of a commonplace throng.

Unfortunately the arguments pro and con have not been presented at full length or with sufficient clarity and conviction. I cannot think of another important man of letters about whom there is so little to read, of any interest. In both the praise and the blame a few conventional terms keep appearing, as in a kaleidoscope around and around; and in the past decade or so the blamers have shown more verve and self-assurance than the praisers. Our diligent book reviewers, perhaps having written themselves dry about him long since, have reacted lassitudinously to the almost annual succession of his books. Certain of our noteworthy serious critics (Edmund Wilson for one), offended in taste or dissatisfied in intellect, entirely lost their patience with this or that recent volume and seemed peculiarly to be trying to shame the rest of us out of our enjoyment.

As a rule perhaps one ought not to take cognizance of this kind of adverse opinion, or of the group thinking and conversation of intellectuals which it may be taken to reflect. It cannot be replied to in any detail without giving it emphasis and further circulation. But in the instance of Maugham at present it seems worth while because he is to be blamed for some of the confusion and the repetitiousness.

In all his confidential expository writing he has presented himself, or, one might say, typed himself, as having only a limited specific talent; as not knowing or thinking much about anything outside his field of professional dramaturgy and narration; as having no vision of the state of the world, no psychological science, no profundity; and as not admitting any intention in his writing except to entertain. "The purpose of art is to please." He should have been warned of the riskiness of oversimplification and understatement in an age of advertising.

For his least favorable critics have borrowed a good part of his representation of himself, even parroting certain phrases and epithets, belittlingly, and to the advantage of their preferred school of modern writing, whatever it may be. In their aggressiveness, his defense position has been turned around; as if it were some bit of Maginot Line with forces of the enemy established in it by mischance or by mistake. The confusion is great, quid pro quo; and those who disapprove of him attack one so fiercely, in the regular uniform of his thought turned inside out, and with the passwords— writing is a livelihood, fiction is a pastime, the mixture as before —that one often feels obliged to fight him too, before one can give him his due praise.

Some people of course are real believers in unpopularity, mistrusters of success; and the recently booming market for whatever bears Maugham's signature, and the adaptations of the motion-picture industry, and all the publicity and the publicizing, have made these people disrespectful. His detractors have him on their minds a good deal, and feel romantically about him in their way; they are anti-fans. In ordinary social intercourse one hears far more talk of any sort of relative failure on his part—when a given novel can be said to have fallen short of the standard set by some previous novel, or perhaps has sold a few hundred thousand copies less— than of the successes of other writers. I may seem sarcastic, but it is not my intention to suggest that the opponents to Maugham are all of a superficial or unreasonable spirit. Certainly they are not. Among my best friends there are three or four whose opinion of authors as a rule tallies with mine, whose cultivation and judgment I appreciate exceedingly, with whom I cannot have a civil conversation about this one author, so zealous or jealous have they become, in their resolve not to have him overestimated.

But the poor criticism and the captious momentary talk have only increased Maugham's general celebrity, emphasized his unswerving strength of mind in his own way, and given further advertisement to his tranquil, uninfluenced, unceasing production. The fact is that the anti-Maugham party have not really been able to put up a candidate of their own for the specific position in contemporary letters—the combined artistic and popular position—which they are so impatient of his continuing to hold, decade after decade. All these years they seem never to have found themselves in agreement with the great public about any contemporary writer, nor succeeded in bringing the collectivity around to the style of writing they do care for.

❖

Now here let me cast my vote with the majority, for Maugham, beginning with a general statement of admiration, a profession of faith. I believe that his best books, perhaps eight or ten volumes, will endure for posterity and be read with continuing benefit and pleasure. Except for the extreme jeopardies facing Western civilization as a whole, I feel no uneasiness whatever about his having his sufficient fame in the outcome of the century; his share of what is called, in rather old-fashioned writers' parlance, immortality.

In the meantime a really considerable slump of his reputation is to be expected; something more than the restlessness against him in literary society and the carping of professional critics. It is normal, melancholy though it must be for any author who has lived to see it. Presently, a great many of those who for years have delighted in him above all other storytellers will have had their fill, and they will forget to recommend him to the younger generation. Already his imitators have somewhat coarsened and debased the forms and devices of his fiction, so that one looks upon certain of the beauties of it with a dull, dissipated eye; he no longer gets credit for uniqueness.

And meanwhile his successors, it is to be hoped—those who are not too idle or freakish or unfortunate—have been getting set with types of literature to suit themselves, with departures from his way of thinking. In subject matter especially, various frontiers have been opening up continually: new ruling passions in the ascendant,

and up-to-date strengths of mind and weaknesses of character, which
Maugham in old age could not be expected to understand very
well, which his perfected forms and practiced techniques would not
have suited in any case; concepts of what is desirable in life, and
what is hateful or insufferable, differing radically from those he has
exemplified in a hundred various tales and indeed in his own life
story.

Do I make him seem older than he is in fact? Never a muscular,
sanguine, egotistical man, for many years he has been acutely
conscious of his age. Infants born when he first began to complain
of it, in *The Summing Up* (1938), have grown to manhood, and he
is still producing books, only a little less regularly and ambitiously;
still enjoying his life to some extent; but still dwelling on the
solemn theme, the note of farewell. I think this is a trait of literary
artists; as work of art does actually offer the possibility and degree
of survival after death, it is apt to lead to some imagination of
the time far ahead. My impression is that as life has worn on, and
his career has seemed to be drawing to a close, Maugham has often
wondered how posterity was going to view his career and collected
works, though I have never heard him speak of it.

With praise of him by serious critics so insufficient in these last
decades of his life (a mountain of clippings indeed, but more than
half of it quibbling, unimpressed, or unenlightened) and the word
of mouth of the intellectuals so little in unison, likely to make only
a weak, jangled reverberation in the period to come, and no very
remarkable record of official or academic honors—for he has not
been greatly indulged in this way either—what is going to lead the
good reader of posterity to take the trouble of procuring and reading and re-evaluating his books? Curiosity, I suppose, above all.
What made this man so beloved by the unliterary, unofficial, unaca-
demic humanity of his time? And as it has been a crucial historic
time, what can his popularity have signified, and what good or harm
was there in it? So few contemporary men of letters have kept their
public for three decades, with a continuous production and increasing sale of books the while; attention will be attracted to him by
this. He will be part of a history lesson.

And when it comes to reading for pleasure or for any personal emotion or edification, he will not have, in (let us say) the middle of the twenty-first century, all the competition that appears at present. A quantity of literature, especially fiction, vanishes in thin air. Some of the work of famed contemporaries of his has already been shelved; and in almost all of it we can see the ephemeral and perishable elements. Any little random enumeration and review of them is suggestive of the relative soundness of his narrative art, indicative of its greater staying power. In the various ways in which they have proved weak, he took the trouble to develop particular strength. The mistakes they made, the predilections they indulged in: these were what he most severely forbade himself and guarded against. I gather that in his formative years he studied everything they were doing; then considered, in his reading of all the still-valid fiction of the past, every sort of parallel; carried the lesson forward in speculation upon the future; and regularly applied it to his day's work, most earnestly desiring not to have written in vain.

H. G. Wells, for example, so hard-working and serious, so influential for many years, wrote like a newspaper; and since he rashly prophesied things in every volume, what he got right will seem platitudinous and what he got wrong, absurd. At the other extreme, the fine fiction of the period has been characterized by a certain remoteness of subject matter, elusive and allusive; and obscured by linguistic innovations, a playing with words, like poetry. It is hard to foresee how so luxurious a fabric of writing will endure; there is not much precedent in literary history. Half the work of wonderful Joyce surely will revert to the universities; recondite crossword puzzles. Not a learned type of reader myself, I feel that the best novels of Ford Madox Ford and Maurice Baring might be appreciated if they were read at all; but they are likely to be overlooked, their careers in their lifetime having gone so modestly. As I remarked just now, there is more than the pecuniary advantage in having sold like hot cakes; readers long afterward wonder why. E. M. Forster will certainly last; only five novels, and (what a mystery it is) none at all since 1924!

Thus very naturally, with so little early twentieth-century literature that will still seem readable, the wondering future reader will turn to the wide shelfful of the collected works of Maugham; the one of all his generation the least like a genius, the one most emphatically disavowing any such pretension. Down out of the attic of literary history his narrative art will be brought, as though it were some piece of inherited furniture that had gone out of fashion for a time; comfortably functional, solidly constructed, with not much gilt on it but finely carved.

And the use and the enjoyment of reading him many years hence, I believe, will not be very different from our own at present—precisely because he has been sagacious and cautious in his handling of themes of the day which grow commonplace or obscure; because he has been content to write a pure prosaic prose without any remarkable invention of new ways of expressing things; because he has written a great amount, so as to constitute a distinct Maugham-world into which his readers can enter, of which they can learn the idiom and the implications, each volume helping them to understand the next, building up their response to the next; and because he has discovered and devised story after story worth telling for the story's sake, the one and only thing he has boasted of himself. The love of narration as such evidently is elemental and permanent in human nature.

◆

If you have been following Maugham's own line about his work too ingenuously, or reading the current criticism with entire respect, you may have assumed that it is, if not altogether thoughtless, of a very limited intellectual interest. Now I will dispute this, and give you some illustration and analysis of the kind of thought I find in his fiction, or (as I suppose Maugham would prefer to have me say) the kind of meaning I read into it.

Without exaggeration! I maintain only that in all his best stories and novels there is an underlying, somewhat hidden significance, pervasive spiritual sense, and important moral counsel, and general view of life and vision of the present world—supplementary to that sole purpose of entertainment continually announced by him—which will repay whatever trouble of intellect you may take in your reading. You will be the wiser for it. Presumably he is not aware of all that he puts in a work of fiction; but I feel sure that he is always conscious of more than he cares to talk about.

In his lifetime he has had an extraordinary range of experience of the world, often in contact with great personages of his generation, sometimes concerned with historic events. Also year after year all sorts of persons, struck by the tolerant spirit and sagacity of his writing, have kept bringing him their report or confession of those extreme occurrences of private life in which modern human nature so often strangely manifests itself, unveils itself. He has a reading and speaking knowledge of five languages, and has read everything, including all the classics of religion and metaphysics, studiously. He is the most serious of men, seeking the general truth in all things, holding himself responsible for his every belief or disbelief, never fooling himself or others, thinking hard. It would be odd indeed if his production of books, even unpretentious stories, were as light-weight as the common estimation has it.

To be sure, he has a strict sense of the different literary forms, putting limitations upon his content in each of them accordingly. Not only *The Summing Up* but various other volumes of nonfiction have been somewhat in the vein of autobiography, therefore not appropriate for any display of intellect as an end in itself. In many a story he has made use of the first person singular; and then, quite as modestly, as though it were reminiscence or truthful expository writing, he has allowed himself only that extent of thoughtfulness, intelligence rather than intellect, which could be referred to his own character, within plausible radius of himself. In a novel of course there is always something or other subject to interpretation in terms of economics and the social sciences, psychology, and so on. But he has kept all this somewhat out of evidence, according to his dear tenets of simplicity and clarity; in any case kept it out of vocabulary.

Now, some readers depend a great deal on verbal associations and style in general, as indications of seriousness of thought: massive abstruse specialized words, complicatedness and elaboration in other ways as well, and a mysterious solemnity. There is never anything like that in Maugham. He irately disapproves of it in others' work, even in the writing of technical philosophy and the accounts which scientists give of their research and speculation. Years ago, I remember his taking the matter up with certain eminent professors and a biologist or two in person, advocating a less self-indulgent style. In all his mature period his own way of expressing ideas has been direct and plain and pithy, somewhat in emulation of Dryden and Swift and their followers, but with constant observance of the rhythm of informal modern conversation and with some easy colloquialism.

If you are looking for deep thoughtfulness in a story or a novel by Maugham, you cannot expect to have it underlined for you as such. You must use your head, in order not to mistake simplicity for insignificance; and you must learn to recognize his idea in that envelope of reality in which ideas do actually generate, in incident and in dialogue and in little sequences of cause and effect. Also you will need to read somewhat slowly, pondering as you go along, and to bear it all in mind for some time afterward, weighing it against your own experience and ideas and feelings. Otherwise Maugham is not the author for you, and may never be.

If, on the other hand, you are the more natural, easy-minded, unreasoning man, and what you want is the mere spinning of a yarn, now a kind of myth against some exotic background, now a pitiful or exciting bit of low life, now a humorous scene of high life, to pass the time—with perhaps just a little inspiration or revelation incidentally adhering to your mind when this or that feature of the plot chances to correspond to some recollection or present preoccupation of your own—well, you have Maugham's explicit blessing. You are the reader he writes for, by his own account.

For my part, I like works of fiction to have meaning, the deeper and the more consequential the better; and unless I find this to my satisfaction, fiction reading amuses me very little and leaves me discontented. Story form can convey a greater and more accurate truth

—as to human nature in its various manifestations and inhibitions, and general human fate of the day and age—than any abstract or generalized literature, dogma or dialectic or deduction of science. The actual perusal of a book is only a part of the literary experience. By mere mechanism of the mind, the time I pass in recalling and reflecting upon what I have read is greater than the time it takes to read. When, with no difficulty or superfluity or prolixity, I have been given something worth thinking about, I love the writing in question, and the writer; this is my chief reason for admiring Maugham.

The thought in Maugham's novels is mostly ethics, religion, or the psychology of creative endeavor. *The Moon and Sixpence*, for example, has to do with the strange compelling destiny of the artist ahead of his time, to whom moral defects, unkindness toward others, even brutality and megalomania, may prove helpful in becoming great; as in the case of Gauguin. *Cakes and Ale*—which I once heard Maugham himself recommend as his own first choice of his novels —gives a picture of the literary life, with assorted types of men of letters, the celebrity and the young novice, the real creator and the parasitic literary journalist, and others; it also shows the essential goodness of a sexually loose woman and her benign influence on the men around her. *The Painted Veil* is a portrayal of the unhappiness resulting from irresponsible adultery; the beneficial psychotherapeutic effect of doing good to others; and the appeal of Roman Catholicism when one is unhappy.

To be sure, none of this will greatly impress or entirely satisfy any true intellectual. It is not that absolute learnedness and virtuosity of mind which Thomas Mann, for example, in the novels of his old age, exercised almost as proudly and far-rangingly as Santayana in his eclectic philosophy or Toynbee in his world history. On the other hand, what Maugham has to offer is not frivolous matter; and the point of thinking, I take it, is not quantity of thought but rightness, relevance, and indeed helpfulness.

◆

Christmas Holiday is unique in Maugham's fiction in that its theme is sociological and political. It is the one of his fifteen-odd novels that has meant most to me personally. As you may recall, it is the tale of a happy-natured and fortunate English youngster named Charlie, holidaying in Paris. He has a less fortunate friend there named Simon, who introduces him to a pathetic Russian-refugee prostitute calling herself Lydia. Presently she confesses her true identity—she is the wife of Robert Berger, a notorious murderer— then, little by little, narrates their love and his evil deed.

Upon its first publication in 1939, I think that the majority of Maugham's readers did not respond with their customary enthusiasm; as though determined to shut their eyes a few more months to what its entire plot and all its characterizations portended. Also those who wrote the criticisms of it missed its grave implications, not stopping to think. Which is no final matter; books of the greatest importance, even masterpieces, even classics, often have had to wait awhile for their high rating and proper interpretation. For example, take the case of Stendhal.

Nineteen hundred and thirty-nine, the end of the great lull in modern history; the moment of awakening from the sweetest, most heedless sleep humanity ever indulged in! As of that date, *Christmas Holiday* had greater significance than any comparable reading matter, I think: social significance. The phrase is outworn, I know, but here we have exactly what it was meant for.

Maugham in this slight volume, less than a hundred thousand words long, with his air of having nothing on his mind except his eight characters—how they came together and what happened and what they said and how they felt—explains more of the human basis of fascism and nazism and communism than anyone else has done: the self-fascinated, intoxicated, insensible character of all that new leadership in Europe; the womanish passivity of the unhappy masses dependent on it and devoted to it; the Anglo-Saxon bewilderment in the matter, which still generally prevails; and the seeds of historic evil yet to come, not at all extirpated in World War II but rather multiplied and flung with greater profusion in no less receptive soil farther afield, even beyond Europe. Europe the starting point, the womb and the cradle, as in fact it has been for millenniums.

It is a political allegory as plain as *Candide;* though far tougher and less pleasant, less cocksure. Our part of the twentieth century is harder to diagnose than the eighteenth ever was. Young Charlie is a representative of that prosperous and liberal middle class which, prior to World War II, was the predominant governing class of Europe. Robert Berger typifies the new dictating class which developed out of World War I and has had a setback in World War II but apparently still has a future, with ex-middle-class Simon attached to him as brain-truster and propagandist. Lydia personifies the desperate and infatuated common people.

All of us in the remoter and temporarily securer part of Anglo-Saxondom, are Charlies; and how can we help shivering, as he does, when we hear Simon's propaganda and apologia and forecast—to my mind, the most brilliant pages Maugham has ever written—and, worse still, when we sense the relatedness and the awful understanding between the multitudinous Lydias and increasing Robert Bergers in the world? Paired off everywhere: the hopeless and the ruthless, the victim and the victimizer, Duce and dupe, Fuehrer and follower, commissar and worker, hero and hero-worshiper, villain and villain-worshiper; antithetical mortal types! Somehow each appears to be the other's fate, the other's mate; in a kind of complicity, in cahoots. Is it a different humanity from ours? Or only a different stage of the same great reign of terror?

It is painful reading matter, I tell you, that midnight when in the excitement of having murdered, Robert Berger makes love to Lydia so passionately and insatiably that he seems to her godlike; and as she tells it later on—when she is leading a degraded, woebegone life, with her notion of atonement—we sense that she thinks it was worth it.

Robert Berger of course is amorality personified, because he has found that it pays well, and out of overweening conceit, and for the fun of it. But be not sentimental! Lydia is amoral too, in her grand passion and her despair. She has no belief in anything except love:

the more extravagant the quantity of love the better. Call it romantic if you like, it is a state of spirit almost exactly corresponding to
a convulsion, or animal reaction of the body. Harmless and well-
meaning as she is, observe how complacently she yields herself to
his excitement of evil derivation, flattering herself with it, asking
nothing else of him. She merges her soul with his. Indeed Simon is
the only character in this book who has a distinct feeling of right
and wrong, or any sense of the consequences; and Simon is half-
crazy, in self-pity based on his boyhood and in bitterness against
authority, no matter what, come what may.

It is not a propaganda novel. No mention of Germany, for example; or of unfortunate Italy; or of Russia, for that matter, except
what Lydia remembers of the bygone days of Lenin's revolution.
No particular criticism of the tumbledown ancient structure of Europe; no blueprint of ameliorated future. Only the human equation:
the fortunate and innocent youngster who has his little vision of evil
but not the remotest notion what is to be done about it; the un-
healthy-minded intellectual who believes in evil; the girl of the
lower depths who endures evil and apparently always will, utterly
discouraged and incorrigibly inclined to mysticism; and Robert
Berger the evildoer, born evil; and the old woman who because she
gave him birth blames herself forever, and lies and cheats to save
him.

Add it up and draw conclusions from it if you like, as best you
can: add and subtract and multiply and divide and subdivide! In
various staff headquarters and foreign offices and peace conferences,
better heads than yours and mine are aching with the emergency
and the mystery of it still, today, this minute; and I hope to God
that some of them have read this book. On the continent of Europe
which is, after all, the most consequential portion of the world, at
least half the women and the homosexuals are Lydias, hundreds of
thousands of the men are Simons; and what of the Robert Bergers?
Law and order have been, more or less, restored. A good number of
the worst ones, the mass murderers and super-thieves and the more
impassioned liars, have been caught red-handed, repressed, impris-
oned, executed; that much the victory of 1945 accomplished. But the

unlucky unwholesome multitudes upon whom they battened—and by whom they were given their strength—are still the same, in a plight worse than ever, with daydreams wilder. They are more to be pitied than blamed, yes, but none the less dangerous for all that. Passive to their passionate ones, in maleness and femaleness entangled, in the European mood of love-death, Liebestod, presently they may once more bring forth the leaders appropriate to their circumstances, the types whom the weak love and the morbid admire; and then what?

The last line in *Christmas Holiday* is: "the bottom had fallen out of his world," that is, the holidaying English boy's world. Now naturally almost all Europeans say as much; and Americans echo it. For evidently Europe is the bottom of our world also; but an echo is never a sufficient answer.

Now, with no intent of sophistry, to you who have followed my Maugham interpretation and my little thread of argument almost to the end, I say this.—Never pretend to have made more sense of a novel or to have found more meaning in it than your actual experience of the reading of it has entailed. Never attach more importance to a novel than you feel. Let me not bully you about this novel that I love.

I remember that when it first appeared, and my friends were reading it and more or less enjoying it, and I spoke of its dread allegory and prophetic sense, a number of them said they had no idea what I was talking about. A year or so later I brought the subject up in conversation with Maugham. As a rule he dislikes listening to anyone's opinion of his writing. I think this is not just shyness but also a kind of contrariety. If you quibble with him, he wants to fight back, even unfairly, haughtily. The least excess of praise, on the other hand, only stimulates in him the artist's deep and painful discontent with everything he has done to date. Which is one of the important nerve centers of art. But upon this occasion he did not shut me up. I outlined all the significance of his book as it appeared to me; I alluded to the various disagreeing or obtuse readers.

Maugham said, "Certainly I had those things in the back of my mind while I was writing it. But if I had insisted on them I should have spoiled my story. It is not the business of a novelist to tell his readers what they are to think of his characters and his plot. If you want your work of fiction to be read, and you have some point that you wish to make, you must bring it in discreetly. Your reader may not take your meaning, or it may not interest him. You must let him read for his pleasure."

◆

Now I want to examine one of his short stories, still with my characteristic fervent interest in what it signifies or points to; a very different thing from the dread allegory of revolutionary Europe. It is my favorite story, at least for the moment: "The Treasure." May I point out that it was written in 1942, a time when Maugham's powers of creation might indeed have been expected to be dwindling, running on at their ease in mere competence, upon accrued reputation—as he himself would sometimes remark, with others echoing?

It is an incident of sexual intercourse between a middle-aged celibate gentleman and his perfect domestic servant, just one night and the morning after; an indiscreet and yet, as it turns out, harmless romance. Behold them, in the slightest and quickest possible account of the matter, like a snapshot with the light evenly diffused, not an ugly shadow of a single feature, not a line out of focus: the good mild man, Richard Harenger, habit-bound, but worthy of our respect in many ways; and the faultless, quiet, and somewhat mousy woman, Mrs. Pritchard, the treasure.

Though it has a charming humor, you might call it a lonely kind of thing to read; you feel as isolated with them as they are with each other. They do not speak of the other inhabitants of their world, that is, their two worlds: the men he works with, the people she goes back to when she is not working. This indeed they have in common: both of them are of that order of human beings who have to be judged primarily on whether they are good at their jobs or not, and they both are; it is an important premise. Having read to

the end—average reading time about twenty minutes—you are perhaps as well acquainted with them as they are with each other; although, as employer and employee, they have lived together a good
while before the quick exceptional impulse of manhood and
womanhood comes to them, that one night. The morning brings a
little panic, at least to the male breast. Companionableness of the
body in the midnight hour is all very well, but they are not in the
least kindred spirits. How could they be, stationed in life as they
respectively are? But she says nothing, and he thanks his stars.
According to your morality and your recollections, it may give you
a lump in your throat or it may make you blush.

On its very small scale it is a perfectly formed story, as it were
Chopin in words, though the words are all so prosaic: the briefest
prelude, then the nocturne for four pages, then the aubade for a
page and a half; all in perfect pitch, and in exact contemporaneity,
and pertinent to everyone or almost everyone in some way.

A couple of no particular interest, no oddity at all: what charms
us? what gives them their breath of life? I think it is the fact that
each of them has a particular morality, that of the male and that
of the female, that of the property holder and that of the wage
earner, and perhaps other dissimilarities besides; and in spite of
the conventions and the selfish considerations and the points of
pride fixed in their minds, it is not static in either case. You feel it
trembling in the balance; you observe its positive and negative
poles, prosaic realities in the morning, relaxation and risk in the
dead of night.

The humor of it—need I say?—is the matter of the classes and
the masses, in the particular small unorganized category of domestic employment. In the more disclassed and democratic time to
come, they tell us, such a man as Harenger, if he requires the particular service that Mrs. Pritchard rendered so exemplarily that
night, may have to marry her; which may or may not prove a
happier arrangement. This is a kind of joke rarely offered by
Maugham; what the French call pince-sans-rire, that is, pinching
without laughing.

When a characteristic contemporary incident is as well told as this—no matter how slight and smiling and pastime-like—it can be compared to one of those clocks which need no winding up. It takes its movement from the general current of the day and age, alternating current indeed; and with its silvery tinkle exactly on time, of its time, you hear also a regretful echo and a prophetic echo.

Twenty minutes of reading matter for pleasure, it expresses other things as well: that very modern hypocrisy about sex the point of which is to avoid responsibility, to save oneself trouble; and a form of virtuousness of which many people are quite proud, though if the truth were told it amounts only to lack of sexual energy or lack of fancy; and that state of late middle age when we lose hope of love, perhaps even the faculty of loving, when a little pleasure is all we have a right to expect, and a little goes a long way, and (let us face it) even pleasure does not mean as much to us as convenience and comfort. It is as expressive of homosexual relationships as of heterosexual, perhaps more so.

◆

When I began this essay I fancied that I might refrain from writing about *Of Human Bondage,* the novel that first made Maugham famous as a novelist, having come to the conclusion that everyone I know appreciates it just a little more than I do. A good many men of letters pride themselves on their not liking this and that; not I. But if I were to disqualify myself and skip over so famous a work, who knows what conclusions my readers might jump to. In fact I am well aware of its great qualities, and its shortcomings seem to me significant. Published in 1915, it is now regarded as a modern classic, and rightly; but whereas Maugham's other mature novel writing is definitely characteristic of the twenties and the thirties, the modernity of this is questionable in some way, might almost have been done at the turn of the century. It is naturalistic and convincing in the way of George Moore and Gissing and Hardy, indeed the way of Maugham's own early *Liza of Lambeth* and *Mrs. Craddock;* but at the same time it is a narrative of mood and neurosis and symbolism. But, although it is a spacious and copious work, life does not seem to flow through it freely or completely. It is somewhat willfully composed, according to preconception and thesis. It has, as you might say, north light in lieu of sunshine, and a sort of blackness here and there, as a substitute for shadowy depths and real mystery.

In theme and plot it comprises several elements of very general interest and emotional appeal. First and foremost, it provides an image of youth. In epochs of social transition and readjustment of morals, a type of self-important immaturity is apt to appeal powerfully to the imagination of the younger generation; for example, Saint-Preux, Werther, Lord Byron (all Hamlets, in a way). Because they were so representative and influential in their time the historian will always have to consider them, although they are perhaps more dead than alive on our bookshelves. Correspondingly in this century we have had Buddenbrook, and the Shropshire Lad, and just lately the suicidal and mystical Glass boy. Maugham's Philip Carey comes in between.

The device with which the work concludes, that of an aesthetic object with spiritual connotations—as the poor limping and victimized protagonist's understanding of himself develops, he likens it to the design of a Persian carpet—is reminiscent of Henry James, is it not? (This observation might irritate Maugham or it might make him laugh.)

The weakness of *Of Human Bondage*, at least from an American standpoint, is the class consciousness that runs all through it. Philip never, never forgets that Mildred is lowlier-born than he; but then (it seems to me) the reader never forgets that he is lowlier-born himself than quite a lot of other people. It is an atmosphere not of dog eat dog, but of dog snub dog. Perhaps this is not an outworn theme in England. The welfare state and the opening up of education have brought on a slight recrudescence of snobbery and counter-snobbery, which the success of the so-called angry young writers and the new cult of D. H. Lawrence illustrate.

The great thing in *Of Human Bondage* is the love story: an impassioned mutual misunderstanding and stranglehold of two pathetic young persons, as painful as cats, as awkward as dogs. The relationship never altogether explains itself, but it seems very real, and it is unforgettable and instructive.

Although the outer reality of the book was all obviously drawn from Maugham's remembrances of his own youth, I have never sensed anything particularly autobiographical about this main matter of the relationship between a loving booby and an unrequiting strumpet. Perhaps he came upon it in Hazlitt, along with many other germs of fiction incidentally expended, unwritten.—"The contempt of a wanton for a man who is determined to think her virtuous. . . . He officiously reminds her of what she ought to be; and she avenges the galling sense of her lost character on the fool who still believes in it."

Maugham's particular admiration of Hazlitt is excellently expounded in the essay entitled "On Style" which I have already recommended; but with little or no portraiture of the great Romantic essayist, no retelling of his ill-starred love life, in which, as between Philip and Mildred, the distress of sex was complicated by class prejudice.

Certainly the subject matter of unpleasurable, unbeneficial, hopeless love, roughly speaking sado-masochistic, transcends in importance the more sentimental and idealistic contents of *Of Human Bondage:* the egocentric immaturity, the numinous aestheticism, the social tension, and it is less apt to seem old-timely and inconsequential to future readers.

The style of *Of Human Bondage* is unsatisfactory to me. It is neither relaxed and conversational, which, roughly speaking, has been Maugham's later way of writing, nor finely measured and embellished; it is only eloquent and copious. Rarely indeed is any sentence fitted to the thought in question, drawn tight, and sent swiftly and airily, arrowlike, to its target. Instead, this is the kind of prose that just keeps encircling its content, sincerely and tirelessly, until of course at last the reader understands, without really having to concentrate or make an effort, and without the particular pleasure of illumination or disclosure at any point. Did Maugham at that time lack dexterity and definiteness? Certainly in his later novels, even those that followed *Of Human Bondage* in short order, he demonstrated every sort of skill and precision. This one major work he seems to have composed for readers of a somewhat slow and passive mentality, needing to have things spelled out.

❖

With reference to the lifelong labor of literature Maugham has said that he was greatly influenced by a fact about Darwin which, at an impressionable age, he read in some book or heard someone tell: Darwin never worked more than three hours a day. Reflecting on this—ambitious but reasonable youth that he was—he came to the conclusion that if biological science could be revolutionized and a great deal of the ideology and the ethics of the era altered at that comfortable rate of daily endeavor, surely it would suffice for him to earn a living and make a name for himself as a playwright and story writer and novelist.

A willful man, he seems to have persisted in this as well as other plans of those early days. He rouses from sleep at dawn or soon after; but he brings no manuscript or even notebook into his bedroom, and does not go to his writing room until he has read awhile and breakfasted at leisure. Just before one o'clock he steps into the living room, ready for his cocktail and lunch; pleased with himself if the work has gone forward, clear in his conscience anyway. Approximately Darwin's three hours . . .

But in order not to set him up as a dangerous example to any ambitious but lazy literary youngster—and not to give aid and comfort to those of the intelligentsia who maintain that he has had it easy, and all his renown is but good luck—I will give a little more information. Listen to this, and try to imagine yourself working as he does. Week in and week out, year after year, in whatever circumstances—though surrounded by frivolity, though assailed by bothers and anxieties, and touched upon occasion as all men are by exceeding affection or pity or self-pity or anger—regularly every morning he goes to his desk and labors at his writing. For months at a time he will not skip a day. One day I did see him in the living room before lunch, grumpily seated by the fireplace; he had a bad toothache, and even then he was engrossed in a heavy laborious tome, preparatory to the composition of something theological or historical.

Indeed in his middle life he made some voyage every year or so, notably to the Orient and around the South Seas, in what must have seemed a carefree manner. But think of the cargo of fiction he brought back upon each return voyage! He was not wasting his time. To this day the spirit of travel for travel's sake (and story's sake) has scarcely calmed down in him. Even in the city, with details of publishing or other commitments of his career to attend to, also when he takes vacations in the summer or weekends with friends— except when actually in transit, in the train or in the plane—regularly almost every morning he goes to some desk or substitute table and works awhile.

This is not drudgery, I know, but it is something that for my part I should find harder to endure and sustain: control, inner tension, and in fact, faith, and faith in oneself—and I dare say it is more to the purpose of literature in the long run than that way of pent-up ambition occasionally overflowing, rushing, making up for lost time, which gives one the feeling of being a genius, or that way of desperate engagement and deadline with stimulants and sedatives and hell to pay, which is the habit of so many contemporary authors.

Furthermore, in Maugham's case, the time he spends at his desk is only a part of the labor. All his stories and novels have been worked out in his mind before he ever takes his neat pen in hand. Someone has told him an incident of real life, perhaps no more than an impressive utterance or gesture at some crucial moment. That is the commencement, as it were the grain of sand in the bivalve. But real life never seems to him as good as imagination, at least not as good to write about. Therefore he ponders, and sometimes years pass before he is able to devise the fulfillment and change, the different ending, the superstructure of moral implication, which will make all the difference between reality and art.

Then he begins searching for the bits and pieces of everyone he has ever known which can be molded into fictitious beings capable of doing or experiencing whatever it is that he has to tell; adding subordinate episodes as they may enhance or clarify the main matter, and drawing all into one unit; regulating whatever faults of implausibility or contradiction may develop; and deciding upon the order of narration most natural to it, most effective for it. All this goes on in his head; not in Darwin's three hours but in the other twenty-one, when he rouses too early in the morning, when he sits by the fire, when he is taking short salubrious walks.

There is a touching page in his memoir of the beginning of World War II, *Strictly Personal,* bearing upon this matter of the advance preparation of his fiction. In the disaster of France he was in personal peril; the Germans having learned from his volume of stories entitled *Ashenden* that he had served as a secret agent in World War I, or something on that order. As he was escaping to England on a miserable coal boat, seated with fellow passengers on the deck—as a kindness to them, to pass the deadly tedium and to relieve their collective fear and shock and loss—he told them stories. He began with some which he was in the habit of telling, which he had learned to rely on to amuse people. But he ran through his repertory of these little set pieces; and so he went on and gave his unhappy audience the benefit of certain plots and projects of fiction which he had borne in mind through the years, and never been willing to tell, lest the bloom of his own interest in them be worn off before they were ready to be written. The reason for his willingness, then and there, on the vessel of refuge, was the shadow of death hanging over them, environing them. They expected to encounter a submarine or perhaps a flight of predatory planes; therefore the aging storyteller felt that he could spare some of his fondly hoarded material. Even in the event of a safe homecoming, he fancied, he would not live to cope with it all.

This must be the most interesting and individual aspect of his vocation of letters and his career: his planning and planning, major matters and minor matters alike; his constant looking ahead and budgeting every faculty and every opportunity, with due unflattering consideration of the probabilities for and against him; his sense of a significance and a form in the story of his life, beginning and middle and end, as definite as in the construction of any three-act play or short story or shapely short novel; and his constant thought of death, the indelible finis on the unfinishable page.

Even in his reading of the works of other men, I have noticed that he keeps to a sort of schedule. Detective stories are to kill time when he is sleepless or in some pain. Novels that friends have sent him can be sufficiently perused, in kindness and out of curiosity, in half-hours of relaxation. Usually he devotes an hour in the afternoon or evening to rereading one of the classics of fiction, Goethe, Fielding, Cervantes, and the rest; and he keeps certain volumes which mean a great deal to him on his night table, against the difficult hour of daybreak.

As to the great old masters of fiction, remember that it has always been his hope and intention that the best of his books should entitle him to some place in their hierarchy of world fame and centennial duration, though a modest place. His requirement of himself has never changed in the fifty or more years; perhaps not to be great, but to be good, according to the proposition of their greatness. They are the objects of his devotion, as it were the inspiring and interceding saints. Also each of them is exemplary to him in some particular of the art; and he still constantly turns to them when he has come upon any little problem of his own writing, to consider what solution one or the other may have found in a parallel case. When anything in his work in progress has reference to a learned or abstract matter, he researches tirelessly. He has been known to study as many as forty volumes for one short and easily readable chapter.

Naturally, as a fiction writer, his principal research is just learning to know people, getting them to tell him what they have experienced, probing their minds, observing their emotions and their morals. In this he has been tireless, too; also patient and relentless, teasing and combative and kind—whatever the human instance may call for—and nothing that does not infringe upon the Darwinian hours seems to him too much trouble; not a detail of humanity is too small for his acute and impartial eye. Often as he goes out to dine he has a question ready to put to someone he expects to meet; the answer to which will fit into the morrow's page.

He is, as nearly as can be, a single-minded man. Some years ago he confided to a friend that, within his remembrance, he had never gone anywhere or cared to have any new person introduced to him —except for one of his diversions, for example bridge playing—or pursued a particular acquaintance with anyone, unless he had some idea of a function or utility for his literary art in so doing: some study of the narratable world up to date; or a search for types of humanity, in the way of a painter needing models to pose for him; or a glimpse into strange ways of living; or an experimental discussion of ideas important to him with reference to work coming up.

Naturally the friend, upon hearing this, felt a pang of self-consciousness and pride; but later he remarked that of his observation over a period of years he believed it to be true enough. In appreciation of his friendship in the time he spent in this country during World War II, let me say that I think it is no longer true. Every sort of ulterior motive and craft and documentary sense seems to have waned out of his various human interests. His kindness toward young people has a character of benign, humorous fatherliness, without any very intense urge to understand them. In society he seeks especially those who can tell him of philosophy and religion. As the years pass, the shadow of mortality grows no lighter or smaller, no, not in any man's life! Once in a while he recognizes new subject matter as such, when he hears of it or comes upon it, and points out to some young writer its interest and feasibility, and the proper way to handle it. But, even more certainly than on the perilous refugee boat, he reminds himself that there will not be time for it to rise and swell in his mind, to ripen for his neat final manuscript and printed best-selling page. He makes way for us, he leaves it to us, with his blessing; but also with a certain challenging, sardonic, mistrustful sense. He is easy to please but not easy to satisfy.

Let us not have, in praise of a man so realistic and judicious, any mixing of the classifications of men or any sentimentality. He is not a saint or a sage or a hero; only a true and greatly accomplished literary artist. But neither let us forget that art has its virtues, and they are rewarded in more ways than one. I remember that one day he came in from his writing room, visibly happy—with a light step, the strong downward expression of his mouth softened, his eyes in their delicate crisscross wrinkles perfectly clear—and remarked, "I will tell you, as it may not have occurred to you, that there is a particular drawback in the career of writing."

Upon our inquiring what the drawback was, he answered, "When you have finished the day's work, and you have to take your leisure and wait for your creative gift to be restored next morning, anything you can do in the remaining hours of the day seems a little pale and flat."

To have commenced literature two thirds of a century ago, and still, in spite of life—and by life I mean disillusionment and unlucky affections, increase of pain and worldly losses, and the shames of human nature, along with horrible war and civil war, and the ruin of nations, and the failure of a whole structure of delectable usages—still to enjoy writing so much that nothing compares with it, and to write to the end, is a grand and enviable thing, and a spiritual thing. There are a number of good reasons for dedicating oneself to the art of writing; surely this is as good as any.

Chapter Four

An Introduction to Colette

I have a passion for the truth, and for the fictions that it authorizes.
— JULES RENARD

Upon publication of *Mitsou,* her love story of World War I, Colette received a letter from Proust. "I wept a little this evening, which I have not done for a long while."

Mitsou concludes with a passionate communication from a little musical comedy star to her lieutenant in the trenches; and this impressed Proust especially, but he quibbled: "It is so beautiful, it even verges on prettiness here and there, and amid so much admirable simplicity and depth, perhaps there is a trace of preciosity." He could not quite believe in the sudden elevation and refinement of *Mitsou*'s style, educated only by love. And how characteristic of the very neurotic great man! The chapter of the lovers' dining in a restaurant reminded him dolefully of an engagement to dine with Colette which he had been compelled to break, it unfortunately having coincided with one of his illnesses.

Upon publication of *Chéri* she received a letter from Gide. He expected her to be surprised to hear from him; and perhaps she was. While Proust was a great complimenter, Gide was known to be somewhat chary of endorsements. He had read the tragical tale of the youngster in love with the aging courtesan at one sitting, breathlessly, he said. "Not one weakness, not one redundancy, nothing commonplace!" Why in the world, he wondered, had none of the critics compared her young hero or villain with Benjamin

Constant's "insupportable" *Adolphe?* "It's the same subject in reverse, almost."

On the whole, this was higher praise than Proust's, and deservedly higher; for in the three intervening years Colette had extended and intensified her art. Gide quibbled also, or rather he suggested that with his natural uneasiness and malicious humor, if he took a little more trouble, in all probability he would find something quibble-worthy. "I'd like to reread it but I'm afraid to. What if it were to disappoint me, upon second reading? Oh, quick, let me mail this letter before I consign it to the wastebasket!"

It is pleasant and, I think, appropriate to begin with a glance at these two little documents of literary history. For, when Proust and Gide were dead and gone, it seemed to me—and to a good many other readers in France and in foreign parts—that Colette was the greatest living fiction writer.

I know that in critical prose, as a rule, the effect of the superlative "greatest" is just emotional. It is not really susceptible of analysis, at least not of proof. Even the comparative "greater" is unhandy in any limited number of pages, as it calls for some examination of those who may be thought comparable. Greater than Mauriac? Greater than Martin du Gard, Jules Romains, Montherlant, Sartre? Yes, I say, though I have not had the zeal to read or reread that entire bookshelf for the present purpose. Let me not pretend to be able to prove anything. Let me just peaceably point to those of Colette's merits, here and there in her work, which I regard as components of greatness; going upon the assumption that in the essentials, as to general literary standards, the reader will agree with me. Easy does it!

I may state that, beginning about a decade ago, I have familiarized myself with Colette's work in its entirety. My nearest and dearest friend, with characteristic munificence, made me a present of the collected edition, fifteen volumes, seven thousand pages, two million words, in that handsome format which finally crowns the French literary life: laid paper with margins, red ink as well as black; and had it handsomely bound for me in Holland. That spring I read everything that I had missed in ordinary editions in the past, and reread all the masterworks that I had loved so dearly for many years. I go on rereading every so often; and thus I know whereof I speak. I have it all fairly fresh in my mind.

I wish that I could illustrate this essay. From childhood and girlhood on to the day of her death, Colette photographed entrancingly. The first written description of her that I ever read was an entry in Jules Renard's *Journal*, November, 1894: her appearance at the first night of Maeterlinck's translation of *'Tis Pity She's a Whore,* bright-eyed, laughing, "with a braid of hair long enough to let the bucket down a well with"; Melisande-like.

Rebecca West has described her in her middle age, out for a walk with her bulldog, a rich silk scarf looped through its collar in lieu of a leash. That most gifted and intrepid reporter's principal impression was of animal energy and fierceness; to such a degree, she declared, that it almost frightened her.

I first met Colette in 1935, when she and Maurice Goudeket, her third husband, came to New York on the maiden voyage of the *Normandie*. Her American publisher invited me to a cocktail party in her honor. She was not expected to speak English, and as I had lived in France long enough to speak French fluently if not correctly, it was thought that I could facilitate the sociability. It thrilled me to meet her.

I remember her strong hands—serious writing is a manual labor! —and her fine feet in sandals, perhaps larger than most, rather like the feet of Greek goddesses. I remember her slightly frizzly hair fetched forward almost to her eyebrows, because (as she has told her readers) she has a square boyish or mannish forehead. I remember her delicate nostrils and her painted thin lips.

The conversation that I had been invited to engage in was not really very witty or deep. She extolled the great maiden ocean liner; how safe it seemed, how imperturbable upon the waves! She gave it as her opinion that there was nothing at all surprising about skyscrapers; man having been all through the ages a mountain climber, a tower builder. I then expressed my pleasure in the little conversation I had had with Goudeket, a distinguished and interesting man.

"He is a very good friend," she said, and she emphasized friend little. As I recalled certain bitter pages about her first marriage —the bitterest were still to come—I supposed that the designation of "husband" seemed unromantic to her.

Now I will furnish a sort of biography in rough outline and ré-umé. I wish that, instead, her autobiographies—the half dozen ittle volumes that, taken together, are perhaps her most important work: *La Maison de Claudine, Sido, Le Pur et l'Impur, Mes Ap-rentissages, L'Etoile Vesper, Le Fanal Bleu*—were all available in ;nglish. What I shall do is flutter in and out of that noble repository nd treasure-trove, picking out bright bits, like a magpie. Though he has many reticences, grandeurs of style, and sometimes little rid-les, she seems not to have left much for other narrators of her life o do, except to simplify and vulgarize.

Sidonie Gabrielle Colette was born on January 28, 1873, in a illage in Burgundy, Saint-Sauveur-en-Puisaye. Her father, Jules oseph Colette, was a pensioned-off soldier who had fought in North Africa, in the Crimea, and in the wars of Italian liberation, and lost leg at the second battle of Marignan. Her mother, Adèle Eugénie idonie Landoy, born in Paris, was a young widow when the ex-ouave loved and wooed and won her. It was a good marriage. She as an octoroon. Blessed France! where it may seem to handicap ne in a career of serious authorship to have commenced with a eries of slightly raffish best sellers, or to have divorced and gone on he stage, as Colette did; but where race prejudices are few and mild. Never have I heard any mention of that sixteenth part of Negro lood in the famous authoress's veins; only her own statement.

Mme. Jules Joseph Colette—Sido, if we may presume to use that bridged name which, her daughter has said, "sparkles amid all my nemories"—was a woman of real force of character and unusual aind, with a gift of expression from which, doubtless, for the most art, her daughter's genius derived. As a young girl Colette must ave felt overwhelmed by her. The first independent action of olette's life, marriage, rash and premature, was in specific rebel-ion against the better parental judgment. Thereafter Sido must ave sensed the wrongness of impinging too closely upon her daugh-

D

ter's difficult life; she stood upon a certain ceremony, kept her dis
tance.

La Naissance du Jour (Break of Day) (1928), the novel of the
renunciation of love in which Colette portrayed herself under her
own name, and as approximately the age that she had reached in
reality at the time of writing it, testifies to the fact that the thought
of her mother was still a challenge to her, sixteen years after her
death. On page after page she studies herself in the mirror of her in
heritance, measures herself against Sido's stature; and true bereave
ment echoes all through it, slow and impassioned, like the ground
bass of a passacaglia or a chaconne.

She began her filial tribute long before that. The best of the little
chapters of *La Maison de Claudine* (1922), which is an account of
the home from which the author of the Claudine novels came—not
otherwise connected with the best-selling series—are portrait sketches
of the dear progenetrix. *Sido* (1929) is a more formal portrait, but
still entranced and entrancing. Even after thirty-four years, in
L'Etoile Vesper (The Evening Star) (1946), there are sudden touch
ing souvenirs: a fragment of a blue dress of Sido's, a miniature of
Sido's mother—to whom Sido's father, the quadroon, was notori
ously unfaithful—one of Sido's recollections of another of her chil
dren, and a severe motherly criticism, of neglected and disorderly
cupboards. And in this text, as elsewhere, whenever assailed by fear
or bitterness or any other serious trouble, she evokes the great strong
spirit, and despite her own age, threescore and ten—threescore and
nine, to be exact—clings almost like a child. The filial devotion
half of it posthumous, was the mightiest strand in her entire being

The next most important strand was coarse and incongruous
and seemingly weak; nevertheless, it held her a long time. At twenty
she married the noted journalist and hack writer, Henri Gauthier
Villars, known as Willy. She was then, as he remarked some year
later of her heroine, Claudine, as pure and unsophisticated as "any
little Tahitian before the missionaries got there." He was, to char
acterize him in his own manner, the opposite of a missionary. He
was a bad, clever, corpulent, somewhat crazy man. He was only about

ifteen years older than she, but already the worse for wear, physically as well as spiritually. "Worse than mature," Colette said.

"The day after that wedding night I found that a distance of a
thousand miles, abyss and discovery and irremediable metamor-
phosis, separated me from the day before." What a painful sentence!
What a beautiful sentence! All of her portrait of Willy from memory years later is perfection. "The shadow of Priapus, flattered by
the moonlight or lamplight on the wall"—then, little by little, the
traits of the mere middle-aged man coming out from behind that
image of newly espoused male—"a look in his bluish eyes impossible to decipher; a terrible trick of shedding tears; that strange
lightness which the obese often have; and the hardness of a feather-
bed filled with small stones." He was nervous, disgraceful, and
shameless, foxy and comical and cruel. He was thought to resemble
King Edward VII; but in spite of his carefully dyed, extra-thick
handlebar mustaches, his wife noted also something of Queen Vic-
toria.

The term "hack writer," as applied to Willy, needs a little explaining. He was, as you might say, a wholesaler of popular reading
matter: music criticism and drama criticism; and in book form as
well as journalism, revelations of his own everyday life and night
life in the somewhat side-splitting way, sometimes verging on the
libidinous, with verbal pyrotechnics, especially puns; and all sorts
of light fiction, something for almost every type of reader; and once
in a while, dramatizations. Hacking indeed; but he himself did
scarcely any of the writing! Doubtless he had what is called a psychic
block to start with, but he made it work. He employed writers, several at a time, for his different types of production. "Willy *have*
talent," said Jules Renard. He was not lazy. He helped his helpers.
Sometimes he seemed to want to fool them, pretending that the
work of one of them was his work, and getting another to revise it,
and so on. He may or may not have given them a fair share of the
income from all this; they never understood his finances. Some of
them had literary careers on their own in later years: Messrs. Vuil-
lermoz, Curnonsky, Marcel Boulestin.

Young Mme. Colette Willy's literary career began with her telling little tales of Saint-Sauveur; tales of childhood, girlhood, and school girlhood. One day Willy suggested her trying to get some of these memories down on paper. She tried, the result disappointed him and he discouraged her. But one day when he happened to need money he picked up her manuscript again and thought better of it. Could she not work on it a little more? he asked her. It needed only a detail of psychology here and there, a specification of emotion. Why not develop her little heroine's crushes on her girl friends just a little further?

Immature female writers, as Colette remarked years later, are not notable for their moderation; nor old female writers either: "Furthermore, nothing is so emboldening as a mask." Before long Willy's reminiscing young wife was his favorite ghost writer. He paid her too; well enough, it seemed to her at the time, enabling her to send little presents to Sido, woolen stockings, bars of bitter chocolate. He would lock her in her room for four-hour stretches while she inked up a certain number of pages with her heaven-sent and profitable phrases, sentences, paragraphs.

In her recollection of all this Colette has expressed mixed emotions, doubtless impossible to unmix: pathos, furious resentment and toughness toward herself—Willy locked the door, but, she had to admit, there was nothing to hinder her from throwing herself out the window—and in spite of all, a certain appreciation of the way destiny worked to her advantage in it, amor fati. For thus in servitude, page by page, volume by volume, she became a professional writer. Regular as clockwork: *Claudine at School* (1900), *Claudine in Paris* (1901), *Claudine Married* (1902), *Claudine and Annie* (1903); and then a new series, *Minne*, and *Les Égarements de Minne*. Willy took all the credit and signed them all.

Claudine, all four *Claudines*, had a fantastic success. Shall I attempt to say what it was like, with American equivalents, for fun? Rather like a combination of Tarkington's *Seventeen* and Anita Loos's *Gentlemen Prefer Blondes*. Also there was the factor of personal notoriety. Suppose Anita Loos had been married to, let us say, Alexander Woollcott, and he had posed as the author of it and given the public to understand that it was the true story of her life! Also in due course it was dramatized and acted by a favorite actress, Polaire, who was, as you might say, a cross between Mae West and Shirley Temple. The name "Claudine" was bestowed upon a perfume, indeed two perfumes in competition, and upon a form of round starched schoolgirlish collar, and upon a brand of cigarettes and a flavor of ice cream. It makes one think of the old story of the sorcerer's apprentice, with a variation: young Mme. Willy not only brought the broomstick to life, she was the broomstick.

No wonder she has shown a divided mind about the merits and demerits of those early volumes. As a rule her references have been rather shamefaced, disdainful; and critical commentators on her work have followed suit, even I. But in truth almost any writer who had not gone on to write something very much better would be quite sufficiently proud to have written the *Claudines*. To be sure, here and there they put us in mind of that once popular periodical, *La Vie Parisienne*. They are a little foolish but not at all false. They are wonderfully recreational, with all the assortment of approaches to romance, and with small talk, sparkling every instant.

A part of Colette's talent appears in them all right: her warmth of heart, brilliance of the senses, command of language; only none of her genius. She surely appreciates them as well as they deserve, for all her little promulgations of sackcloth and ashes. She fought hard to get the rights away from Willy; for a while both names appeared on the title pages, then hers alone; and she devoted two and a half volumes of the proud definitive edition to them.

While she was writing, writing, writing, for Willy, intimate relations between them went from bad to worse. Halfway through the miserable marriage, or perhaps three quarters of the way, she suddenly felt unable to stand it; collapsed in her own mind about it. She began to believe that perhaps Willy was not simply wicked but insane; a furtive kind of insanity, venting itself in little sadisms and in whims and frauds of one kind and another. She tried to pity him but she found herself unable to pity him. Presently she realized that the reason she was unable to pity him was that she had begun

to be afraid of him. She wrote of this with somber moderation
with a sort of good nature, which gives one gooseflesh. "Healthy
young people do not easily open their minds to fear, not altogether
not constantly. The worst tormentors have their hours of clemency
and gaiety. Perhaps even a mouse finds time, between one wound
and the next, to appreciate the softness of the cat's paw." And on
another page there is an allusion to something that happened fi
nally, that she resolved never to tell; worse than anything that she
had told!

Whereupon she retreated to the country, to a little property in the
Franche-Comté called Monts-Boucons. Willy gave it to her, but
afterward seized it back. She told him that going away would en
able her to get on faster with her work, his work; but there appears
not to have been any vagueness in her own mind about it; it was for
the specific purpose of suffering. It was what in our American life
is so common or, I should say, what we have so common a term for
(the French have none): nervous breakdown. It was the turning
point of her life; anguish, the first phase of independence!

In her account of this, years later, I note one of those components
of literary greatness which I have undertaken to indicate when I
came to them; a sort of contradictoriness in the working of her mind;
manifoldness. When reticence would seem to have closed down on
her, because she is ashamed to tell the whole story, and no wonder;
when her thought has failed, no knowing any longer what to think;
when she feels obliged in all honesty and modesty to specify that
she cannot really specify anything—then! then more than ever, com-
pensatorily, her power of expression of emotion reaches its peak, by
means of images and verbal music.

There in retreat in the Franche-Comté countryside, having on
her mind day and night her problem of oversophisticated, broken-
down psychopathological metropolitan home life, suddenly she discovered, not the meaning, not the moral, but the metaphor, in
simple nature around her; in the painfulness of nature. Metaphor
singular? No, metaphors plural! all over the place; but all saying the
same thing.—A superb serpent pecked to death by hens. Dark pain
ful wasps slumberous in the ground like a tiny buried bunch of

grapes. Her cat undeterrably murderous without even any excuse of hunger, and the bird on its nest optimistic but obstinate as the cat approached. Her old horse so badly mistreated by its previous owner that, when she went riding, it had to be bandaged as well as saddled . . .

By means of these observations she expressed the dread and disgust to which her married life had turned, more than by any outspokenness or outcry. And none of it really could be said to be, for the creature concerned, error or bad luck or injustice; in each case it was according to the given nature. Oh, likewise in her own case as the wife of Willy! She was justified in forgiving herself for her weaknesses of the past. On the other hand, she could not be expected to repress in herself indefinitely a certain dire strength of which she was beginning to feel the stirrings. Both things were in her nature, in her attitude and reaction to the rest of nature and to others' human nature: awful compliance for a while, but power of rebellion after a while, even power of hatred.

But never, for her, indifference or obliviousness! This is what I call the contradiction: the creative mind embellishing what it hates; winding around what it is escaping from; rendering everything, as it goes along, in so far as can be, unforgettable. For example, that reptile and the barnyard fowl and those predatory insects and that beat-up horse; Colette kept them stored in her head for about thirty years, along with the more general concepts of early sorrow, early philosophy. As she has expressed it in the way of aphorism: "By means of an image we are often able to hold on to our lost belongings. But it is the desperateness of losing which picks the flowers of memory, binds the bouquet."

Nervous breakdown had done her good, as it often does, or so it seems: something in the way of a liberating effect. In some way suffering outweighed her natural conservatism. As she expressed it in later years almost cynically, she had monogamous blood in her veins by inheritance, the effect of which was a certain enfeeblement in the ways of the world. There by herself in Monts-Boucons, bloodletting! What year was that? Perhaps 1904. Now and again the chronology of her memoirs disappears in the poetry. She did not actually, entirely, leave Willy until 1906. Why the delay, when she had seen all and foreseen all, and as they say, found herself?

In more than one text Colette has declared, and no doubt sincerely thought, that it was mainly on her mother's account. From the very first day of her marriage and metropolitan life she had painstakingly prevaricated in every letter back to the provincial town. Perhaps Sido read between the lines, but she replied only to what her daughter chose to tell. Little by little Colette felt bound by her own spiderweb. Given what our sociologists call vertical social mobility, it is a frequent crisis in the lives of gifted young persons who have ventured to the city in search of fortune, to no avail, and then have to consider giving up and going back home prodigal sons or daughters not even remorseful, nobodies with not even a cent or a sou. The prospect of burdening Sido in the financial way troubled Colette especially. Must she not have been inhibited by another point of pride also? In Sido's instant perception of the miserableness of Willy, and prediction of the martyrdom of being married to him, had she not felt some possessiveness, bossiness? It is a matter of observations that daughters often very nearly perish rather than admit that mother knew best.

But at the close of a life and career so felicitous and successful, let us not glibly say that at this or that point things were misconceived or mismanaged. Nowadays one is apt to make too much of the spell cast by parents, and the fixation of first marriage, and everything of that sort. Especially in the lives of literary persons, planners by their temperament and training, the feelings of ability and ambition may be of more decisive effect. What caused her to set her bizarre young heart on the odd older man from Paris in the first place, if it was not the fact that he was a literary man? And after she came to hate him with her whole heart, probably it was the muse which kept her there beside him a while longer, faithful to vocation rather than to the marriage vow; only seemingly shilly shallying, while accumulating the materials for a great piece of literature decades later.

Willy was her job as well as her husband and her subject matter. She remembered to tell us how—doubtless sensing her restlessness the gradual unfolding of her wings for flight, also the sharpening and tensing of her beak and claw—he opportunely raised her wages. The *Minnes* were more remunerative than the *Claudines*. It does seem to me that if I had been the author of those six volumes at the rate of one a year I should have felt quite confident of being able to support myself by writing—also my mother in the provinces, forsooth, if called upon—even without an accustomed consort, slave-driver, agent, and front man. But Colette did not feel confident. She was like someone learning to swim, someone who has learned, who can swim, but still depends on water wings. And the fact is that, when at last she got up her courage and left Willy, and continued writing—an excellent volume in 1907, another in 1908—there was not a living in it. It must be admitted that she did not, perhaps could not, certainly never wished to, write any longer in the previous half-humorous best-selling style, Willy's style. She went on the stage instead.

◆

I feel a little embarrassment about the theatrical interlude in Colette's life; which let me deal with summarily. I have not gossiped with any old friends of hers, or questioned my Parisian friends of that generation for the outward aspect and general public impression of her life on stage and backstage, or researched concerning her in the drama criticism and gossip columns of newspapers or news weeklies which perhaps exist in French libraries, yellowed but not yet moldered away.

Even in her lifetime, surely, Colette would not have minded my doing so. As a rule when literary folk manifest a dread of gossip, horror of investigation, like the ostrich in the adage, one reason is an exasperated proprietary sense. They want to do their own telling in their own way with due applause and profit. Colette told all about her career on stage quite soon: two theatrical novels, three if we count *Mitsou*, and a volume of sketches, as well as various passages in her autobiographical works.

But, having read all that, I find myself in a quandary which (I think) may derive from ambiguity or at least uncertainty in her feeling. So much of it seems to me funny, but apparently to her it all bore connotations of resentment, misfortune, sorrow. Even when the theme is the picturesqueness of something, or eccentricity of someone, when obviously she means to make it as entertaining as possible, it is in a minor key or upon a sharp or harsh note. The theatrical way of life is lonely, and it was especially so in old-fashioned vaudeville or music hall, with brief engagements in a hundred towns. Perhaps in young womanhood loneliness, lonesomeness, loneness, is as hard to bear as unhappy marriage. Perhaps, with a vocation as absolute as Colette's for literature, working at anything else seems an outrage.

And literary persons especially mind the impermanences of the interpretative arts, musical performance as well as acting and dancing. In Antibes on the French Riviera there is, or used to be, a little Roman tombstone bearing the inscription: SEPTENTRION AET XII SALTAVIT ET PLACUIT. Have I remembered the Latin as it should be?—Someone named North, or perhaps someone *from* the North, aged twelve, danced and gave pleasure. In Paris in the Musée Guimet there is, or used to be, a little Egyptian mummy; within its angular tight leathery arms appear some dried bits of something else: it is a dancing girl clasping upon her bosom her last bouquet. Which is said to have inspired Anatole France's *Thaïs*, Massenet's *Thaïs*, and indirectly, Somerset Maugham's *Rain*. Such are the personifications of the theatre, vanishing out of men's minds in no time, unless memorialized in writing or one of the other fine arts.

Colette's stage career began more or less by chance, in semi-public, upon occasions of that elaborated, almost laborious sociability which is peculiarly Parisian: masked balls, soirées littéraires, amateur theatricals. She has given us an account of a great afternoon in the garden of a noted and lovely young American woman, sapphire-eyed Miss Nathalie Barney, when she, Colette, and another lovely young American woman, red-haired Miss Eva Palmer, costumed as, respectively, Daphnis and Chloe, performed a playlet by Pierre Louÿs. That same afternoon there also entered, upon a white horse, costumed as patient Griselda, that young Dutch or perhaps Asiatic woman, Mata Hari, whom the Germans later employed as a spy and whom the French detected and executed. Come to think of it, I do not believe that Colette's old friends have gossiped about her much; not in my time, not interestingly. As acknowledged elsewhere, years later I had the honor of acquaintance with the red-haired Chloe just mentioned when she was Mrs. Sikelianos, and expounded the dualism of Greek religion to me; but never a word about that gala garden party.

Presently Colette got beyond the fashionable and sophisticated orbit and took for her partner a good capable man named Georges Wague, who made a professional of her. For several seasons they appeared in various pantomimes, ballets, and sketches, most of the time on tour around the provincial cities. One of their numbers was first entitled "Dream of Egypt," which a certain police commissioner, goodness knows why, obliged them to change to "Oriental Reverie." Their greatest success was entitled "Flesh," and it ran for an entire year. Then there was "The Bird of Night," in which Colette wore rags and tatters, rather Sicilian-looking, with a third performer named Christine Kerf, and they all three went about glowering at something.

The iconography, especially the photographic archives, seems more evocative than the literary or journalistic record. Somewhere in a scrapbook I have pasted a reproduction in rotogravure of an early news photograph in which Colette is making an entry, perhaps on stage, perhaps at a ball, with a panache of what appears to be real peacock tail, borne upon the shoulders of four young strength-and-health men in jockstraps. In recent years, in magazines and in popular little monographs, there have appeared a number of such shots, a little less comical and a little more poetical with the passage of time: one as a black cat, in woolly tights with inked-on whiskers; another in repose, propped up on a taxidermized head, showing to advantage those fine feet which, a quarter of a century later, impressed me. A certain art study reminds us who was the most famous, most influential dancer in the world in those days: Isadora Duncan. In at least one action photograph we are able to glimpse something of Colette's talent; a tension and a kind of blissfulness in the holding of her head and the outflinging of her arms.

The upbringing and formation of a writer as such: that is the significance of everything I have had to tell thus far. Even follies working out better than one could have calculated; even mere drudgeries serving a dual purpose, future subject matter as well as present livelihood nothing to be regretted unless the fatigue is too great or the lifetime too short! For, as a rule, the development of talent into mastery, or even genius, is not a matter of studying to write or training to write, but of exercising as greatly as possible the entire being, senses, nerves, excitements, emotions, thoughts; only two or three habits of mind making the difference, leading on specifically to literature: the recollective faculty, conversational power, including the power of making others talk, and of course studiousness of the classics of literature and the other arts.

As we look back on Colette's life, indefatigable beyond anyone's, and not short, certainly we see that her odd, hazardous, almost scandalous young womanhood, even the years of hack writing, even the intense unhappiness, even the years of hack acting and dancing, all of it just as it happened was almost ideal for the future writer's purpose.

◈

Now please look with me at some of the result and the outcome, the writing itself; particularly the works of fiction. I will point to things and underline things, with a good bit of quotation and paraphrase, with commendation to my heart's content and very little adverse criticism. The two novels of the theatre, *La Vagabonde* (1910) and its sequel, *L'Entrave* (1913) made a reputation for Colette, quite distinct from the success and notoriety of the *Claudines*. Renée Néré, the protagonist of both, is also in some measure self-portraiture, analytical, spiritual, and not without self-consciousness. Perhaps Colette felt that this somber presentation would counteract the foolish, girlish mask she had put on for Willy.

The curiosity about the life of Thespians evidently is international and ever-recurrent, but as a rule has not inspired novelists very profoundly. Colette, for her part, played down all the glamour of show business, reduced it to realism, almost dispelled it. Theatre is merely Renée Néré's livelihood, while she rejoices in, then suffers from, love-relationships. I think the appeal of these two novels must have been not particularly to the stage-struck but to career women in general. Those were the early days of feminism, with a little host of women even in France seeking to wean themselves from domestic unhappiness by means of various labors out in the world, with very little written by way of guidebook for them, to say nothing of consolation.

It was *Chéri* (1920) which made Colette famous. Though she did not get around to writing *The Last of Chéri* until six years later, they really constitute one and the same work. It requires an unusual ability to hold a theme in mind for so long a time, ripening it, resolving it, perhaps depending for some of its elements on one's further experience as well as developing artistry.

Colette's first pairing off of novels, *Minne* followed by *Les Égarements de Minne,* was just upon order from Willy; and as soon as they became her property she combined them rather imperfectly in one volume, *L'Ingénue Libertine* (1909). But perhaps this effort of reconstruction inspired her serious interest in binary form. The connection between *La Vagabonde* and *L'Entrave* is more than just the further developments in the life of Renée Néré. Over and above the explicit continuity there are recurrences of emotion, like echoes in the transepts of a large building, back and forth.

In *Chéri* and *The Last of Chéri* the double construction is handled much more decisively and strongly. There is an entire shifting of key and change of tempo from one to the other, and a somewhat different proposition in morals and psychology; yet the reader feels that all this was a part of the writer's knowledge and plan in the first place. A sweeping and agitated, sensual, humorous love story ending in farewell, then a concentrated and solemnly instructive account of psychopathology, they are structurally perfect together, with an effect of not simply chiming echoes but of polyphonic music; with clear perspectives both in the passage of time and in the way the mind of each protagonist focuses on the characters of the other protagonists, and all according to human nature and fatality from start to finish.

Said Laurence Sterne, of all men of genius perhaps the least masterly, "I begin with writing the first sentence, trusting to Almighty God for the second." Have you observed and compared the odd beginnings of the various great novels? It is pleasant to do so, and it often illumines the deep-laid aesthetic and particular personality of the novelist in question. Both of Sterne's own first sentences are famous. There is a thrilling solemnity about the four and a half syllables of *Moby Dick,* "Call me Ishmael"; and the rest of the paragraph meandering along, "the watery part of the world" and so forth. The dozen words of *Anna Karenina,* thoughtful, universal, and yet simple, give an instant impression of narrative genius: "All happy families resemble one another; every unhappy family is unhappy in its own way." In due course there was struck the new note of American literary art; in Hemingway's first book, for instance, "Everybody was drunk . . ."

Now turn to the opening page of *Chéri,* the voice of the spoiled youngster addressing his aging mistress, an absurd outcry: "Léa! Let me have your pearls!" Do you see? it is rather like theatre, sudden, in order to prevail over the incredulity and metropolitan nervousness of the audience; and poetical in the way of the stage, with more paradox than sentiment.

It is not unlike the fine opening scene of *Der Rosenkavalier,* first thing in the morning, with the dramatic soprano in or on her grandiose eighteenth-century bed, and the mezzo-soprano uttering the clarion notes of the pledge of everlasting devotion which in fact only lasts out that act. I wish that in the course of one of my conversations with Colette I had thought to ask her whether she had seen the music drama of Strauss and Hofmannsthal (1911) before writing *Chéri* (1920). She had always been appreciative of music, and indeed in Willy's day helped with his music criticism and went along to Bayreuth.

No matter. The theme of an oldish woman in love with a very young man or a boy, and vice versa, is an old and fairly familiar

theme; natural, insoluble, therefore persistent—except perhaps in
the United States. We seem to take our matriarchy straight, in the
proper context of family relationship, and more often analytically
than for the expression of heartache or heartbreak.

"Léa, Léa, you're not listening to me!" the heartbreaking French
youngster continues. "Let me have your string of pearls, Léa! It's
as becoming to me as it is to you. Are you afraid of my stealing
it?" And there, swiftly and simply, you have the three or four
moral factors upon which the entire sad story turns: Chéri's
childishness; and his exceeding good looks and corresponding self-
admiration; and that constant concern with cash value, which was
practically all the education he had been given, prior to this love
affair; and his resigning himself to having a bad reputation, not so
much cynicism as defeatism.

Mauriac, a strictly Roman Catholic writer, having written a
biography of Racine, situating the glorious dramatic poet in relation to baroque theology as well as classical theatre, emphasizing
his profoundly troubled Christianity, inscribed a copy of it somewhat surprisingly: "To Colette, nearer than she thinks to this
periwigged man."

If we give this a second thought, even in the opera-like or operetta-
like first part of *Chéri* we find something of Mauriac's meaning: the
suggestion that mere human nature, natural human happiness, is
hopeless, that there is original sin, et seq. None of Colette's unhappy
mortals, whether like puppets jerked to their death by pride and
error or just drawn to it by time in the ordinary way, seems to have
the least sense of the eternal life, or any feeling of having to choose
between salvation and perdition. But often their undeluded, un-
reconciled attitude as to the condition of humankind here below is
quite Catholic. In the mentality of *Chéri*, in his plight of psyche
if not within his will power, is a readiness for religion.

Interviewed by someone, in *Les Nouvelles Litteraires* if I remember correctly, Colette stated the subject of this pair of novels in
plain terms without a hint of religion or even of philosophy, as
follows.—When a woman of a certain age enters into a relationship
with a much younger man, she risks less than he. His character is

still in a formative stage, and therefore the more likely to be spoiled by their love, deformed by the failure of it. After they have parted he may be haunted by her, held back by her, forever.

This of course is what reminded Gide of Benjamin Constant's *Adolphe*. I am tempted to quote from the famous commentary which Constant added by way of preface to the third edition: as to those degrees of passionateness which a young man may think he can arouse in his mistress without feeling them himself; which nevertheless little by little take root in him also, and injure him terribly in the uprooting. It would require very lengthy quotation and perhaps new translation.

Chéri is younger than Adolphe. Léa is older than Ellénore. Shall I tell you the plot? It is simple: the life and love and death of one Frédéric Peloux. Chéri is his pet name, as we should say darling or dearie—the French word is not quite so belittling, as it means, literally, cherished one. The protagonists of the older generation are all courtesans, or so near as makes no matter; and all rather super-annuated and retired. The cleverest and least pleasant of them, Charlotte Peloux, Chéri's mother, has contrived, or at least facili-tated, his attachment to her old friend, Léa, born Léonie Vallon, known as Baroness de Lonval. Léa was in her forties; in all walks of life women were expected to retire early then. Chéri was nine-teen. It suited Mme. Peloux to have him kept out of mischief, and schooled and exercised for his future marriage, and at someone else's expense the while.

It worked like a charm. It continued for six years, quite peace-ably and dignifiedly, in good understanding and good health and powerful enjoyment of sex. You may look down at it, as a kind of mutuality of the commonplace and the materialistic—bourgeoisie gone wrong—yet in its way it was love. At any given moment it must have seemed to everyone that Chéri was playing the inferior part. He always took that wrongly suggestive tone; his requirement of the pearls, for example. Oh, probably his love never attained any particular height or powerfulness, except in intercourse. On the other hand, it never really diminished or altered, until the day of his death. Only his young body detached itself from Léa's old body, and only when ordered to do so.

How remarkably we are made to see and feel that, although she has begun to age quite rapidly, Léa is still physically, sexually attractive: blue-eyed and rosily blonde, with long legs, and that very flat back which you may also observe in Renaissance sculpture, with dimpled buttocks and somewhat exceptionally elevated breasts, long-lasting.

Colette lets her do most of the emphasizing on age herself. With one eye always on the mirror—as a normal and necessary part of the discipline of courtesanship—evidently, a good while before her intimacy with Chéri started, she had learned always to think of herself as gradually growing older. That was what the passage of time, every day, every hour, every minute, meant to her. She had accustomed herself to the prospect of finding herself, one fine day, really old, disgracefully and decisively old; and she had resolved to call a halt to love life and sex life before that happened. Thus, in her sorrow when it came time to lose Chéri, time to let him go, time to help him go, there was a factor of submissiveness to fate; long-prepared, philosophical.

The gerontophilic devotion—the feeling of a young person for someone definitely not young—is a very genuine, earnest, and passionate devotion. Who has not experienced it or observed it? Only as a rule it is not to be depended on; it is short-lived, subject to sudden coldness and indeed sexual incapability; it is a fire in straw. It was not exactly like that in Chéri's case. The elder person, beloved in that way, very naturally skeptical to begin with, nevertheless as a rule is almost certain to get enthralled little by little. But if you have any common sense, good education, or worldly wisdom, you will keep your skepticism in mind even after it has ceased to have any currency in your heart. For you must be prepared to yield your young person to some other young person or persons one fine day, upon a moment's notice. Was this not what happened between Léa and Chéri, when young Edmée came on the scene? Not exactly.

For we feel quite certain that Chéri would never have decided upon, nor lifted a hand to procure for himself, that pulchritudinous well-schooled impeccable creature; not in a thousand years. It was all managed by the matriarch, Mme. Peloux, more managerial than anyone, and more mercenary. Edmée was the daughter of the courtesan noted among them for having put away the most respectable amount of money. It was a case of gerontocracy's having prevailed over gerontophily. And in the essentials Léa functioned as one of the gerontocracy. She co-operated in the transfer of her darling back home, back under his mother's control, and into that holy state of matrimony which, as the French conceive and practice it, certainly is a mother's province.

Miserable young man! his emotions are pathetic and profound, as we see terribly by the outcome. His heart is in the right place but he has scarcely any head. Whether in happiness or unhappiness, he has not even observed exactly what his emotions were, until too late; until someone else has decided things. To all intents and purposes he is inarticulate. His talk—his explanation of the beauty and singularity of his eyelids, for example—is a kind of play-acting, like that of infants at a certain age; sound rather than sense. In more ways than one he is a kind of infant. In the very first instance, his passage from his mother's malicious and avaricious salon to Léa's bed and board—oh, blissful bed and sumptuous board!—was but a bewitchment. Now back again, as it were the dream of an infant not yet born, from one part of the womb to another.

The comedy of the aging courtesans is as well developed, and perhaps as important, as Chéri's misery. And in their scenes together the malicious, almost joyous tone and brisk pace of the first volume continue into the second: satirical vivace even amid the funeral march. Once in a while we laugh at them, but more often *with* them, in appreciation of the fun they make of one another. It is not all unkindness. In this class of womanhood one has to be careful of old friends, in view of the difficulty of replacing them. Their main objective in their youth and in their prime having been to please men, now it is rather to find various ways of conciliating other women; talking amusingly is one way. Sense of humor keeps up their courage, and serves another mutual purpose also: helps them pretend that those compulsions which constitute their morality—competitiveness, avarice, cruelty—are not really heavy upon them; that a part of their evil is not evil at all, but only a convention, affection and clowning.

Léa is the least amusing, but partly in consequence of that keeps our sympathy from beginning to end. Note especially her first encounter with Mme. Peloux after the marriage of Chéri and Edmée. Upon previous readings I seem to have missed this passage; now it delights me. After absenting herself in the South of France for a season, by way of discipline and therapy, Léa has returned to town with her heartbreak not remedied, but anesthetized, scarred over. She has reached that decision so long meditated: farewell to men, once and for all, and at once. Naturally she has been feeling dull and nervous, listless and slack.

Then, without warning, she is called upon by Chéri's mother, Edmée's mother-in-law; triumphant and infernally inquisitive, and, yes, at the same time sincerely friendly. For an hour Léa sits and gazes at that all too familiar face and form, the short and tight and tirelessly bestirring body, the large inhumane eyes and the glib lips; sits and listens to that lifelong chatter, petty but savage, detail after detail of the skillful, almost mechanical futility of her existence, the organized heartlessness. All of this, Léa reflects, with self-commiseration for a moment, is being visited upon her as a test of her strength of character.

And the next moment, exultantly, she realizes that in fact her character is strong enough. In the time to come as in the time gone by, she will be able to strike back. She knows, or can soon figure out, what well-turned phrase will hurt, what practiced and well-timed smile will worry. And upon the instant she feels less discouraged about herself. From her dreaming of love, and nightmare of the end of love, and sloth of sorrow, now animadversion and contempt and resentment have waked her up. She feels her heavy-heartedness, her sense of having nothing to live for, lifting and dispelling. What she will have to live for is simply self-defense. Her terrible old friend, old enemy, will keep her on her mark. In the strain of losing Chéri, and in the spirit of general renunciation, she has been living at a somewhat higher level and greater tension than was good for her. Mme. Peloux has brought her down to earth. She is grateful.

Here in a small way we have a philosophic mystery: the vision of evil as giving opportunity for an exercise of virtuousness of a sort. I realize that my comment upon this is longer than Colette's telling. In incident as in aphorism, along with the stimulation of our senses, acceleration of our sentiments, she has the power to set our brains to work. As Montesquieu expressed it in a maxim: "A great thought is one that puts us in mind of a number of other thoughts."

Meanwhile the process of Chéri's death has started, though it does not happen until 1919. As noted above, a certain lack of intellect has been ominous in him all along, predisposing him to demoralization. Stupid, or if you like, innocent, apparently he has taken it for granted that he will be able to resume amorous intimacy with his old beloved after the necessary term of concentration on his young wife. He attempts it one night; and perhaps, if he had not then noticed certain new ravages of her age, devastated nape of neck, weightiness or weightedness of cheek—he pretends to be asleep, and peeps at her with only the narrowest beam of morning light between his beautiful eyelids, through his thick eyelashes— and if she had not noticed his noticing, perhaps, perhaps!

Indeed they are tempted by one another even after that; later that morning, for just a moment, there glimmers between them a further hope of the recommencement of love, a lunatic hope, "such as may be entertained by persons falling down out of a tower, for the time it takes them to reach the ground." That is the conclusion of the first novel; a thrilling chapter. What difference would it have made if they had recommenced? Only the difference of a few more months of enjoyment, or perhaps a year, perhaps two years; downhill enjoyment, of course. But is that not the best that is ever offered anyone on this earth: prolongation, with deterioration? Also, for Chéri, the difference between suicide and a gradual ordinary death.

As it happens, his suicide is gradual too. The entire second novel, *The Last of Chéri,* is devoted to it. No suspense; the very first page indicates to us, with many tiny touches—I count seven suggestive words, set in odd cadences—that he feels condemned to death or has condemned himself. But he finds it a strange hard task to carry out the sentence. Even his self-absorbed wife senses something wrong with him: "white shirt-front and white face hanging in a darkness." One thing he has to overcome is his self-esteem, his narcissism; that more than anything might have inclined him to spare himself. Every time anything or anyone reminds him of his good looks, the prospect seems to brighten.

The outbreak of World War I is wonderfully timely for him, just two years after his marriage; and as long as it goes on, his morbidity does deviate into heroism. And when peace has been restored, will that not, we ask ourselves, serve at least as an acceptable substitute for happiness? No, it is the ignobility of the postwar life which strikes him; ignoblest of all, his own parent and his own spouse. Of course the real trouble, or perhaps I should say, the true pretext for the real trouble, is just his inoperative and irremediable feeling about Léa. Not infrequently, I believe great love gets one in a habit of procrastination; so that one's grief at the failure or loss of it also rather maunders, loiters, creeps.

Notwithstanding Colette's deftness and forward-moving rhythm, she has allowed *The Last of Chéri* to be, doubtless wanted it to be, her slowest book. It has called to my mind the catch phrase of a comedian in old-fashioned burlesque years ago, one of those endlessly patient, absolutely pessimistic types prone to more or less comic accidents: "No hope, no hurry."

Nothing that really deserves to be called accident happens to Chéri, scarcely even incident. We are given a fantastic feeling of being with him morning, noon, and night, while all his life is in a kind of quiet decomposition, unraveling and discoloring. We watch him as he seems to be deliberately experimenting with himself, with singular little techniques, little exercises, to turn his mind backward, to deaden himself to the present, to withhold himself from the future. It is all quite harmless behavior; only entirely unenjoyable and without true motivation.

At the last he spends most of his time with an awful little old woman, the oldest of all the courtesans, called La Copine, that is, the chum or pal, who knew Léa well in her heyday. Comedy again, but this time it is not vivace or even allegro; La Copine is like a death's-head wearing a wig, reminiscing all through the night, largo. She has a great collection of photographs of Léa, studio portraits framed and snapshots just thumbtacked up. In one of the snapshots she is escorted by one of her young lovers; not the one before Chéri, but the one before that. In another snapshot there appears in the background an elbow which La Copine declares must have been Chéri's own elbow; but he knows better, and it is only a blur anyway.

And then suddenly, when it has become almost a bore—in the scenes with La Copine, Colette has lulled our minds along with a soft, almost listless humorousness—suddenly we have reached the end. Chéri has reached the point of real readiness for the little flat revolver which he has had in his pocket a long time. He bolsters it up between two pillows so that he can stretch out at ease, his ear pressed to the barrel. In his freakish fatigue of life, at the last minute he seems almost unwilling or unable to make the effort of dying. We have a feeling that his laziness might almost have saved him. The worst and most rudimentary of the forms of will power, stubbornness, has destroyed him. We mourn over him very little.

Instead our minds run on ahead to what might possibly furnish a third volume: the reactions of those who have loved him. It is a gauge of the verity of Colette's characterizations that we can conceive their suffering in a circumstance she has not written—the thunderclaps in their several minds, especially the punishment of Mme. Peloux, and the ghastly bafflement of Léa, realizing how stupid she was ever to let him go, how conventional, how lazy; and of course for them both, for all the courtesans, fear! The sudden needless passing of one so young sounds the knell of everyone older, deafeningly.

❖

Glancing back at all the above synopsis and commentary, I have a troubling impression of having imposed on the story of Chéri an extra sordidness somehow; accentuation of the immorality, diminution of the charm. No wonder! For what, in fact, have I had to offer? Only some of its bones, no flesh and blood, nothing in the skin of the language in which it was written—none of the beauty of the way Colette wrote, which is often like a conferring of her own personal physical beauty upon the fictitious creatures she writes about, even unfortunate old satirized macabre creatures like La Copine. By means of diction, syntax, cadence, she gives them all something like complexion, milkiness and snowiness, rosiness and amber, and something like sheen of hair, sometimes raven and sometimes golden, and sinew in one place and bosom-softness in another, and every single lineament of things in accord with every other, according to all five senses; that is to say, verbal equivalents.

Style! it is what Colette is most celebrated for, in France, in French; or perhaps I should say, what first brought about her celebrity. Even in the early volumes, perhaps not in the *Claudines* but surely in the *Dialogues des Bêtes* (1904) and *Les Vrilles de la Vigne* (1908), she wrote like an angel; handled the language to perfection, or almost to perfection, in an inimitable, influential way.

And of course the sensuousness which I have tried to suggest is only one aspect of it. Elegance, brevity, and clarity are other aspects; and those turns of phrase, speedy and forceful and neat, and with a sense of fun, for which the French have the word "esprit." Expressiveness above all! In the first place, the expression or at least implication of the mentality of the author, in passages where the theme or construction of the particular work requires this to be restrained or held back; connecting it, therefore, with the lifework as a whole, maintaining some coherency of thought and correspondence of emotions throughout. Colette's great characteristics of mind and heart are an odd form of pride; serenity; thankfulness; stoicism; and a kind of sharpness or asperity.

And in the second place, more important for the novelist as such, the rendering of nuances of the particular subject matter, minutiae of characterization, instantaneities of the plot, with almost imperceptible touches, subtle selections of vocabulary, small patterns of syntax, even little calculated disorders. When a manner is as fine and intensive as Colette's, it can hardly be distinguished from the action or emotion or thought it has to convey. On many a page her meaning really resides in the mode of utterance rather than in the terms of statement; the nuance is all-signifying, as in poetry; and it loses heartbreakingly in translation, as poetry does.

Having mentioned in passing certain subtleties of this kind in *The Last of Chéri* I wish that I could examine passages in the other novels with the like or even closer application. But I know that, alas, writing about the detail and texture of writing is a mug's game, especially in English. We are short of technical terms of the art, English and American literature never having been as painstakingly wrought and self-conscious as the French. Academic critics of course invent technicalities and teach them to their pupils, but neither the general reader nor, indeed, the creative writer understands them very well. Perhaps on the whole the best way is just to express enthusiasm simply, as one would any other feeling, rejoicing in the artistry in question, marveling at it, pondering, with imagery more or less in the manner of the artist under consideration, and with borrowings from the phraseology of the other arts if they seem to suit.

In this way, for my part, I often compare Colette's prose to dancing. That was at the back of my mind when I declared that her years on the stage had been helpful to her in the development of her greatness as a writer. I borrow an exquisitely apt term, not, to be sure, from the kind of dancing Colette did, but from the old Italian-Russian-French tradition: absoluteness, as applied to the perfectly trained and entirely experienced female ballet dancer, *assoluta*. A discipline and indeed muscularity altogether disguised by gracefulness, so that the eye of the beholder is deceived, the sense of reality set aside—for a split second, the ballerina assoluta is emancipated from gravity; she pauses and reposes in mid-air, stops to think in mid-air! Does this seem altogether farfetched, as an analogy of literary style? Believe me, I could prove it, with plentiful and suitable citations, with perfect phrases suspended in mid-paragraph, and never for a split second failing to keep time to a general music.

❖

Twice, a quarter of a century apart, Colette undertook a most difficult or delicate theme: triangularity in marriage, by which term I mean something more than chance infidelity, something different from the regular sinfulness of adultery; an involvement of the marriage partner sinned against, condonation or acceptance for whatever reason, or perhaps inclusion somehow—in *Claudine Married* (1902), which is the third in the *Claudine* series, and in *The Other One* (1929).

In the very early work the involving element, connecting link, is some measure of homosexual responsiveness between young Claudine and a strange young woman named Rézi, who presently turns out to be Claudine's husband's mistress. He encourages their attachment, with intermingled amusement, kindness, and lustfulness. To be a good novel, with this oddity and crisscrossed compounded feeling, it would have had to be very good. In fact, it is only pleasant and interesting.

For one thing, there is the dubious, perhaps illegitimate but irresistible biographical interest; the mirroring of Colette's own youth in the immature and surely distortive creation. In those days when *Claudine* was not only a best-selling book but a successful play, played by Polaire, Willy persuaded Colette to bob her wonderful long hair to match the bizarre and entrancing little actress's. In a popular edition of *Mes Apprentissages* Colette let us see a photograph of them, out of doors somewhere, at the races or at a garden party; unhappy young ghost writer and moody young matinee idol in strikingly similar white ruffles, like twins, escorted by their notorious elderly employer. Perhaps Willy intended only a bit of good publicity. We cannot now entirely accept the conclusion to which an excitable Parisian public undoubtedly jumped. In one of her most beautiful miniature narratives, Colette made her feeling about

Polaire quite clear, as of great importance in her life then, in another way; no triangle. Possibly it was public misapprehension, wrong gossip, which provided her with that part of the plot of *Claudine Married* in the first place. Accident is sometimes inspirational.

But in spite of her great lifelong use of experience of her own in her work of fiction, on the whole she was less inspired by the turn of personal events, the impulse to explain or to justify her conduct, than most authors. Her life provided her with knowledge, but in the handling of it she has been extraordinarily objective, with pride of aesthetics rather than of reputation, and with unusual educability and severe critical sense. I am inclined to think that even in her early work, when any self-indulgence or frivolity appears in it, it is because, at that time, she could do no better; she had not learned how to write those pages more seriously. *Le Blé en Herbe* (1923), her masterly novel of young love, youngest love, initiation and defloration—the modern *Daphnis and Chloe*—recapitulates one of the themes of the not quite successful *Ingénue Libertine*. I think that dissatisfaction with *Claudine Married* may have been one thing that moved her to write *The Other One*. Alas, once more, she somewhat missed the mark. If she were to live long enough, she might try it again, in still another volume, perhaps a masterpiece.

Certainly the autobiographical factor has ceased to amount to much in *The Other One*. Farou, the husband in it, bears not the slightest resemblance to Willy. He is a playwright but rather, if I may say so, like Henri Bernstein. He is a great bull-like, hardworking, tireless and tiring creature. He loves his wife Fanny very well, though he has been unfaithful to her in the way of a little relaxation now and then, as it has happened to come in handy. She has always forgiven him and relaxed about it; and now relaxation, even laxness, laziness, is a part of her nature. She seems just not capable of not forgiving, though this time it is under her own roof, under her nose. The mistress this time, Jane, Farou's secretary, has become her good friend and comfortable companion. Fanny is not young; neither is Farou, but he still seems rather excessive in her life, too much for her. All things considered, she feels the need of Jane; and Farou needs her, rather more in the secretarial capacity than the amorous capacity. Fanny gets to thinking of Jane no longer conventionally as interloping mistress, rather as an assistant wife; and the book comes to a close in this way, which is a kind of happy ending.

As a whole, *The Other One* lacks vitality. Perhaps this subject matter lay fallow in her mind too long. It does not lack plausibility or function or general human interest; only it is not intensely interesting. It lacks chiaroscuro: no brilliance anywhere in it, no deep sort of obscurity either. Or perhaps I should say, the lights and shades, the several contrastable elements, are not arranged to set each other off to best advantage. The date of it puzzles and fascinates me: 1929, the year after the avowedly autobiographical *Naissance du Jour*, sumptuous with landscape-writing, grievous with frustrated and stoical amorous feeling, haunted by Sido's ghost. Perhaps wearied by that, she went to the other extreme in the story of the Farou family; overdid the objectivity. And after it, not another volume for three years—then a spate again, the most remarkable sequence of all: *Le Pur et l'Impur* (1932), the boldest of her reminiscences, all about various singularities of sex, then *The Cat* (1933), and then *Duo* (1934). When we consider *The Other One* in its place, in relation to the lifework, it is mysterious. In seemingly shallow, limpid, even glassy waters we discern greenish and bluish tones; something sunken perhaps, wreckage or treasure.

❖

Duo (1934) also is a story of marital irregularity, but not condoned at all, quite the contrary; and it has an unhappy ending, as unhappy as *Chéri*, except that the denouement comes about more promptly. The marriage of Michel and Alice has lasted a decade; a good marriage, with no lack of sexual responsiveness thus far, a happy, hardworking life, working more or less in double harness in various theatrical enterprises. But, recently while he was absent in the South of France on some business venture, she gave herself to one Ambrogio, a business associate; a silliness, a mistake, to which she called a halt after about two weeks. And, indiscreetly, she has kept some improper letters from him, in a purple letter case; and she carelessly lets Michel catch a glimpse of this, then tries to persuade him that there is not, never has been, any such object; and thus the deadly trouble starts; jealousy, the unpleasantest conceivable subject, the shame and disgrace of humankind, from the beginning of human history. No, not from the beginning, but ever since Dante or ever since Catullus!

"I do not believe in denouements," Balzac made one of his high-brow great ladies say. Literature can do as well as chance, if the literary man tries hard enough. "But," she concluded, "if we reread a book it is for the details." Colette's details are a marvel. For example, turn to Michel and Alice's breakfast on the terrace. It is the morning after the first evening of his wild jealousy and her evasiveness and defiance; after a night of extra-deep sleep, in avoidance of intercourse. Our concern about them has been well worked up, in behalf of both the justifiably but exorbitantly aggrieved husband and the culpable but regretful and well-meaning wife. "Man and woman, close together, disunited, languishing for one another." We hope that they may soon make peace.

Wifely, there on the terrace, to make him as comfortable as possible, she reaches across and turns the coffee pot and the cream pitcher, so that he shall have the handles on his side. Without comment! A good part of matrimony is in that gesture. Then a still slumberous bee comes clumsily to the honey pot, and she will not let him swat it with his napkin. "No, let it go," she cries, "it's hungry, it's working." And the mention of those two fundamentals, work, hunger, bulking so much larger in her womanly mind than jealousy—that male mania, negative form of eroticism, which is tormenting him, destroying their marriage, destroying him—brings tears to her eyes.

Note Colette's probity in this particular: she informs us of Alice's being the healthier-minded of the two, having the more constructive purpose. Michel is the sympathetic one, we suffer for him; but she is rather to be approved, less disapproved. And subtlety as well as probity! Writing as a woman, with wisdom explicitly womanly always, Colette enters further into Alice's mind and motivation than into Michel's. She seems to hint at various extenuating circumstances, excuses for her infidelity. Also, I think, she makes it quite clear that, if asked, as one woman moralizing with another, she would agree with Alice that infidelity was no such terrible thing, per se.

In due course, remembering and understanding everything about Alice, her background, family, upbringing, and all, Colette also added a sequel to *Duo—Le Toutounier* (1939).—Alice widowed, back in the family studio apartment in Paris; a conversation piece with two of her sisters, Colombe and Hermine, somewhat woebegone bachelor girls, career women. Their fond curiosity brings out Alice's defects, inadequacies; their psychology mirrors hers with the greatest animation of little lights and colors. And here we note that those characters Colette knows best, and perhaps loves best, put her under no particular obligation of indulgence. Here we learn why we did not like Alice better in the former novel; what it was about her that, almost more than the fact of her infidelity, contributed to her husband's desperation. For example, a certain conceit not unusual in women, but especially brought out by tactlessness in her case; and a kind of bravery that is not real courage, only false pride and defiance. Think back! how she frittered away Michel's patience and good will by changing her story every little while: admixture of truth and falsehood, unkinder than either. How self-indulgent she is, doubtless always was; therein she trespassed in the first place. Worst of all, her lack of imagination; therefore she fails to say the things that might possibly have consoled the poor creature trespassed against; therefore at last she lets him have it, the entire documentary truth, crude and exciting.

Note how I have mingled tenses in all these sentences, turning from the one book to the other; years apart in the writing, only months in the chronology of Alice's life. Here once more the binary form is impeccable; the division of the material very precise and meaningful. For one thing, at the end of *Duo* we are alone with Michel when he is planning to drown himself; whereas in *Le Toutounier*, Alice allows herself to believe, and convinces her sisters (and the insurance company), that it was an accidental death.

Nevertheless, she blames him, even for misadventure—hah, the fool! stumbling into the floodwater, forgetting the slipperiness of the red-clay riverbank—because she loved him, still loves him, and terribly misses him. There is often a factor of anger in great bereavement. Do you remember Schumann's song cycle, *Frauenliebe und Leben?*—"Now for the first time you have hurt me, hard unmerciful man, by dying, and that struck home!" She also blames him for his proneness to tragical feeling, darkening those last few days before the so-called accident; much ado about nothing, a trait of maleness.

But even in bitter widowhood Alice does not blame him as Colette blames him, and as we blame him. Colette shows us his abysmal pessimism, his self-destructive ardor, from the first word of the trouble. And at the end, Alice's impatient stupid entire revelation, with documentary evidence, which maddens him: he himself insisted on it; he would not take no for an answer. Neither to the right nor to the left would he turn or even look; nothing else touched or excited him, only his determination to know more than he could bear knowing. The sin of Psyche! he would commit it if it killed him, and it did.

Let me also call attention to the pages about the singing of the nightingales, once to each of these miserable mortals whose love is failing. The nightingale is a bird very dear and personal to Colette. *Les Vrilles de la Vigne* (1908), one of the first works of her own sole devising, without Willy, begins with a sort of allegory or fairy tale, two or three pretty pages. A nightingale falls asleep in a vineyard in the burgeoning springtime, and when it wakes up, has a bad fright; for the tendrils of grapevine have begun to wind around its feet and wings. Therefore, thereafter, it sings and teaches its young to sing, "While the grapevine is growing, growing, growing, I'll stay awake." In French this is a near enough approximation of nightingale rhythm. It expresses her feeling of escape from marriage—thirteen years of tendrils!—and of blessedly finding that she has voice and song of her own; that is, literary talent and something to express by means of it.

Here in *Duo,* in the prime of that talent, we have nightingales once more. The poor adulteress leaves the room, and the poor cuckold, sitting there by himself, begins to pay attention to a number of them, singing their hearts out, but softly, remotely; and then to a soloist, a much greater voice than the others, or perhaps only proximity makes it seem so. But how sad! how sick! Michel is not able to take any pleasure in any of it. It is as though his thoughts partly deafened him. How can a man so sad and sick partake of glorious nocturne? Only by withholding his breath, then trying to breathe in time to the music, which suffocates him a little and keeps him from thinking for a minute or two. And afterward—one of Colette's characteristic touches, with her sense of physiology keener than anyone's!—he feels a burning thirst.

A couple of pages further on, he goes out of the room; Alice comes back. It is her turn to listen, especially to that one loud tenor voice seemingly wasting itself away in brilliance, in repetitions so insistent and variations so farfetched that it scarcely suits her troubled heart; it seems to hinder all emotion, except its own emotion, if it can be called emotion. But, but, when the soloist pauses for a moment to catch its breath, there arises the soft chorus of the faraway singers, each for himself, each at the same time in harmony with the others—"accordés" is Colette's word, which means reconciled as well as harmonized; which also means matched, mated, betrothed. And unhappy Alice is reminded of the great spring labor going on along with the spring concert; assembling and weaving the nests, laying and hovering and hatching the eggs, feeding the fledglings; labor of the females for the most part. But not lonely; as long as they must labor the males will not fail to serenade them!

It is one of those metaphors, extended and, as you might say, dramatized, bearing as great a portion of the author's thought as her dialogue or her action—for which I love her. Do you not? Do you see what it signifies, suggests? The woman listening to those male birds, thinking of those dutiful female birds inarticulately nesting, is childless. In her joint life with Michel now stricken suddenly, in their hapless marriage unbalanced, toppling, hopeless, that important cornerstone of civilized heterosexuality is lacking: no egg, no fledgling, no real nest! Therefore, perhaps she thought of herself as free to lead a little double life for a fortnight, entitled to partake of modern single-standard morality; thus she erred in idleness, with not even watchful conscience, not even sufficiently troubling to keep it secret. Therefore, therefore . . . Go farther with this theme if you wish. Colette always knows when to stop; here she has stopped with the metaphor.

A bad thing about jealousy is the element of pornography in it: the stimulation of visualizing one's darling in someone else's arms, with the consequence of desiring somewhat more than usual just when one is expected to content oneself with somewhat less—or as in extreme and morbid instances, as in Michel's case, looking backward, crying over spilt milk, desiring the past. How clearly Colette has marked this, though with no stress or scabrousness! Michel himself admits it, in a single painful exclamation, after Alice has let him read all Ambrogio's letters: one of the games of love played by those two happened to be, ah, something the miserable husband has especially delighted in, more than anything, more than life.

Another detail: whereas Alice is Parisian, Michel is a Southerner, meridional—even as Sidonie, née Landoy, and Jules Joseph Colette. Make no more of this parallel than it is worth; it doubtless furnished their daughter with observations of the contrast of temperaments. From the first page of *Duo* it is suggested that Alice is somewhat the more intelligent or more civilized—or rather, the other way around: Michel is the more instinctive, primitive. Perhaps I oversimplify this. The point is that he is not at all the type of man for whom it is normal or natural to forgive a breach of the marriage vow. But for the grace of God, but for a generation or so, and a veneer of twentieth-century morals, this story might have ended in murder instead of suicide. It would have done Michel good to give Alice a beating, would it not? Yes, but perhaps he would not have known when to stop. Indeed, this might quite plausibly be given as his excuse for committing suicide: to prevent murder, or to punish himself for murderousness.

As representations of suicide, a subject most important to us, important in the symbolical or anagogical way especially, psychologists having shown us how frequently misdemeanors and misfortunes partake of the same dark frenzy, only a little less dark—the same desire to die but less determined, the same unwillingness to live, dilatory—see how the case of Michel compares, contrasts, with the case of Chéri! This is but a momentary violence, though the result is forever; an act almost of aggression, though the point of departure is true uxorious devotedness.

Whereas Chéri is bemused and benumbed, torpid, unmotivated. Would that he had been capable of a bit of violence! Colette has given us, as one of the gravest indications of his state, the fact that he feels no jealousy of Edmée. That might have waked him up and saved him. Or, alas, he might have relapsed into his slumberousness again, gone sleepwalking away in some other realm no less lonely. For there is a curse upon him; and we feel that if he had not turned it into the channel of death it would have developed in another direction: imbecility or worse.

The Last of Chéri, from the first page to the last, is a representation of that famous so-called sin of the Middle Ages, rampant again in this century in more ways than one: acedia, that is, horrible languor, malignant listlessness, irremediable boredom, paralysis of soul; the intolerable sorrowfulness when even the specific sorrow keeps slipping one's mind. And this is the greatest portrayal of it in modern literature. Michel is not in this classification at all. If the engaging circumstance of Alice's infidelity had not befallen him, or if Alice had kept him in blessed ignorance of it, he would have been all right.

See the mystery of morals! Although Chéri's background is so bad, all those old courtesans constituting so gross and mean and base a society—and Michel and Alice and even Ambrogio are just average inoffensive humanity—the opprobrium upon him is slighter; for the most part we think of it as sickness. Michel is the wickeder.

E

In case of suicide we cannot moralize upon the act itself—we do not know enough—only upon the attitude of mind, heart, and soul just prior to it. What was in Michel's mind, heart, soul? Possessiveness, punitiveness, intermingling of lust and prudery, deafness and blindness to all the signs of Alice's love, rejection of her. In Chéri's. Only disappointment, disappointment in himself and in the crazy bad sick world—many a saint has felt as much—and fatigue and loneliness and stupor; nothing very bad, nothing unfair.

And see the indivisibility of morals and psychology! in *Duo* Alice is the healthy one. In so far as Michel's wicked intention is to make her suffer, he miscalculates, it miscarries, she is too strong for him. Wherein lies her strength? In her dullness of mind as well as her robustness, lack of imagination as well as good nature. Her salvation and Chéri's perdition are correlative in some way, but impossible to correlate. The fact is that neither of the two sets of values by itself—neither right versus wrong nor sickness versus health—will serve to explain or to save humanity. We have to try first one and then the other. And in the last analysis of course there is no salvation: everyone is deathward bound, the road has no turning. God is not mocked.

◆

It occurs to me that I have taken *Duo* out of chronology, for no particular reason; not far out. *The Cat* (1933) is another of Colette's masterpieces, made of rather similar materials of middle-class humanity, matrimony again; matrimonial misunderstanding and mischance and fiasco. Approximately of the same length, the same shortness, I think you will agree that, because it is more poetical it tells more and signifies more per page. It has no sequel, needs no sequel.

The marriage of Alain and Camille scarcely deserves to be called a marriage; it lasts only a few months, a trial and a failure. We first see Alain still living at home with fond parents. He has a most cherished, most beautiful cat named Saha, a thoroughbred Carthusian, grayish-bluish. After the honeymoon he takes it to live with them. Marriage does not make him any the happier; neither does he make his wife happy. He lets her realize his vague sense of having made a mistake, vague longing to be back home again, infidelity of spirit. The cat seems to Camille emblematic of all that. She tries to kill it, does not succeed. But Alain cannot forgive her, nor she him.

Do you observe how this constitutes a sort of diptych with the story of Michel and Alice? And here also, how strong and sure Colette's sense of justice is; how deft her communication of it, though never passing specific judgment! Is it by instinct, or with intellect like a precision instrument? I think it is a part of her femininity, and an attractive part, to seem to set aside claims of mere cerebration. As in *Duo* she has presented the wife somewhat more understandingly than the husband, that is, more explanatorily, with an extra perspective, a brighter light. But by the same token, the more critically! We are not in the least obliged to love the female; we are allowed to love, and to feel that Colette herself loves, the male.

Indeed, peering a little more profoundly into creative coincidence than it is proper to do, we may remark that we have heard of only one other person on earth as devoted to cats or to a cat as this young Alain; that person is old Colette herself. And as she conceived this story she may well have arrived at a part of the tension between him and his bride by asking herself, What if I had to choose between my cat and some such vain, disrespectful, disturbing new young person?

Alain's young person really is a terrible girl, a type that may sometimes incline one to despair of the epoch; so very nearly in the right about almost everything, but just missing the point; so self-righteous but so lacking in self-assurance; possessive without strength, destructive without deadliness. She has energy to burn but somehow very little warmth, except perhaps in the specific conjugal connection. With a certain fatuity, as to her importance to her husband, which gradually gives way to sadness and bitterness, in the realization of her unimportance, she seems to have nothing else to live for.

Indeed we sympathize with her as to her resentment of the cat. We see that it is less exorbitant and less abstract than Michel's jealousy in *Duo*. The trespassing of Ambrogio against him was a thing of the past; and even at the time of its happening he felt no injury, not the slightest pang, no deprivation. Whereas Saha is an ever-present rival, lauded by Alain with every other breath, and established by him as a permanent feature of their married life. But why, we wish to know, why could she not somehow gradually vitiate and exorcise the childish magic it has for her dear husband? Is there ever any point in a vain, violent iconoclasm, loudly denying the tabu and pushing down the sacred image? And if it came to the point of violence against her will, if her husband in his aelurophily suddenly maddened her, why so inefficient about it? Why defenestration, instead of poisoning or drowning? The folly of just giving it a push, hurting it, and arousing its hatred, paroxysm of hissing and explosive yellowish eyes, which is what betrays her to Alain!

The worst of this kind of female character, we say to ourselves, is that even in violence it falls between two stools. It results not even in disaster but in muddle and mess and absurdity. But, beware! this kind of objection is valid in aesthetics, if you really prefer tragedy to comedy; but in morals it is evil nonsense. Falling between two stools is better than successfully killing cats. The reason for Camille's weakness and coarseness and confusion, and even loss of husband, is fundamental and creditable. To express it in the sentimental style, she is on the side of life. It not only enables us to forgive her, it necessitates our forgiveness.

Her dear husband really is a maddening youth, though attractive. He is as fatuous in his feeling of unimpeachable male supremacy as she in her feeling of absolute female desirability; as self-indulgent in his daydreaming and voluptuous frivolity with his pet as she in her vain commotion and pursuit of pastime. We can never feel quite happy about him, even when he is perfectly happy himself, even when he gets back home where perhaps he belongs. In the very first chapter we observe how recklessly his parents have spoiled him; marriage to Camille seems the only hope for him. At the end of the story we cannot see into his future at all; it seems all beclouded and scarcely even tragic, just harrowing. He is a type that may sometimes incline one to despair of France.

Two thousand years ago St. Paul decided that it is better to marry than to burn; a way of stating the case which seems to start marital relations off on the wrong foot. Psychologists nowadays, scarcely less severe, have added that it is better to be infantile—better to disappoint a wife and concentrate on a cat and give up marriage altogether, as Alain did—than to commit suicide. If we agree, we are constrained to admire this young man more than the poor hero of *Duo*. Colette seems not to have reached any absolute decision upon this point; no aphorism that I can recall. But certainly she expects us to take Alain's cat as an emblem of child life, home life, childish home life, and of its compromise and consolation in secret: autoeroticism. No pettiness about this; nothing belittled or made sordid or left sordid—not ever, in the writing of this good woman and liberal writer!

Let me call your attention to her description of Saha at night, at the beginning of the story: one night just before Alain's marriage, on his bed, thrusting her claws through his pajamas just enough to worry him, with a pleasurable worrisomeness; then giving him one of her infrequent quick kisses with her chilly nose; then seating herself on his chest while he falls asleep; and until morning, vigilant perfect superhuman creature, seeming to fix with her hard eyes, and to follow around and around in the darkness, the fateful zodiacal signs, lucky and unlucky stars, which in unknowable time and in incomprehensible space dance to and fro over sleeping humanity. Two things at once—it is that manifoldness in Colette's mind which I have mentioned, as of the time of her great fit of depression in Franche-Comté—a very slight instance, Alain's mere inconsequential self-provided soporific pleasure, and at the same time a very great concept, great eternality and destiny, even as personified by Bashet, the cat-goddess of the Egyptians.

Toward the close of the story there is another little picture of Alain and Saha together. He holds her in his arms, rejoicing in her entire contentedness and entire confidence in him. With the peril of Camille's rivalry happily averted, Saha has, Alain reflects, a life expectancy of perhaps another decade; and he winces at the thought of the brevity of life, the brevity of love. In the decade after that decade, he promises himself, probably he will want a woman or women in his life again. He does not specify Camille; he is not such a cad as to expect her to wait for him. But in any event, he promises Saha, he will never love another cat.

Yes, this love scene of childish man and almost womanly cat seems almost too good to be true, too pretty and tender and humorous. It is a kind of happy ending. Any valid commentary upon a work of narrative art has to be in some measure a retelling. Now suddenly I realize how much less cheerful my retelling of this has been than the text itself. The loveliest of love stories; at the same time a serious study of modern matrimony, yes, indeed! But the true love in question is that between Alain and Saha; the true marriage is theirs. Camille is the troublemaker, the interloper, who makes a fool of herself and is successfully driven back out of the way. It is almost an allegory or a fairy tale; and what truth there is in it I certainly cannot state, in the way of either ethics or psychotherapeutics.

❖

In *Gigi,* the most successful of Colette's short narratives—metamorphosed into an American play and into two motion pictures, one French, with perfect performances by two illustrious elderly comediennes, one American, with music—two of her chief lifelong themes are entrancingly and significantly combined: the crossing of the border between girlhood and womanhood, and the ordeal of growing old, with due sagacity and tenderness and vicarious power. Gigi is the darling child of a family of unmarried women, all (or almost all) courtesans. Her mother has been unsuccessful, and therefore is reduced to singing small parts at the Opéra-Comique. Therefore her loving and tyrannous, realistic and pessimistic grandmother and her wealthy and conceited and didactic great-aunt Alicia have taken her in hand, to train her for, and launch her in, the only way of life they know.

It is, for the reader as well as the pretty and promising girl, educational: how to sit becomingly with one's elbows close at one's sides and one's shoulder blades flat on one's back, how to smoke without getting the tip of one's cigarette wet or even moist, how to negotiate difficult foods such as soft-boiled eggs and broiled or roasted small game birds; and questions of still graver consequence, for example, which jewels may be accepted as a sufficient token of esteem, and which, on the other hand, are virtually an insult.

By the miracle of Colette's handling, her gift of romanticization, her profundity of human kindness, none of this is cynical or squalid. The details of petty and even funny realism do not obscure the sad reality of old age, most notable in cases of extreme worldliness like these superannuated charmers, in whose range of vision there is no eternal life except ever-recurrent youth, generation after generation. Nor does the social satire detract from the romantic happiness of the ending, when Gigi is wiser than they; when all their calculation of making a living by being lovable suddenly gives way to love itself, love requited, and wedding bells.

Perhaps the reader has begun to have enough of being escorted through Colette's enjoyable lifework from page to page by me, and will willingly go on now independently, with references to his own experience and applications to his own problems. For my part, at any rate, I suddenly feel almost ashamed of stating and interpreting so much, topsy-turvy and wrong end to.

For, truly, slight pure narrative itself ought to be given precedence over any meaning that one can read into it or any moral that may seem attachable to it. Is not this the profound thing about narration, the almost mystic belief of the true narrator? Incident, description, characterization, dialogue, are the means of expression of truths that are greater, more affecting, truer, than anything that can be put in general or theoretical form. Perhaps a great narrator like Colette only pretends to be thinking about her characters, coming to conclusions about them, pointing morals—the supreme narrative device, to convince us of their reality! We are able to moralize about them, ergo they exist.

◈

I will tell you something of the latter part of Colette's life, with a particular appreciation of the extraordinary love story which is reflected in her autobiographical novel, *La Naissance du Jour* (Break of Day); then conclude this long fond essay.

Colette's later years do not lend themselves to lively recapitulation as her venturesome youth did. Somewhat as it is said of kings and queens, that happy reigns have no history, it will be understood that very great labor of authors and authoresses—fifteen short novels and fifteen long stories and scores of very short tales and sketches and half a dozen volumes of nonfiction in this authoress's case—is bound to curtail the more obvious materials of biography.

Just prior to World War I Colette married Henry de Jouvenel. She bore him a daughter, Bel-Gazou, of whom she wrote enchantingly, enchantedly, at the age and stage of growth when a little human being is most like any other immature animal: *La Paix chez les Bêtes* (Peace among the Animals). Jouvenel was a distinguished and successful newspaperman. Therefore, very naturally, Colette forsook the stage and also took up the career of journalism, and after their divorce continued in it for many years, indeed never discontinued; presumably had to depend on it for a part of her livelihood until almost the end of her life. The literary art, in the present half-revolutionized world, does not as a rule feed its practitioner, though world-famous. While more Frenchmen read more books than we, they pay less per volume.

Thousands of pages of Colette's collected works were first printed in, if not conceived for or commissioned by, various newspapers and periodicals; including five solid years of drama criticism, in the second-thickest volume. No one has written more gravely than she of the waste and fatigue of hack writing, though without plaintiveness or pretension. But, on the other hand, I think no one has managed it so well, with so much to show for it in the end. After her autobiographies have grown familiar around the world as one great work, perhaps her greatest, then surely some editor will select and assemble from all her reporting, column writing, and familiar essay writing the equivalent of an important diary, notable especially for terse, intense aphoristic passages, which surely a great many readers will appreciate.

All her life, she confided to us, she suffered from two recurrent bad dreams: one of the presses rolling, and no copy; and another of coming out on a vast vacuous platform or stage to sing, and her song lapsing. In those old days of her acting and dancing, did she also sing? I do not recall any mention of that. Which reminds me: just for the pleasure of it, in 1924, she went back on the stage in Léopold Marchand's dramatization of *Chéri,* in the role of Léa, with the famous comedienne so near and dear to her, Marguerite Moreno, in the role of Mme. Peloux, Chéri's mother.

In 1925 she met Maurice Goudeket, and, before long, entered into the great understanding and intimacy with him which continued for the rest of her life. As I have said, an early stage of that relationship is reflected, but *not* (Goudeket has assured us) truly narrated, in *Break of Day.* Both in content and in form, this work of fiction is especially meaningful and central. Central even in the way of paper and printer's ink, it is to be found in Volume VIII of the *Oeuvres Complètes,* with seven octavo volumes before it and seven after it. In our understanding of her narrative art as a whole, it is impressive as a kind of divide, or watershed, halfway between her storytelling and her vein of autobiographical subjectivity, and indeed between fact and fiction; halfway also in her life, between the influence of her unforgettable mother and her exemplary and helpful third marriage. Even her style in it is transitional and momentous, a matter of echoing, reminiscing effects and of little clarion notes of surprise and prophecy here and there; befitting that time of life which has been called the old age of youth and the youth of old age, a time fraught with heartache and youthful tensions.

An almost careless admixture of autobiography in her various forms of fiction was characteristic of Colette even in her salad days, when her first husband, Willy, bullied her into writing, and she let him sign her books temporarily. The heroine of *L'Entrave* and of *The Vagabond*, the sad divorcee bravely earning her living as an interpretative dancer in vaudeville, is obviously a self-portrait. Upon occasion she mingled things the other way round, carrying elements of her yarn-spinning over into the early volumes of non-fiction: for example, the most important of her tributes to her mother is entitled *La Maison de Claudine*, as one might say, The Home that Claudine Came From.

In *Break of Day*, which is in story form, nouvelle form, the mingling is stranger than ever. It frankly purports to be an experience of her own, and she portrays herself not only in the throes of it but with pen in hand, fountain pen in sunburned, garden-hardened hand, all through the summer night and in the dawning blueness of another day, day after day, writing it. The name she gives herself in it is the same as on the title page: "Colette." Furthermore, she surrounds herself with known unfictitious friends: Carco, the successful novelist, Segonzac, the famous painter, Thérèse Dorny, a beloved comedienne of those days, and others. Only, evidently, Vial, a young man whom this "Colette" loves and decides not to go on loving, is fictitious.

Most nouvelles, which somehow take place in a perpetual, mobile present, with continuous updating of the past and continuous glimpsing of the future, have simple plots. What could be simpler than the plot of *Break of Day?* A literary woman in her fifties has been enjoying an amorous intimacy with a man in his thirties. Into the picture comes a strong young woman who has made up her mind to marry him. Thus far, he seems not to have fallen in love with the young woman; he still loves the older woman; but she is ashamed to compete, perhaps afraid to. She gives him up and sends him away, and resignedly dedicates herself to an independent way of life, with her good friends and beautiful cats, with her garden and orchard and vineyard, with her literary subject matter (including what has just happened) and her sense of style, decisive in morals and mores as well as in literature.

What necessitated this renunciation? That is suggested to us by the secondary sense of the title, *La Naissance du Jour:* the birth of the day, the coming of the light, revelation. In the pattern of her intimacy with the young man—altered, though only slightly altered, by the marriageable girl—it has been revealed to her that he will not be able to make her happy much longer; neither will any other young or youngish man. Worse still, it is going to be impossible for him to keep from making her unhappy. To suffer from ill-founded expectations of love at her age is beneath her dignity. It is her duty, she thinks, to avoid unhappiness of that order.

In his tender, distinguished memoir, *Close to Colette*, Maurice Goudeket states that Vial was not modeled upon him in any essential. Certainly, let us take his word for this, although the dates and overlapping circumstances to be noted in two recently published volumes of Colette's letters are striking and must have meaning. When Colette and he drew close to each other in 1925 they were aged, respectively, fifty-two and thirty-five. She wrote *Break of Day* in her house in Saint-Tropez, which is the scene of it, and in a hotel nearby in Provence (when Goudeket was in Paris) during the autumn of 1927 and the following winter.

We often thoughtlessly say that art takes a long time, whereas life is short, "Ars longa, vita brevis"; which saying seems to relieve the embarrassment of unenergetic artists, but is not necessarily true. In fact it may be quicker and easier to write a story than to love or hate, settle down or run away, marry or part. The creative faculty is able to do some experimenting with the creator's life, which may be to his or her advantage.

Certainly, for Colette, the renunciation of love accounted for in this fiction of "Colette" and Vial was, in actuality, the road not taken. Her loving companionship with Goudeket went on uninterruptedly; she refers to him in almost all her letters from 1925 on. In 1935 they got around to a formalization or legalization of their relationship, and he was her perfect helpmate, watchdog, adviser, editor, and (as she customarily called him) "best of friends," until her death in 1954. It is hard to think of Goudeket as ever having been a mere lover and beloved (like Vial), so greatly did he transcend that youthful role in the successive decades. He has not written boastfully of the transcendence; but pages and pages of her elderly autobiographical writing have a marvelous aura of appreciation of him.

The most moving of her self-portraits is the opening chapter of *L'Étoile Vesper,* which is all interspersed with dialogue of husband and wife, the least wordy dialogue in all literature, as their conjoined minds at that late date scarcely required words. When the Germans were in France, with a weak French government to do their bidding, Goudeket, being of Jewish descent, was taken in a general roundup of about twelve hundred various unfortunate persons and kept in the concentration camp of Compiègne for a while; and after his liberation from that hellhole, had to live half free and half in hiding, here and there in the provinces, preyed upon by the bureaucracy and the evil police, for another eighteen months. Colette's account of this is terse and stoic, and her account of his home-coming, at last, proud and reticently tender.

In the course of those war years Colette was gradually stricken with extreme arthritis, and for the last decade of her life was confined to wheel chairs and to bed. I do not see how she could possibly have accomplished the latter part of her lifework without Goudeket's affection and surveillance and help.

All this is a far cry from the discouraged realism and renunciation of *Break of Day.* We may conclude that it was a hypothesis which did not come true, and that Vial was a personification. What Colette had to say farewell to in 1927 and 1928 was just a part of herself, and just one aspect of love; the fierce and fearful narcissism of always wanting to mirror oneself in the beloved, the weak possessiveness, the hopeless, unnecessary jealousy, and the point of pride. Indeed it is a wonderful simplification to be able to attribute all one's happiness to someone and to blame that same someone for all one's unhappiness; but there are other simplifications for us as we grow older.

The word "love" in a love story—and in almost any criticism of fiction, unless the critic spells out his meaning—is apt to connote only that magic realm in which, as Sir Thomas Browne expressed it, two people "so become one that they both become two." Perhaps there is, or can be, some truth in this in young manhood and young womanhood; certainly it grows false and fatal as the years pass. Farewell to it, Colette said in this story; never again! And if she had not exorcised and uprooted the romanticism in herself by some such creative effort as this broken-off romance with imaginary Vial, she might not have had the courage to entrust the rest of her life and her lifework, and the first part of her posthumous reputation, to Goudeket.

The glory of the true history, and the crowning of their two lives with the *Oeuvres Complètes,* makes one almost impatient with the melancholy tale. Here we may see a disadvantage in the combining of real and personal materials with the composites and embodiments of fiction. Knowing the rest of Colette's life as she lived it, we cannot take the somberness of her narration as literally as she intended. But the somber implications last, and may serve the reader well, in his own thought and feeling. Any piece of authorship that ends in leave-taking and in the solitude of the one left behind (though left behind to write, as in this case) touches upon everyone's loneliness and the universal anxiety. It reminds us of the one really hateful thing about life: that we must all depart from it eventually, or to state the matter more exactly, that it must depart from us, is departing from us.

But Colette's melancholy writing is saved from dreariness and desolation by her stoic sense. It is a somewhat nobler and, I may say, better-natured form of stoicism than the mere endurance of distress. Though she never jokes, there are gleams of humor, bitter mischief, and brilliancy round and about her every sad saying and every poor prospect. Having said things or portrayed things, she rather simply forbids herself to be distressed by them any longer. She forces the distressing matter, disappointment or injustice or bad luck, all the way down inside herself, into depths of literature, profundities of love, and other almost mystic depositories of her thinking; and she gives us to understand, induces us to believe, that she is strong enough to be able to do this without too many of those cross-purposes of the mind and the nervous system which we call neuroses.

Break of Day begins with a letter from her mother, Sido, to her second husband, Henry de Jouvenel, declining an invitation to visit them in Paris, the year before her death; other maternal letters, in whole or in part, are interspersed in the text; and Colette handles a good many of her fictive incidents and arguments as it were in a musical composition, variations on themes of Sido's life and Sido's thought; notably, an intense responsiveness to physical beauty, which is not often characteristic of the female sex; fastidiousness and pride, especially with regard to the imperfections of the body in the decline of life; and great work-morality. It makes a strange immortal atmosphere: a ghostly presence, handing down feminine ideas from generation to generation.

The reason Sido declined to visit Colette and Jouvenel was that a pink cactus which someone had given her was in bud. In untropical France, she explained, it was apt to blossom only every fourth year. If she missed it this time, she might not live to see another blossoming. This is on the first page, and on the second page, Colette imagines her mother's joyous concentration, with an enraptured expression smoothing all the wrinkles out of her old face, bending down and watching the place in the midst of the knife-edged plant where the promise of the flower was thrusting—"a woman who, like a flowering plant herself, had gone on indefatigably unfolding and opening for three quarters of a century"—and on the third page, we have Colette's acknowledgment of the similarity of her own almost perverse, blissful gaze at her Vial as he slipped out of her bed, out of her house, at daybreak.

When Sido, in her mid-seventies, played chess with a little shopkeeper in her village, she kept on the alert for any sign of her senescence. "When I become too disgraceful and impotent at it, I shall renounce it as I have renounced other things, as a matter of decency."

In still another letter the solitary old woman, though in danger of fatal illness, objected absolutely to a family plan of hiring someone to spend the night in the house with her. No poor substitute companionship in the wee small hours for her! she protested, and itemized the miseries involved: the rumpled bed and the unpleasant toilet bowl, alien inhalation and exhalation in the dark, and the humiliating prospect of having to wake up with someone else in the room. "Death is preferable," she said, "it is less improper."

No wonder that the daughter of such a woman minded the compulsions of love as she began to feel un-young. Goudeket has told us that, even as an octogenarian, with every excuse of arthritic immobility and last-minute literary endeavor, his wife would not admit him to her room in the morning until the tasks and technicalities of her toilet and make-up and wardrobe had been completed.

Colette's father also had cherished a packet of letters written to him by Sido when she had been obliged to spend some time in a nursing home after an operation. After his death she found them all in his desk, and expressed a sort of disapproval. "What a pity that he loved me so much! It was his love for me that annihilated, one by one, the fine faculties that might have inclined him toward literature and science. He chose to keep dreaming of me instead, tormenting himself about me; and I found this inexcusable."

It is what I call work-morality. According to the idealism that the strong-spirited mother and the gifted emancipated daughter had in common, it is wrong to pride oneself on any mere greatness of love or mere intensity about it or mere continuation of it. Let us ask ourselves, instead, what results from it in the other areas of our lives, lifelong: perhaps a strengthening and steadying of the various functions of head and heart, perhaps not; possibly a tribute to it in some way, by means of intelligence and talent, or it may be, alas, nothing but inhibition and vapidity.

Break of Day is a story of literature as well as love. When Colette declared in it that she felt duty-bound not to subject herself to untimely, unnecessary unhappiness, the duty that she had in mind was her vocation of letters. As of that date, the time had come for her to lay in a supply of her customary lifelong pale-blue paper, to take pen in hand, to rediscover in her memory the great traces of nature and human nature, the pleasures and sorrows of the prime of life, and to convey them to others' minds, readers' minds, by means of well-focused language and logical grammar and clarifying syntax and sweet euphony; and never again to be distracted from literature by life. "Cold with emotion is the bronzed hand, which races upon the page, stops, crosses something out, and starts again; cold with a youthful emotion."

From that time on, pride and courage and vocation were to be the predominant moral concepts in her work, and pantheism was to be its principal emotion, transcending individual or intrapersonal feelings. I find the imagery of nature worship in *Break of Day,* even in English, enchanting. Turn the page now, and see for yourself: the ripening color of the Saint-Tropez afternoon, after the siesta, with a cat also rousing from its siesta, yawning like a flower; and then the descent of the north wind, the mistral, anesthetizing all that part of the earth between the Alps and the Mediterranean; the early-morning seascape, blue-black, and scarcely awake yet, when Colette went wading out into it, then trudged back up the beach with a load of seaweed, to make a mulch around her tangerine trees; the beautiful child holding a rose, on the threshold of Sido's sickroom, afraid of her because she was dying; even Vial's naked beauty—his body somehow more exact, more aroused, more expressive than his face—with antique patina of sunshine and salt water, and a bluish light shining on his shoulders, a greenish light girding his loins. Death and sex also subordinated to a general concept of the rightness of nature. . . .

If one is religious at all, in the pantheistic way, when the fateful farewell time comes, it may be easier to forfeit and to take leave of things beloved, things more or less perfect, at their peak—the pink cactus in bloom—than of any lesser thing, worn away or overblown. In case of the more acute and tragic deprivation, one can at least keep, for remembrance and for a kind of worship, a godlike image, a concept of heaven on earth. So, at the time of writing *Break of Day,* Colette evidently thought.

◊

Beginning in 1948, continuing through 1949, concluding in 1950, the illustrious old publishing company of Flammarion issued the collected edition to which I have kept referring in this essay;

prepared for the press, as its colophon specifies, by the author's husband. "Thus, at the conclusion of a long career," wrote the collected one in a tiny general preface, "thus and only thus is the writer enabled to compute the total accumulated weight of his life-work. At this point only is he entitled to rejoice in his own good opinion; also his real anguish commences." Anguish of unrevisability, irremediability—fundamental though much ignored principle of ethics as well as aesthetics!

In other brief sentences scattered all through the collection she sounded the same proud, uneasy note; glanced back disappointedly but dispassionately upon every work in which she could detect unworthiness, frivolity, mannerism. So many pages having been written in a great rush, of dire necessity, she was afraid of their seeming not polished enough. Here and there, alas, had she not failed to discover the absolutely suitable word, to form the perfectly felicitous phrase? As she had been dependent on incidental inspiration so frequently, with this fortuitous commitment and then that, perhaps her entire lifework lacked cohesiveness, which the younger generation, and in due course posterity, might notice and deplore.

Let no one laugh or even smile at her unnecessary humility, fastidious and fretful apologia. Instead, let the multitude of fellow writers hang their heads in, relatively speaking, shame; and let the shameless, the unhumble, the uneducable, despair and cease and desist from writing altogether; and let the very young with any talent, in high school, at universities, at writers' conferences, on newspapers, wherever they may be, dedicate themselves with stricter and fonder vows than the usual! It seems to me that the time has come—a part of the twentieth-century revolution being against culture—to speak out in this connection with some portentousness and intensity. In the more serious sects of religion perfectionism is a sin: and according to the present science or semiscience of psychology, no doubt it is psychopathological. But in the literary art it is just method; the one and only good and sound method.

It is an essential feature of the artistic temperament: pride of greatness—and heartbreaking ideal of greatness for those who know

that they personally are second rate, which keeps them from declining to third rate or fourth rate—taking all that has been done
already as a matter of course, a matter of no further interest; climbing up on the previous proud accomplishment, not to glory in it,
just to see what may lie beyond, perhaps accomplishable, if one
lives long enough. From which must derive for aging artists a
certain chronic bitterness, and for second-raters, a sickness at heart.
For we never do live long enough. "Ars longa, vita brevis."

It can be justified in religion, come to think of it! Bossuet, the
glorious baroque theologian and preacher, explained it in someone's funeral sermon: "We are inevitably less than our thoughts,
God having taken pains to indicate by means of them His in-
finity." Without changing his saying much: artists, by the great
pains they take and by the extent of their intelligence, always
greater than their ability—along with other voices in the enormous
concert of the world, cacophony of the cosmos—indicate and celebrate infiniteness. And surely there is not in the world at present
a greater exponent of this than Sidonie Gabrielle Goudeket, née,
and known as, Colette.

We know how the aesthetic conscience and high, tender, and
constant virtuosity began in her case. She recalled a very early, very
significant slight incident for us. It is in a commissioned text, ac-
companying some fine color plates of exotic butterflies, hack writing
—an account of the butterfly collecting of her two adolescent
brothers; over-nice and wasteful. Every evening they would sit in
judgment upon the day's catch and relentlessly eliminate every
unworthy specimen. "Thus, aged seven or eight, I learned that
only beauty deserves preservation, and that the sons of men in
their vainglory are never altogether satisfied with anything."
Neither, it may be concluded, are the daughters of women; least
of all, the daughter of Sido.

Supreme rememberer! how frequently, and with what youthful
sensitivity until the very end, her mind turned upon those early
days! Perhaps I have laid too much stress on her dissatisfaction with
the style and form of this and that small part of her lifelong creation. Certainly she regretted its incompletions more than its im-

perfections, looking longingly at certain mysterious untouched themes, unarticulated messages, especially things about her mother. She specified in the final preface to *La Maison de Claudine* in 1949 that, when Sido died, she seemed not to have departed upon any remote path into abstract eternity; instead, she said, "she has made herself better known to me as I have grown older." Perhaps the extraordinary matriarch had deposited things in her mind that she had not yet discovered. "I began this discovery late in life. What better could I conclude with?"

I remember thinking, when I read this page, that she might still find time to paint one more filial portrait. She gave it up, or perhaps put it off too long. Almost everyone in the shadow of death likes to plan something up ahead; it gives one a feeling of a certain extension of one's lease of life. But not extremely fearful, certainly disregarding her bodily desuetude and the unabating pain and the increasing awkwardness, she kept on with her exquisite journalism. Often, in the past, photographers had concentrated on her strong hand with well-fleshed and tapering fingers and unprotruding fingernails, poised over pages of her work in progress, or reposing amid sulphur-glass paperweights and other bibelots and small useful objects in elegant disorder. It appeared not greatly changed in the last photographs. It always either held, or was about to take up, one of her accustomed extra-thick pens.

She lived out her life in the heart of Paris, in the Palais-Royal, that extensive rectangle of not very palatial architecture built by Louis XV's cousin Philippe-Egalité who was not opposed to the Revolution, whom the revolutionists decapitated nevertheless. It is said to be the first apartment house ever erected; that is, the first conglomeration of fairly small sets of rooms designed to be rented to independent individuals of middling income. Inside the rectangle is a colonnade, a playground, statuary, flower beds, a little melodious uplifted water, and an orderly plantation of modest trees.

It suited Colette. The bed in which she lay bedridden was placed alongside of the window, with a mobile desk that she could pull up close over her knees. She slept very little, troubled by the usual nervousness of the aged as well as by the caprices of unrelenting arthritis and by her genius, and often worked at night. Over her head hung that electric light sheathed with blue paper referred to in the title of her memoir of 1949, *Le Fanal Bleu* (The Blue Beacon). To nocturnal strollers in the colonnade and the arbitrary garden area down below it became as familiar as that star referred to in the title of her memoir in 1946, *L'Étoile Vesper* (The Evening Star), the folding star of shepherds, Sappho's star. Colette's modesty about her authorship was not constant, thank heaven; it was traversed by almost youthful gleams of natural and joyous importance and by the sense of immortality looming. And, especially when she worked late, she must often have thought of Flaubert, who more than anyone else influenced her in the matter of style, verbal workmanship, justness of diction, melopoeia; Flaubert who kept such a regular nocturnal working schedule that the bargemen up and down the Seine used his study window as a lighthouse.

There is a text expressive of her belief in the literary art, which let me now translate, carefully, not without vanity of my own style, as a somewhat more appropriate tribute to this writer whom I love than any 10,000-word exegesis. In her young womanhood she made friends with the noted courtesan, Caroline Otero, known as La Belle Otero; a sort of friendship of curiosity to which writers naturally are inclined. When she came to write *Chéri,* apparently this world-famous beauty—with thorough changes, from brunette to blonde, and from Spanish to one hundred per cent French, and so on—posed in her mind for certain aspects of the characterization of wonderful Léa.

Years later, sixteen years later, she wrote a description of Otero, in *Mes Apprentissages,* and brought into it with seeming casualness, with little touches in sentence after sentence, and with wondrous authority at the close of the second paragraph, an article of creative faith: "That beautiful body, so arrogant in its declining years, defiant of every illness and evil frequentation and the passage of time, that well-nourished body, with plumpness drawn smooth over its muscles, with luminous complexion, amber by daylight, pale in the evening: I vowed that someday I would describe it, painstakingly and disinterestedly. We can never produce perfect likenesses of the faces dearest to us; we slip into passionate deformation somehow. And who ever will undertake to set down faithfully all the traits of true love?

"Instead we record, with words as with paintbrush, the flaming redness of outworn foliage, a green meteor amid the blue of midnight, a moment of the dawn, a disaster. . . . Spectacles not notable for their significance or their profundity, but charged by us with premonition and emphasis. For the time to come they will bear the imprint of the four numerals of a given year; and mark the culmination of some error, the decline of some prosperity. Therefore, it is not for us to say with any assurance that we have ever painted, contemplated, or described in vain."

Chapter Five

A Call on Colette and Goudeket

Love is a secondary passion to those who love most, a primary passion to those who love least.
— WALTER SAVAGE LANDOR

When I went abroad in 1952 and called on my old and dear friend Cocteau, who was Colette's neighbor in the Palais-Royal, he told me that it had been one of her most dolorous weeks; her arthritis clamping down tight and chiseling away at her. In spite of which, he thought, surely she would receive me, especially if he telephoned and asked her to. For various reasons, I scarcely wanted his powers of persuasion so exercised in my behalf.

Later in the week I found Anita Loos, the dramatizer of *Gigi*, dining at Florial's, out beside the fountain under the honey locusts, and she confirmed the bad news of the arthritis; nevertheless, she encouraged me. "Don't write," was her advice. "M. Goudeket, the guardian husband, will think it his duty to ward you off. Just take a chance, ring the doorbell. At least you will see him, or you will see Pauline, the perfect servant. They're both worth seeing."

But I could not imagine myself standing all unannounced on their doorstep, nor think of any suitable initial utterance to the doorkeeper. Then I recalled the fact that when my young friend Patrick O'Higgins wanted to get in and take photographs of her, he armed himself with roses. With neither his infectious half-Irish gaiety nor his half-French manners, perhaps I could afford an even more imposing bouquet, to compensate. I sought out the major florist near the Palais-Royal, and asked if they knew which size and shape and shade and redolence of rose Mme. Colette favored.

They knew exactly: I forget its name; it had a stout but not inflexible stem, and petals wine-red on the inside, brownish on the outside.

In the doorway the perfect servant gave me a good look and concluded that she had never laid eyes on me before. I held the roses up a little; I thrust them forward. It brought to my mind an encounter once upon a time with a fine police dog when, thank heaven, I had in hand a good thick slice of bread for the purpose of conciliation. I made polite statements about my not really expecting Mme. Colette to see me but, on the other hand, not wanting her to hear from M. Cocteau or Mlle. Loos or anyone of my sojourn in Paris and departure without having paid my respects. Pauline evidently regarded this as all hypocrisy but appreciated the style of it. She took the roses, forbade me to depart without being seen by M. Goudeket, ordered me to sit down and be patient, and went away very neatly.

The Palais-Royal is a quiet building. I could hear a heavy chair being pushed back somewhere; I could hear footsteps along a corridor, certainly not Pauline's footsteps, heavier and not so neat. Facing me was a double door composed of panes of glass backed by permanent light-colored curtains, which made everything there in the hallway rather bright but nothing really visible.

"What is it, Pauline? Who is it, Pauline? But no, but no, not that vase, not for roses. Oh, they're magnificent, aren't they? So long-legged and in such quantity! Leave them here on my bed, for the moment."

Though the farthest thing in the world from a young voice, it had a sound of unabated femininity, and it could never have been livelier at any age. It was slightly hoarse, but with the healthy hoarseness of certain birds; nothing sore-throated about it.

"Who brought them, Pauline? What young man? The one of the other day, the Swiss one? But, my poor dear Pauline, if he's gray-haired, what makes you think he's young? If only you'd remember names, so much simpler."

Thus she sputtered or, to be more exact, warbled, and I gathered that Pauline withdrew from the room in mid-sentence; the hoarse and sweet phrases murmured to a close. Presently I heard a manly mumble of M. Goudeket, meant for me not to be able to under- stand; and presently there he was with me in the hallway, wel- coming, at least half welcoming.

He declared that he remembered me, which, remarkable man that he is, may have been the case. "As for Colette," he added, in a sort of aside, "I am afraid she is not in good enough health to see you."

Using his arm like a great wand or baton he motioned me into a room which appeared to be *his* room, where there was a display of bibliophily and an important desk.

In France I always observe a great difference between politesse and just politeness. Politesse is stronger and can be made quite un- comfortable for one or both of the participants. M. Goudeket seated himself at the desk, assigned me a chair vis-à-vis, and questioned me for half or three quarters of an hour until he became convinced that I truly, unselfishly, loved Colette's work and would continually do my best to further a general love of it in vast and remunerative America.

I told him what I thought: a number of the most interesting titles for export to this country had not yet been translated (still have not)—especially her reminiscences, which ought to be combined in one fat volume, suitable for a large-circulation book club. I went on to say, in a less businesslike manner, that I could not think of any autobiography by a woman to compare with this work of hers. Most women, throughout literary history, have been rather secretive, therefore objective. Not even Mme. de Sévigné is in Colette's class for width and depth of revelation, for fond instructiveness, and for poetical quality. This comparison, though perhaps hackneyed, seemed to gratify M. Goudeket.

Then I mentioned Colette's particular gift of brief wise commen- tary, epigram, and aphorism. As a rule this is not one of the abilities of the fair sex. Logan Pearsall Smith's famous *Treasury of English Aphorisms* included, if I remembered rightly, only two authoresses. This information made M. Goudeket smile.

As soon as cordiality prevailed between us, our conversation flagged. Despairing by that time of seeing the beloved authoress, I looked at my watch and alluded to the fact. that I had another engagement, beginning to be pressing.

This apparently astonished M. Goudeket. "But I thought you wished to pay your respects to Colette," he protested. "Surely you can spare just a few more minutes! Speaking for Colette, alas, I am afraid she will be deeply disappointed if you don't."

He said this with rare aplomb, disregarding what he had said upon my arrival, exactly as though, at some point in our interview, he had been able to slip out of the room and reconsult her about me, or as though she had communicated to him by telepathy.

"Colette has changed her mind about seeing you," he said. "She is feeling in rather better health today than usual. Come, we will knock on her door." He knocked good and hard and then ushered me in. He addressed her as "dear friend" and he called me "M. Ouess-cotte."

Let me not flatter myself that the great writer had been primping for me all that half or three quarters of an hour; but certainly I have never seen a woman of any age so impeccable and immaculate and (so to speak) gleaming. Let me not try to describe her: her paleness of enamel and her gemlike eyes and her topknot of spun glass, and so forth. There was evidence of pain in her face but not the least suggestion of illness. What came uppermost in my mind at the sight of her was just rejoicing. Oh, oh, I said to myself, she is not going to die for a long while! Or, if she does, it will have to be sudden death somehow, burning death, freezing death, or thunderbolt of some kind. The status quo certainly is life, from head to foot.

She arched her neck back away from me and turned her head somewhat circularly, though in only a segment of circle. She worked her eyes, staring for a split second, then narrowing them, then staring again, so that all their degrees of brightness showed. She gave me her hand, strong with lifelong penmanship as well as gardening and the care of pets.

"Please sit on my bed," she said. "Yes, there at the foot, where I can look straight at you. Arthritic as I am, it wearies me—or perhaps I should say it bores me—to turn my head too often."

Oh, the French euphemism, which is stoicism in a way! Evidently it was not a matter of weariness or boredom but of excruciation. A moment later, in my enjoyment and excitement of being there, I made a clumsy move sideways, so that the weight of my elbow rested on the little mound of her feet under the coverlet. She winced but did not scowl. I apologized miserably, which she put a stop to by pulling the coverlet up above her ankles, in a dear humorous exhibitionism.

"Do you see? I have excellent feet. Do you remember? I have always worn sandals, indifferent to severe criticism, braving inclement weather; and now I have my reward for it, do you not agree?"

Yes, I did remember, I did agree. She exercised the strong and silken arches for me and twinkled the straight, red-lacquered toes.

On the whole, I must admit, our dialogue or trialogue was not very remarkable. I had been warned of her deafness; indeed the beautiful first page of *Le Fanal Bleu* is a warning. Now, as I try to recall things that she said, I find that they were not very well focused on the cues that her husband and I gave her; she only half heard us. She devoted all possible cleverness to mitigating and disguising the vacuum between us, and therefore did not shine in other ways, as she might have done in solo performance.

Naturally her husband knew best how to pitch his voice for her ear, or perhaps she could somewhat read his lips. "M. Ouess-cotte thinks your autobiographies will have the greatest success in America," he said.

"Oh, has he read them? Oh, the Americans are greater readers than the poor French, aren't they, monsieur?"

"M. Ouess-cotte is perhaps exceptional," her husband murmured sagaciously.

"Have you read *Le Pur et l'Impur?*" she asked. "I happened to read it myself the other day and I took pride in it. I believe it to be my best book. It is the book in which I make my personal contribution to the general repository of knowledge of the various forms of sensuality, do you remember?"

I remembered so well that I recognized this last sentence as a quotation from it, almost word for word: *"Le trésor de la connaissance des sens . . ."* It is a work of gospel truth to my way of thinking, and has greatly guided me in my own life and love life.

When we fell silent M. Goudeket gave us a helping hand, a helping sentence. "M. Ouess-cotte suggests that I ought to make a selection of your thoughts in aphoristic form which I should find here and there throughout your work; something like the *Pensées* of Pascal or of Joubert."

"But no, certainly not, my poor friend! You know perfectly well, I am no thinker, I have no *pensées*. I feel almost a timidity and almost a horror of all that. As a matter of fact, thanks be to God, perhaps the most praiseworthy thing about me is that I have known how to write like a woman, without anything moralistic or theoretical, without promulgating."

And she expressed this bit of negative femininism in an emphatic manner, with her sweet voice hardened, sharpened. "I am a genuinely womanly writer," she insisted. "I am the person in the world the least apt to moralize or philosophize."

I felt challenged by this seeming humility. I, as you might say, took the floor and discoursed with eloquence for two or three or perhaps five minutes. I can recall everything I said, but, for some strange reason, I seem to hear it in English, not in French. Is it possible that in my opinionatedness I slipped into my native tongue without noticing? I seem to see Mme. Colette's face turning mask-like, as though she had suddenly grown much deafer; and M. Goudeket, than whom nobody could be less stupid, looked a little stupefied.

It amounted to my giving her the lie direct. Whether she liked it or not, I declared, she was a thinker, she did philosophize. In volume after volume she has enabled us to trace exactly the stages of her development of mind, her reasoning in its several categories and connections. The gist of it may perhaps be called pantheistic; a cult of nature which is no mere matter of softly yielding to it, which infers a nay as well as a yea, and which includes, yes, indeed, with outstretched arms, all or almost all human nature. Of the utmost importance to her is, quite simply, belief in love; the particular passion in due course giving way to general loving-kindness, amor giving way to caritas, amour leading to amor fati. A part of it is just spectatorship and dramatic sense, with no admiration of evil, indeed not; only an appreciation of the part that evil may play in fate, as among other things it occasions virtue, and a willingness to yield to it in the end, when worse comes to worst, when it takes the form of death.

Suddenly hearing myself talking so grandiosely, and mixing my languages, my few words of Italian along with my French and/or American, of course I stopped; and then it was time to bid the great woman and her good husband au revoir. They very kindly urged me to return to Paris before long, and she undertook to rise from her bed when that time came and to lunch with me at the restaurant just down the street, the Véfour, where she had a corner table marked with her name on a brass plate.

I departed with a lump in my throat, with a very natural dread of old mortality. But then I reminded myself of the printed form of immortality, a sure thing in Colette's case. I stopped at a bookstore and bought *Le Pur et l'Impur,* though I have two copies of it in New Jersey, one very cheap, for rough-and-ready reading, and one well bound, for the sentiment and the symbol. I immediately cut the pages of this third copy, not wanting anyone to observe it uncut in my hand and to shame me by the supposition that I had not yet read it. I walked through the Tuileries and up along the Seine hugging it (so to speak) to my bosom.

Chapter Six

Isak Dinesen, the Storyteller

The human imagination is a curious thing. If it is properly fertilized it can shoot up like a fakir's tree in the twinkling of an eye. Tanya knew the trick, and between us we built up in our imagination a future in which everything but the impossible had a place.

The storyteller's husband, BROR VON BLIXEN FINECKE

Baroness Blixen, the Danish authoress who writes in English under the name of Isak Dinesen, came to New York and Washington and Boston in the winter of 1958-59, not just to be lionized, and not to lecture in the ordinary way. In recent years in her native land she has specialized in word-of-mouth narration; and her purpose here was to tell stories to various audiences, and to have some of her storytelling perpetuated—I hope that will prove to be the applicable and truthful word—on tape and film, financed by the Ford Foundation. She had hoped to go on to California and to Wisconsin, which her father had visited before she was born, and written a book about; but she had to give that up.

She is elderly and in delicate health; so slight a figure that, when she walks, someone's strong arm is required to steady her and hold her up. If that responsibility has befallen you, and you relax it for a moment, she is liable to sink to the floor; however, her fall is like a feather's and she never complains of it. She has intrepidity and exquisite energy.

She bears a resemblance to Queen Elizabeth, the Shakespearean or Elizabethan Elizabeth (not the present sovereign). She has that same shell-like, almost skull-like brow, and interrogative eyebrow and aquiline nose. But Good Queen Bess was red-haired and green-eyed, wasn't she? This Danish noblewoman's hair is of sable; and her eyes are dark, with diamond amid their darkness, capable of all the traditional brunette effects: they flash, they sparkle, they brood, they caress.

Europeans of late have been anxious to be or to seem like us; not Baroness Blixen! She is rather a storybook foreigner, despite her mastery of our language both conversational and literary. New Yorkers were charmed by her exceptional, fanciful ways; for example, her eating and drinking. The word went around, specifying what she liked, the same minimal if not simple fare at each meal: half a dozen oysters, a few grapes, and a split of champagne. Later, she found out how coercively beneficial this country can be. Unfair clubwomen in Boston having imposed on her more engagements than she had agreed to, she had to be put to bed in a hospital for ten days, where the doctors decided that the champagne was counter-indicated and prescribed milk instead.

As an honorary member of the American Academy and National Institute of Arts and Letters, she attended the annual meeting of the Institute and there gave what, I suppose, you would call a lecture. It expounded the custom and function of having a motto or successive mottoes to point the way in one's life, instancing those she has made use of herself, and her changes from time to time as her circumstances or aspirations changed. When she was a venturesome girl, cramped in small Denmark, she chose a Latin motto: "Navigare necesse est, vivere non est," which I translate freely: "To set sail somewhere is more important than life itself." This accorded with her emigration to East Africa in 1914, where she owned and operated a coffee plantation near Nairobi until 1931. Her most recent motto is lapidary and tripartite, that inscribed over the gates of a castle in Spenser's *Faerie Queene:* over the first gate, "Be bold," and over the second, "Be bold," and over the third, "Be not *too* bold." This perhaps covers her exploit of traversing the Atlantic so late in life; a calculated risk, with self-knowledge and with safeguards.

Her principal storytelling in New York was done at the Poetry

Center of the Young Men's Hebrew Association, which, with a certain endowment by the late Aline Bernstein, the beloved of Thomas Wolfe, has become the chief platform in the world for poets and poetical prose writers. As she came on stage there, walking very slowly on the arm of a young staff poet named William Jay Smith, then pausing and turning and, by way of salute to the maximum audience including standees, outstretching her fine-boned arm in a gesture of some singularity—as of a hunter beckoning with a riding crop, or as of an actor in the role of Prospero motioning this or that airy creature into existence, or perhaps back out of existence —we all spontaneously stood up and acclaimed her.

As soon as we kept quiet she established herself in an important straight chair, spot-lit, and after catching her breath in physical weariness for a moment, and gazing around the auditorium with a royal gaze, a gypsy gaze, began the evening's narration. She has an ideal voice for the purpose, strong, though with a kind of wraithlike transparency, which she is able to imbue with emotions, but only narrative emotions. She rarely indulges in mellifluousness in the way of poets; neither does she do much Thespian mimicking.

The basic sound of storytelling is very different from that of poetry or drama; you would notice this, I think, even if you didn't understand a word. Dramatic art wants to differentiate everything, for the sake of the confrontation and the impact, and the consequences in subsequent scenes. Whereas the true narrative feeling, as a rule, unifies. The narrator's enthusiasm about his subject matter and fondness for his heroes and heroines, even for his villains and villainesses, somewhat predominate over the various states of mind and fullnesses of heart that the narrated events entail for them.

What especially colors Isak Dinesen's voice, what gives it overtone and urgency, is remembrance or reminiscence. With soft strong tone seeming to feel its way, sometimes almost faltering, shifting its direction as power of evocation sways it, not perturbed by her listeners, perhaps helped by them, she seems to be re-experiencing what she has to tell, or if it is fable or fantasy, redreaming it. She never gives an impression of having memorized a text and recalling the sentences and paragraphs. When I had heard her tell a given story a second or third time, it astonished me to realize that it had been verbatim, or nearly so. "The King's Letter," her pièce de résistance again and again on her little American tour, requires about three quarters of an hour to read; three quarters of an hour by heart, an undertaking comparable to a liedersinger's concert, or indeed to the great roles in the operas of Wagner.

"The King's Letter" comprises a set of wonderful episodes of her life as a colonial landholder, coffee planter, and lion hunter—not fictitious, or not very fictitious—which for some reason she did not include in *Out of Africa*. That volume, her second in order of publication, is an account of her long expatriation in Kenya Colony: the landscape, and famous fauna, and the friendships that flourish exceptionally when one is living in a foreign land, and in greatest detail, her love and understanding of the Africans. It is a masterpiece. The perusal of it, nowadays, is like a medicine, alleviating some of the fever of our minds due to our awareness of the rebellion of the colored races against the white race everywhere in the world.

I think that she and Joyce Cary, the author of *Aissa Saved* and *The African Witch,* in their premonition or prophecy of the atrocities of the Mau Mau and the anarchy in the Belgian Congo, were far in advance of other authorities on the Dark Continent. Certainly no recent book that I know explains so much.

Out of Africa is ravishingly written; it is like a love potion, strengthening us in our enthusiasm about our life, whoever we are, whenever or wherever it may be: appointed small portion of time and space, this earth of ours beyond compare, matrix of the beloved human species, no matter what the color, however the story ends! One of the books that I love best in all the library of the world, it is hard for me to read it with equanimity now, because it was my mother's favorite book, and my mind is not quite healed from the distress of her death.

Let me give you an example of Isak Dinesen's descriptive prose in that volume, a majestic procession of wild animals as it were in the Garden of Eden. Before she had to take over the active everyday management of her coffee farm she had been an ardent hunter and had taken part in many a memorable safari. On one of them, she writes, "I had seen a herd of Buffalo, one hundred and twenty-nine of them, come out of the morning mist under a copper sky, one by one, as if the dark and massive, iron-like animals with the mighty, horizontally swung horns were not approaching, but were being created before my eyes· and sent out as they were finished. I had seen a herd of Elephant travelling through dense Native forest, where the sunlight is strewn down between the thick creepers in small spots and patches, pacing along as if they had an appointment at the end of the world. It was, in giant size, the border of a very old, infinitely precious Persian carpet, in the dyes of green, yellow and black-brown. I had time after time watched the progression across the plain of the Giraffe, in their queer, inimitable, vegetative gracefulness, as if it were not a herd of animals but a family of rare, long-stemmed, speckled gigantic flowers slowly advancing. I had followed two Rhinos on their morning promenade, when they were sniffing and snorting in the air of the dawn,—which is so cold that it hurts the nose,—and looked like two very big angular stones rollicking in the long valley and enjoying life together. I had seen the royal Lion, before sunrise, below a waning moon, crossing the grey plain on his way home from the kill, drawing a dark wake in the silvery grass, his face still red up to the ears, or during the midday siesta, when he reposed contentedly in the midst of his family on the short grass and in the delicate, spring-like shade of the broad Acacia trees of his park of Africa."

Compact with natural, animal, and primitive realities, *Out of Africa* is also studded with tales, some of them fables and parables, some almost myths, and with character sketches and life stories.— For example, the drunkenness of an old Kikuyu chieftain named Kinanjui, a close friend, and toward the end of the volume, his deathbed, like that of one of the Homeric heroes. For example, the poisoning of her cook Esa, who inherited a black cow, which maddened him with happiness, who then took a lascivious young second wife, though he was old; she poisoned him. The frustration of a Swedish professor who wanted to kill fifteen hundred female monkeys, to investigate something about the fetuses inside them.

F

The battle of a rooster and a chameleon, as it were a coat of arms in motion, which happened toward the end of Isak Dinesen's sojourn in Africa, a portent.

Though with not the slightest confession of sentiment or sensuality, a great love story runs through the work like a strong silken thread, like a great warm blood vessel: her friendship with an English gentleman named Denys Finch-Hatton, an Africa-lover like herself, who comes and goes in chapter after chapter. He flew a small airplane, and one day, without previous notice, proposed her going up in it with him, to see the buffalo out feeding in the hills.

"I cannot come," she said, "I have got a tea party up at the house."

"But we will go and see them and be back in a quarter of an hour," he said.

Which they did, and presently found twenty-seven of them, "a long way below us, like mice moving gently on a floor," and then, under the leadership of an old bull with hundredweight horns, stampeding to a small dim thicket in a glade in a hill, where indeed they would have been invisible to anyone coming along the ground; "but they could not hide themselves from the bird of the air."

"When I came back to my tea party," Isak Dinesen concludes this incident, "the teapot on the stone table was still so hot that I burned my fingers on it." And, characteristically—her mind always brimming over with traditional lore, with old imagery out of the treasure-trove of the world—she remarks that the Prophet Mohammed "had the same experience when he upset a jug of water, and the Archangel Gabriel took him, and flew with him through the seven heavens, and when he returned, the water had not yet run out of the jug."

Here and there in the book she explains how she began to be a writer of fantastic tales. (As a girl she had studied painting, even traveling to Paris for the purpose.) For one thing, her African prompted her to turn to authorship, as she could often divert them by reciting poetry: "Please talk like rain, talk like rain some more," they would beseech her—and even in matters of some difficulty and consequence she could sway them by a bit of glamorous or cautionary narrative.

Messrs. Haycraft and Kunitz in their popular reference book, *Living Authors,* quote her about this: "I began to write there in Kenya, to amuse myself in the rainy season. My native servants took a great interest in my work, believing that I was attempting to write a sort of new Koran, and used to come and ask me what God had inspired me to write."

Her great friend also inspired her. "Denys had a trait of character which to me was very precious, he liked to hear a story told. For I have always thought that I might have cut a figure at the time of the plague of Florence. Fashions have changed, and the art of listening to a narrative has been lost in Europe. The Natives of Africa, who cannot read, have still got it; if you begin to them, 'There was a man who walked out on the plain, and there met another man,' you have them all with you, their minds running upon the unknown track of the men on the plain."

The blessed outdoor Englishman "lived much by ear" and preferred hearing a tale to reading one, and when he came to the farm, was apt to ask if she had got a story. So she invented things in his absence, and in the evenings he would make himself comfortable in front of the fire, and she would sit on the floor, "cross-legged like Scheherazade herself." He remembered what she had previously told better than she did herself, and gently chided her for any inconsistency or error.

He taught her Latin and got her into the way of reading the Bible. In Eugene Walter's interview with her in the *Paris Review,* he provided a long list of other favorite and influential reading matter, among other things: E. T. A. Hoffmann and La Motte-Fouqué and Barbey d'Aurevilly and Mark Twain, Voltaire and Scott and Joseph Conrad.

Out of Africa is her only truthful work; I mean, her only factual work. *Seven Gothic Tales,* her first publication, and *Winter's Tales,* and *Anecdotes of Destiny,* and *Last Tales,* are pure fiction, absolute fictitiousness, harking back not only to the above-listed narrators but to the epics and the sagas as they developed orally piece by piece, long before they were ever written down, and to the corresponding unpublished literature fragmentarily persisting in our time, in Ireland, for example, a livelihood for old begging men with an itinerary of illiterate cottages, and in the market place of Marrakech where, in vicarious excitement, without understanding one word, I myself (as related elsewhere) have enjoyed the interminable serial narration of cross-legged Moors or Berbers.

Of course Isak Dinesen must be aware of the strangeness and indeed sophistication of her practicing, for world-wide book readers, so primitive a type of fiction—intended to amuse, to amaze, and to allure the imagination—and she may feel supported by certain tenets of the ancients applicable to it. Aristotle said: "Impossibilities are justified if they serve the purpose of the poetry." Longinus said: "The effect of genius is not to persuade or to convince but rather to transport the audience out of its usual frame of mind." Admittedly, both these philosophers were referring to dramatic poetry; and Isak Dinesen's narrative often leans in that direction and beckons (I should think) to the future dramatist or scenario writer.

In *Last Tales,* an old prince of the church, Cardinal Salviati expounds an aesthetic of the storyteller's story, differing fundamentally from the more modern artistry of the novelist. One of his great lady penitents, sensing underneath his wisdom and humaneness something more than the usual vocational experience, asks "Who are you?" In reply, he informs her of the mystery of his birth, one of a pair of twins; no knowing which one, the other having been burned up. He cannot really identify himself, he tells her, except by what he has done and what has been done to him.

In the modern novel the most important thing is individuality therefore it has to be, above all, explanatory and intimate. The question asked in it as a rule is not *who* but *what*—what is he or she? what are you, the reader? or indeed, as it is often a subterfuge for autobiography, what am I? It is portraiture or self-portraiture, stepping out of the frame only enough to demonstrate itself in action, or to teach a lesson, or to make a point.

Whereas to the storyteller the events come first. Particularity or peculiarity of the personages involved comes second, as their activity depicts it, as destiny has brought it about. In the first book of the Bible, Genesis—which, as Cardinal Salviati points out, is a story, not a novel—humanity does not even appear until the sixth day. "By that time they were bound to come, for, where the story is, the characters will gather."

Sometimes Isak Dinesen borrows or (I suppose one should say) inherits types of humanity from the old collective family tree of Western civilization, such as Scheherazade, Prospero and Ariel, the Wandering Jew, the Barber of Seville, Philippe-Égalité, Stefan George. "The Wine of the Tetrarch," a tale with which she often regaled her American listeners—it has been available to readers for years, as a sub-narration in the first story in her first book—is a bringing together of the Apostle Peter and the man Barabbas, in whose stead, upon whose cross, Christ was crucified. It stirringly expresses the anguished vacuity of the pagan spirit in which Christianity, that most effective amalgam of ethics and superstition, first took place and took hold.

Another story of the Near Eastern past, "Alexander the Great and the Sybil," inherited by a certain old gentleman from his grandfather and told to another old gentleman in *Last Tales*, she borrowed back from that same volume and amplified and changed, as to its meaning and moral, and gave as a sample of her storytelling technique on someone's television program. The Macedonian world conqueror, temporarily in residence in Babylon, heard of a powerful sibyl or sorceress in that city and had her brought before him. He had no interest in having his fortune told, accustomed as he was to shaping destiny for himself by military prowess and leadership, but he thought it would be pleasant to learn the secret and the technique of clairvoyancy, so that upon occasion, either for pleasure or for advantage, he could prophesy for other people.

She consented to instruct him, but in return for every separate step and particularity of her art he had to recompense her with a precious stone out of his casket, first a topaz, then a sapphire, then a ruby, and finally an emerald, which he yielded up most reluctantly, as he had intended to present it to the famous Greek dancer and courtesan Thais.

The last and essential secret lesson, the sorceress or sibyl warned him solemnly, was a matter of life and death. If he learned it from her and, when the time came, failed to conform to it exactly, it would destroy him. Despite this warning he persisted in his desire to learn.

So she recapitulated her instructions up to that point: the selection of the sticks of aloe and olive and oleander and baobab, the right occult pattern to pile them in, the sprinkling with specified incenses and the setting fire to the pile with a torch—and finally told him that, just at that moment, as he gazed into the smoke, it was absolutely crucial for him to refrain from thinking of the left eye of a camel. To think of the right eye of a camel would be dangerous, but the left eye would be fatal.

This appalled King Alexander, and he never undertook the hocus pocus that he had set his heart on and that had cost him four precious stones.

Its meaning, I suppose—having a mind more explicit and utilitarian than the great Danish yarn-spinner's—is that some knowledgeable persons have knowledge for sale; kings have the wherewithal to buy it; and the better part of any such bargain is the positive part: ingredients, arrangements, and matters of invocation and enumeration. The hard part (which indeed may prove impossible) is to nonknow, non-think, non-remember. For the mind, except in certain pathological states, or after prolonged occult exercises, is irresistible to itself, uninhibitable by itself. It is useless to be reminded *not* to think of a thing. The reminder itself is a thought. We human beings are all zombis, in a sense; that is, we are inhabited by a kind of superhumanity, if not divinity: a part of our being superior to the whole, a part not controllable by the whole.

There is sententiousness more functional than this in many of Isak Dinesen's tales; and some strange and disorderly aphorisms. Remember that she is Kierkegaard's compatriot as well as Hans Christian Andersen's. But most of it is fictitious; not opinionated. Neither in the aggregate nor in separate flashes of suggestive intelligence does it constitute one of those systems of thought that authors develop for all the population of their books at once, or for themselves, to stabilize and comfort the artistic temperament. She is not proposing a philosophy of her own; only letting her personages philosophize: mysticism, thanksgiving, anarchism, whatever comes naturally to the lips of those who are having extraordinary experiences, or who have had them in the past and lived to tell the tale.

Often she composes a double or triple fabric: narrative within narrative, interruptingly, and narrations about narrators. One of her storytellers, very professional, having earned her living in this way for two hundred years, ancient and black-veiled and mumble-voiced, says, "Where the storyteller is loyal, eternally and unswervingly loyal to the story, there, in the end, silence will speak."

Indeed, if we examine the production of most fiction writers we find that their message or thesis of greatest consequence, greatest originality, is something that they seem not to have known when they took pen in hand. They learn from their material as the work progresses, from the phantoms of memory and from the powers and accidents of the art.

In a long story entitled "The Roads round Pisa," a young Danish nobleman traveling alone, thinking that he would give a year of his life to be able to talk to a faraway friend, in order to develop a more objective understanding of himself and his plight in life, says, "I wonder if it is really possible to be absolutely truthful when you are alone. Truth, like time, is an idea arising from, and dependent upon, human intercourse." In Isak Dinesen's mind, generally speaking, it evidently always depends upon some interrelationship of persons, by their psychology and by great abstract coincidence assembled and entangled; in a word, plot!

One great charm and strangeness of her work as a whole—at this somber mid-point of the century, amid so much other world literature that is desperate, whining, punitive—is her having almost entirely silenced in it any personal misfortune or depressed state of her own mind. "All sorrows can be borne if you put them into a story or tell a story about them," she has written, in I forget which volume. Yes, yes, if your concept of the story form and narrative style is classic, stoic, non-neurotic. Over all, her narrative mood—or do I mean mode?—is characterized by bravery, sweetness, enjoyment, even when it has reference to tragic factors.

Some time ago, at home in Denmark, she expressed her appreciation of having had an unusually happy life; and an interviewer asked her to explain it; wherein lay the happiness? Her explanation was that all her senses have been very acute and healthy—sight, hearing, taste and smell. "I have never met anyone who could see as well as I could," she said.

Rungstedlund, her house in Denmark, was an inn in the eighteenth century, and the important poet, Johannes Ewald—who wrote the Danish national anthem—lived there at the end of his life, when he had broken almost every bone in his body falling from a horse. According to someone she talked to recently, the lady of Rungstedlund has seen his ghost, or perhaps only heard his ghostly step; and she has put him in a story, in mid-nocturnal converse with Christian VII, King of Denmark at the time.

According to history books, that king seems to have been, on the whole, insane; and Ewald was wild and unfortunate. But Isak Dinesen pitches their talk in a lull of their two minds, complementing each other serenely enough. One subject of their conversation, proposed by the King, is the idea that there is, or can be, perfect happiness on earth.

The poet agrees, and specifies that in his opinion there are three kinds of perfect happiness: (1) To feel in oneself an excess of strength. (2) To have been in pain, and to have it cease. (3) To know for certain that you are fulfilling the will of God.

It has occurred to me that these three happinesses, diffused of course in every existence, appertain especially, respectively, to three classifications of persons: the very young; those in the shadow of death; and creators of literature and the arts. It is the young who are most often excessively strong; and, oh, great analgesia must be the only consolation for having to depart from this wondrous world and our beloved fellow worldlings; and, with due deference to saints and scientists, I think that creative men are most apt to feel sure that they are doing what they were created to do.

Isak Dinesen, in the several decades of her creativity, surely has known this third happiness to her heart's content. She has given us to understand that it has not all been simply euphoric and voluntary. One night in the spring of 1959, just before her return to Denmark, dining at a friend's apartment with the poetess, Marianne Moore, she told a sort of fable of her own life; a fable with a moral or maxim. By that time her fond Americans really had tired her out. In diaphanous black, her physical being made one think of a fever-wasted child; but her eyes were as lively as the diamonds in her ears. She really did no more than haunt the dinner table: only one oyster, perhaps three grapes; but later, in the softest corner of the room, amid cushions, she sat up as straight as though enthroned on stage at the Poetry Center.

Her mingling of formality and ease, intimacy and sense of performance, is characteristic and memorable. Facing an audience, she simply reminisces, unrestrained and trustful. On the other hand, in familiar circumstances, in private, she gives of herself as generously and intentionally as though she had been paid a great fee. Let the writer who scribbles or types or dictates all day long relax as he pleases at the end of the day; a mere everyman among his fellows. In its very nature the storyteller's art is never done. Listening public is much more ubiquitous than reading public.

That night with Marianne Moore, who listens inspiringly, Isak Dinesen told of the time, two or three years before, when, having had two or three operations on her spine, she couldn't sit up, either to write or to typewrite; the post-operative pain was too grievous. Notwithstanding this, she intensely desired to produce one more book before she died. So she lay flat on the floor and dictated to Clara Svendsen, her secretary, day after day. She had never dictated before, and somehow it differed fundamentally from merely telling the stories; she couldn't get things right. There had to be seven or eight successive versions of some pages. She began to despair. Clara Svendsen urged her to give it up, to wait until her health improved, until the pain abated.

"No, no," the recumbent aged authoress answered, "let us work just one more hour; let us compose just one more page. Of course we shall not get the book done, but we must keep on trying to finish a little more of it."

In due course they did get it done; enough of it to be publishable. It is the volume entitled *Last Tales*. She has published another volume since then.

"It taught me a lesson," she told Marianne Moore and the rest of us. "When you have a great and difficult task, something perhaps almost impossible, if you only work a little at a time, every day a little, *without faith and without hope*"—and she underlined the words with her spooky, strong, but insubstantial voice—"suddenly the work will finish itself."

I do believe that the renunciation of those two glorious and helpful virtues—faith! hope!—in certain circumstances may be the saving grace. Despairing absolutely of what we want to do may help us to do what *can* be done.

Not all her anecdotes and gems of conversation are solemn and illuminating. She has an exquisite and (you might say) frolicsome wit. One afternoon at a cocktail party she propounded to her hostess, and to two or three other young women of romantic and fashionable aspect in a circle around her, this question: "Which of the great poets of the past would you choose to have been loved by?"

The youngest of them answered, "Baudelaire," which charmed and amused me, but seemed to horrify the Baroness.

She also expressed horror of Tennyson and Rilke. We then turned the tables on her. "Which poet would you choose yourself?"

"Robert Burns," she answered unhesitatingly.

Someone pointed out to her that she would have had to resign herself to his going away and leaving her to her own devices a great part of the time.

"Yes, but I could always have gone on expecting him to come back," she said. "Furthermore, all my life I have felt a hearty dislike of a one-man dog and of a one-woman man."

In the story entitled "Converse at Night in Copenhagen" from which I have already quoted, the unruly national poet, Johannes Ewald, explained to crazy King Christian that, as our human existence came about by means of the divine creative word, Logos, it ought to be translated by us and given back to the Creator in our vocabulary, in myth and reminiscence, the abiding forms of our gratitude. Terrible, Ewald said it was, to feel this obligation to Almighty God. "Terrible in its weight and incessancy is the obligation of the acorn to yield Him the oak tree."

Many of Isak Dinesen's protagonists say similar things; it is like the music of Mozart in his operas, which some opera lovers find impersonal, as between one character and another, that is, undramatic. Upon this point of the fulfillment of fate, she has spoken for herself, autobiographically, in *Out of Africa:* "Pride is the faith in the idea that God had when He made us. A proud man is conscious of the idea, and aspires to realize it."

By this time, with life concluding, the heat and flicker and ashes of her lovely mind must be all strangely mingled with that proud sense of having realized and incarnated eternal concepts.

Chapter Seven

Thomas Mann: Will Power and Fiction

Without contraries is no progression. Attraction and repulsion, reason and energy, love and hate, are necessary to human existence.

—WILLIAM BLAKE

Thomas Mann, in his famous old age, paying tribute to Schiller, whom he had cared for more than any other writer when he was young, spoke deferentially of "the mountains of learned appreciation and analysis" piled up by scholarship in the century and a half since Schiller died. "In my diffidence," he said, "I am emboldened by only one thing": the kinship of creative experience, and fraternal intimacy of every creative artist with all his fellow artists, "irrespective of stature, epoch, or character."

When I came upon this passage in *Last Essays*, it seemed an encouragement to write about him. I needed to be encouraged because he is more foreign to me than any other great man of letters whom I have undertaken to eulogize or criticize. The difference between us, in epoch, is only one generation; however, it has been a great watershed in history, and may prove more decisive, more revolutionary, than anything that his thinking or mine has encompassed. I too have, or have had, the character of a novelist. I am not vain of my stature, or sensitive about it. I will try to make my modest point of view very definite and consequential; you can discount it all you like.

Definitely, to begin with, *The Magic Mountain* is the only novel of Mann's that I am enthusiastic about. I admire *Dr. Faustus*, but without liking it or greatly enjoying it. Not one of his other long works of fiction pleases me so much as half a dozen of the short narratives and essays. Let me list half a dozen.—*A Weary Hour,* the brief soliloquy-story about Schiller, dated 1905; the earliest instance of Mann's portraying himself and examining himself in the guise of some great predecessor. *Tonio Kroeger,* of course, and *Tristan.* The early nouvelle-like fragment of the *Confessions of Felix Krull;* the swindler's transvestite childhood. Perhaps not *Death in Venice;* it is a fine and powerfully atmospheric story, but the handling of the homosexual theme in it is not true to life, I think. The essay on Frederick the Great, dated 1915, in spite of the history lesson in it, which seems obsolete and certainly is nefarious from a non-German standpoint. *Disorder and Early Sorrow* and *Mario and the Magician,* perfect tales of the twenties. The essay which is a comparison between Goethe and Tolstoi. The short novel about Goethe, *Lotte in Weimar.* The essay on Chekhov, a little production of the very end of his life. Wescott's choice!

Next, let me specify something about my title, "Will Power and Fiction." Does it suggest to you that famous pattern of the philosophy of Schopenhauer, which indeed underlies a part of Mann's thinking? The will as distinguished from intellect, wielding intellect as its mere instrument; the part trying to include the whole, and almost succeeding; the will to live, which Schopenhauer expressed in the sublimest of aphorisms: "The will is the strong blind man who carries on his shoulders the lame man who can see."

That is *not* what I mean by will power. I mean mere resoluteness, even obstinacy; a deliberate manipulation and organization of one's character for purposes of one's lifework, with plans for the day's work accordingly, every day, and an enforcement of those plans upon oneself and upon one's environing fellow men, year in and year out; heroic, Herculean work-morality, which in the end Mann virtually personified, and which enabled him—in spite of all that he enumerated in *Death in Venice* as having been overcome by that most accomplished of his author-protagonists, Aschenbach: "grief and torment, desertion, and frailty of body, vice, passion, and a thousand hindrances"—to bring his talent and his genius to fruition in a heavy harvest of collected works.

In *Mario and the Magician*, Cipolla, who is really not a magician but a hypnotist, and who personifies fascism, says to his victim, a type of foolish common man to whom authoritarian leadership often proves irresistible, "It would be a pleasant change for you, don't you think, to divide up the willing and the doing?"

Mann, during his long life devoted to writing, never divided them up. At times, I personally wish that he had done so. A part of my thesis is that, as to the style and design and dimensions of the late novels, will power entered into his aesthetic more than is usually the case in literature, and that it had a questionable, controversial, even regrettable effect.

Having mentioned Schopenhauer, as to my idiosyncrasy in the use of that one word, "will," let me caution you not to expect too much of me in the abstract way, about either life or art. I am one of those men—more numerous than you might suppose, especially in the United States—who are not only shallowly educated in philosophy, but somewhat incapable of it, and often mistrustful of it and depressed by it.

Why have I not been prompted by this inaptitude, and other limitations that I might mention, to let the subject matter of Mann alone, and to seek some other pretext for my discussion of the several issues in narrative aesthetics—whether a novel ought to be long or short, whether it should deal in profundities or bring everything to the surface, and so on—which his novels suggest, but which other inferior productions of fiction might be found to illustrate also.

Anxiously reading and rereading all sorts of work by him, strenuously beginning to compose these pages, of course I have felt the incongruity and rashness. But, I say, just as the German translators of Shakespeare had to give up as a bad job all the inherently English beauty of the dramatic poetry as such, and still had incomparable dramaturgy left—the plays of Shakespeare are as successful on the German stage as in the English-speaking world—we could expurgate out of Mann's fiction all the abstractions that I find troubling, the Teutonic arguing and loose erudition, and still retain for general enjoyment a large amount of fine, fantastic, and noble narrative; Mann for the easy reader, the simple thinker!

◈

The reminiscences of Mann translated and published in the United States thus far have disappointed me. There has been generalization enough, authorizing us, almost encouraging us, to wonder and to hypothesize and to begin composing a legend, but with a paucity of the data most desirable for the understanding of the personality of a man of genius, the uninventable details—haphazard beams of light and little lightning flashes. I hope that all this is being well recorded in Germany. Even the closest kinsmen and the proudest friends grow forgetful, and presently they die, and their knowledge dies with them. I am not thinking of formal full-length biography. During most of his lifetime, pinned down as he was by his labors, blessed by a great marriage, and in old age, somewhat constrained and embarrassed by his expatriation in America and in Switzerland, perhaps he did not have an especially interesting life to write about in that way.

His own "Lebensabriss," the autobiographical sketch that he wrote for a German periodical in 1930 and permitted Harrison of Paris (that is, Monroe Wheeler and my brother's wife) to publish in a limited edition in Paris in 1932—which for some reason was not published in the ordinary way in this country until 1960—is precious though rather dry and slight. Toward the end of his life he took his diary of the years that he devoted to *Dr. Faustus,* 1943-1947, and reworked it into a memoir of the process of composition of that oddest of masterpieces, in the context of his everyday life in exile in California, and against the distant background of the war in Europe, which he entitled *Die Enstehung des Dr. Faustus* (1949). This does not make lively reading, but it is the rarest sort of document, invaluable to the Mann enthusiast and to the serious critic alike. Its very dullness and the headline-like simplification of every sort of subject matter in it, except the literary enterprise going forward, add to the validity of the portrayal of the laborious aged creative man's character and custom of life. Also there are precious details of the inspiration and the various ingredients of the work, and of his own view of it which kept changing and opening out as it progressed. In glimpses throughout the little volume, there is an interesting, intriguing portrait sketch of the musicologist and philosopher, Theodor Wiesengrund-Adorno, who helped him in every phase of the work.

I have found Erika Mann's memoir of the final year of her father's life endearing and informative, and I hope that she has in store for us a record of other years. I gratefully recall a perceptive essay by Arthur Eloesser. Perhaps others personally acquainted with Mann have not understood what it is that I (and other like-minded but less outspoken readers) want and feel the need of: something like Gorki's thrilling brief reminiscences of Tolstoi, which Mann admired and which he used in his essay comparing the sublime genius of Yasnaya Polyana and the great sage of Weimar.

Over the door of his grandfather's house in Luebeck (I owe this bit of information to Janet Flanner) there was incised this motto: "Work. Save. Pray." And, surely, no grandfather's grandson ever worked harder than he, especially after fifty. In a sense he prayed, too, with anxious self-criticism and impersonal world-wide uneasy conscience all his life. I have not heard of his saving money, but perhaps the massive proportions and redundancy of his principal late novels and of many of his essays reflected a certain old-fashioned thriftiness, even parsimony. The wastebasket did not appeal to him.

As a small boy he discovered the Homeric mythology in an old schoolbook of his mother's, and pretending to be Achilles, dragged his small sister three times around the walls of Troy. I am inclined to read deep meanings into this. For most novelists, even those specializing in subject matter of olden time, the process of fiction is a transposition backward; a matter of their conferring upon personages of legend and history, or upon invented inhabitants of yesterday or of the day before yesterday, their own up-to-the-minute worldly wisdom and self-knowledge. They carry their own present back into other people's pasts. Especially in the tetralogy about the

Jews and the Egyptians, *Joseph and His Brothers,* Mann was more scholarly, in the way of a researcher and a resurrecter. He liked to cast himself in the roles of the past, borrowing for various purposes of his life and his art what he took to be the historic experience and the tradition. When he wrote about great literary men dead and gone, it was not just interpretation of their lives and collected works; it was rather a matter of submitting to their influence, explaining himself in the light of what he found out about them.

In the American Academy's commemorative tribute to him after his death, written and read by Thornton Wilder, there is this beguiling sentence: "He was methodical in work and of great industry, furnishing constant occupation to two secretaries." Did Wilder mean just Frau Mann and Erika, or two salaried persons in addition to them; four in all? The little working methods of prolific writers interest me exceedingly. Often they are more suggestive of the dark reality of their work than anything that they are able to tell us about their theory of literature or the sources of their inspiration.

"I worry only in the afternoon," he confided to Fritz Kaufmann, the author of an important philosophical book about him, *Thomas Mann: The World as Will and Representation;* and I take this to mean that he would not allow his mind to dwell upon any matter of real life, parental anxieties and vexations, social maladjustments and disappointments, or even harrowing events in the wide world, until he had concluded the daily creativity.

I wonder what can have inspired him to make himself the spokesman for disorder and psychopathology in so great a part of his lifework? If any very dissipated man were to declare and expound puritanism, all his life, we should apply hard words to him: hypocrite, pharisee, tartuffe! Here we have the reverse, a lifelong student, burner of midnight oil, meticulous indefatigable craftsman, devoted and dependent family man, polyphiloprogenitive to the number of six, fine gentleman and world citizen, nevertheless advocating decadence and foolishness, at least always expressing the fascination of that side of life. Was this only an echoing of Nietzsche and other such immoralists? I think that he rather exaggerated the priority and the decisiveness of those nineteenth-century influences. After he had made up his mind or yielded to his fate, then, and perhaps not until then, he would hunt around for some prototype or precedent; ex post facto!

Can he have been an immoral fellow at a very early age, or to state the matter more modernly, done things that, as a son of complacent and coercive Luebeck, he had been taught to regard as heinous? Possibly; not probably. In great measure, I believe, his suggesting that this was the case was artifice for art's sake, and for the furtherance of his vocation and career, staking out a claim in the area of human subject matter in which he knew himself to be least developed and least authoritative.

Surely the Thomas Mann whom we saw resident in Princeton and on the west coast during the war years gave not the slightest impression of ever having been dissipated or accursed in any way, or on the other hand, of temperamental mediocrity or smallness in life. Let me humorously call attention to a sentence in "Goethe and Tolstoi," somewhat applicable to the author of that brilliant essay himself: "Through long creative years his [Tolstoi's] marriage was an idyll of family life, full of healthy, God-fearing pleasure, against a lavish economic background of agriculture and cattle breeding." Animal husbandry would not (I think) have suited the Manns: otherwise, to use a new American locution, it figures.

He was physically extraordinary, still youthful-looking in his sixties, when I occasionally saw him: a dignified, almost stately, slow-moving man with intense eyes and an uneasy, portentous expression. He had a way of sitting up very straight even in a soft armchair, not as one ordinarily sits in an armchair, rather as in a saddle; I remember thinking, the first time I saw him, that in his youth he must have borne a resemblance to the famous medieval Rider in Bamberg Cathedral. He was not apt to be talkative, and in casual sociability sometimes scarcely listened to the conversation around him. I don't suppose that he was ever very confidential, in the way of intimate remembrances or expressions of emotion. In his "Lebensabriss," the autobiographical sketch that I have mentioned, he tells us that even as a youngster in Bohemian and artistic circles in Munich, he called only half a dozen friends "du." It would not have occurred to me to ask him any sort of important direct question.

And yet in his expository handling of biographical material about other men of letters, as well as in his fiction early and late, he was apt to emphasize traits that seemed reminiscent of himself, derivations from his own experience. Can this have been somehow compulsive, that is, inwardly obligatory? In any case he was well aware of it. "The autobiographical impulse," he said, presupposes "a degree of brains and sensitivity which justifies it beforehand"; whereas the purely inventive, imaginative faculty "so often rests upon sheer self-deception."

In *Death in Venice,* as incriminatingly as can be, he attributes to the perverse dying writer, Aschenbach, some of his own published writings and unfulfilled literary projects; one of the oddest autobiographical impulses ever! I have a theory about this, not corroborated by anyone.—Must he not have had in mind the famous poet, Stefan George? (There is another reflection of that strange personality in Isak Dinesen's greatest tale, *The Deluge at Norderney.*)

Der Siebente Ring, peculiar lyrical utterance of a creative man's doting on a beautiful teen-ager, had appeared just four years prior to Mann's story. Perhaps, as he was beginning to conceive it, he asked himself: what if the author of *Der Siebente Ring* had been somewhat older and much weaker than he was in fact, and what if the boy Maximin had been much stronger and had not died? And then, as he was not just a ruthless fiction writer but a high-minded, well-meaning man of the world as well, perhaps it occurred to him that the reflection on his eminent confrere would be attenuated and rendered less discourteous if he took some of the suggested onus on his own broad shoulders.

Two birds with one stone, furthermore! As I have already stated, the observation of the psychology of homosexuality in this famous tale is not altogether convincing or significant. Even as he composed it, Mann may have detected in it something shaky and unauthoritative. In his youth and his old age alike, literature took precedence for him over every other value. Certainly his position in society in his native land in the first quarter of the century was strong and privileged enough for him to afford any slight scandalous suggestion. It may be that he deliberately lent Aschenbach those tell-tale books of his own, to prop the characterization up, to validate it and guarantee it.

Elsewhere in the lifework there are other similar instances of sophistry for art's sake. Just when a critic or a confrere might have impugned his grasp of some principle of human nature, his acquaintance with a particular social or cultural background, or his tracing of the distant origin or complex motivation of something that he was writing—the reasons for someone's unreasonableness, the mystery of someone's behavior—he would manage to say in an aside, or to suggest very persuasively, that the complexity in question was in his own character; he himself had thought thus and so, in a previous phase or past period, if not at present; this or that had been his own action, or the near equivalent of something that he had done. To quote Whitman, "I was the man, I suffered, I was there"; or an even higher-ranking, older poet, Virgil, speaking for Aeneas to Dido: "All of this misery I saw, great part of it I was."

True or false, here is an anecdote illustrative of this matter, dating from the early days of his vocation of fiction.—Upon the publication of *Tristan* (1903), someone in Luebeck recognized himself in it, a matter of one of his uniquenesses or at least idiosyncrasies portrayed to the life, and accused the young portrayer of having spied on him, from window to window, with a spyglass. To which Mann is said to have answered that, yes, indeed, he did own an optical instrument of that sort, and had often observed his accuser through it, exactly as specified. But as to the characterization in the famous story, it so happened that the spied-on gentleman had not contributed anything to that; it was self-portraiture.

Generally speaking, and seriously speaking, Mann's "autobiographical impulse"—his willingness to identify himself with key figures in his work, villainous as well as heroic figures, assuming spiritual responsibility for them in some measure, lending them his good traits, aspiration, obstination, work-morality, if anything of that kind seemed called for, taking upon himself opprobrium of their bad traits (or semblance of opprobrium) if necessary—doubtless enabled him to bear with some equanimity the reproaches of people whom he portrayed in his fiction or who recognized themselves somewhere in it.

The chief work of his old age, *Dr. Faustus,* raised this issue in a troubling and controversial way. It is a make-believe biography and violent expressionist portrait of a German composer named Adrian Leverkuehn, a reworking of the Faust legend, incorporating also some of the psychology and (in simplified fashion) the philosophy of Friedrich Nietzsche, and certain biographical facts about him, notably his syphilitic infection and his insanity in consequence. What this modernized Faust and latter-day Nietzsche wants in exchange for his immortal soul and his health is absolute greatness as a musician, indeed the ability to revolutionize modern music; and what Mann did, to make this important lifework real to himself as he wrote about it—and to his readers in due course—was to borrow the actual and specific musical modernism of the famous composer who happened to be his near neighbor in southern California, Arnold Schoenberg.

There was no mystery about this in the published volume. Schoenberg obliged him to append to it a characteristically worded "Author's Note" to the effect that "the form of musical composition delineated in Chapter XXII, known as the twelve-tone or row system is in truth the intellectual property of a contemporary composer and theoretician, Arnold Schoenberg"; that the novelist has "transferred this technique in a certain ideational context" to the hero or villain of his novel; and that numerous "details of musical theory expounded here and there in it have been taken from Schoenberg's treatise or textbook entitled *Harmonielehre.*"

In so far as I can imagine myself in Schoenberg's situation—doubtless a silly thing to try to do—it seems to me that, having revolutionized modern music, and published an epochal treatise on how to write it in my way, I should have taken some satisfaction in the fact that, inadvertently, I had taught a world-famous literary neighbor how to write interestingly *about* it. Quite the contrary: as a fellow exile, presumably not syphilitic, certainly not crazy—or, as the saying goes, crazy like a fox—Schoenberg found himself extremely unsatisfied and dissatisfied, and vented his irateness and sadness in an open letter to a literary review.

I certainly do not believe that Mann intended to insult Schoenberg or even to hurt his feelings. The eminent composer's touchiness seems to us now, and must have seemed to the author of *Dr. Faustus* at the time, shortsighted, if not ungrateful. Mann was the proudest writer on earth, well aware of his permanent high standing in culture and powerful influence, and doubtless he felt that he was making a contribution to that immortality which Schoenberg, with his stubborn, idiosyncratic musical output, obviously desired and was entitled to. Romans à clef, as a rule, in the long run damage no one. In the case of any great creative personality or public figure, posterity is glad to have them.

Furthermore, from Mann's viewpoint, *Dr. Faustus* was a work of introspection, an act of conscience. Its principal point was the symbolical connection and correspondence between Leverkuehn's personal hubris and downfall and the German national tragedy. Mann's own hubris had been an obvious fact of the German literary life for half a century. His having to go into exile in Switzerland and, still farther afield, in the United States doubtless had a humbling, depressing effect on him. Nevertheless, and despite the uniqueness of his talent and the internationality of his reputation, he still thought of himself as the most representative of Germans. In all these essentials Leverkuehn was *his* mouthpiece; to all intents and purposes *he* was Leverkuehn. The mere addition of certain aspects of Schoenberg's career as a musician to the sublime and terrible personification of Germany that he (Mann) had conceived out of his own inner resources and out of the sacred subconscious was a comparatively minor matter. Willingly, always, he himself had played the scapegoat's part, shouldering his share of responsibility for things, more than his share. Now, if he had a mind to use someone else's shoulder, even the famous dodecaphonist's shoulder, for an ounce of the burden, a detail of the work, oughtn't he to be allowed to?

I am on Mann's side. I do not, I cannot, disapprove of any fiction

writer's modeling his hero or, for that matter, his villain, on this or
that recognizable prototype, even a living prototype. It is a thing
that all of us who write fiction have a passion to do, whether or not
we have the courage. It is one of our skills, one of our mysteries and
fecundities. Often indeed it requires a certain fanaticism and hard-
heartedness. Some of us simply fail to imagine, and others refuse
to consider, the feelings of those they write about; and often, in
consequence, their work is more powerful than that of scrupulous
or inhibited novelists.

❖

Now I want to examine certain of the particulars of Mann's art in
that novel which I greatly prefer to the imaginary biography of
Leverkuehn, namely, *The Magic Mountain,* pointing to what delights me especially, and making something of an issue of its imperfections. I will be specific and descriptive in both respects.

Though it has been his most popular novel (in the United States),
and though surely its main theme and setting are unforgettable
—pulmonary disease as an exemplification of the human condition
in general, Alpine sanatorium as a macrocosm—you may not have
kept in mind various details that I attach importance to, or see
meaning in; perhaps you have scarcely noticed them, with so much
else to notice on every page. It is one of the most minute and florid
compositions in all literature, with a forceful sort of homogeneity
made up of many small contrasts, with every thread drawn tight,
every bit of the colorfulness and the highlights and the shadows in
keeping and in order; yet never quite three-dimensional, like an
immense millefleurs tapestry.

Do you remember how it starts, in medias res, with the arrival at
the International Sanatorium Berghof of a young everyman, Hans
Castorp, to visit his tuberculous soldier-cousin, Joachim? Immediately we are provided with a symbol of transitoriness and a suggestion of the disgust of death: he has to wait for his room to be fumi-
gated, because an American lady has just died in it. Swiss altitude
and the stimulation of the environment of sick people affect him

with a certain inverse hilarity, something like a mardi gras, but with a hint of witches' sabbath. He keeps blushing, and perhaps it is fever; he laughs more than ever, and has bad dreams.

Then in Chapter II the strong skillful narrator turns us around and bids us look at Hans's family background and childhood, a small world of the upper bourgeosie, rather like that of his first novel, *Buddenbrooks,* presumably not unlike that of the Mann family in Luebeck; in which, however, disquieting themes of the present work as a whole are predicated, foreshadowed: bygone time, which has a tragic or at least harrowing aspect (certainly it must be bad for one, if one ponders it too constantly and intensely); a sense of the relatedness of love and disease; vaguely homosexual feelings; and a good many inklings of death, death mystical and universal!

For example, there drifts up in Hans's mind, from that half-forgotten life, the similarity, noticed by him at the time, between the odor of his grandfather's corpse laid out in the coffin and the body odor of one of his schoolmates, a somewhat sickly boy; and not many pages later, when Frau Chauchat, the female protagonist of the work, makes her entrance, very exciting to the young bourgeois, what attracts him particularly is her resemblance to another schoolmate, one named Pribislav Hippe. Hippe means scythe, emblem and implement of the Grim Reaper. Liebestod, love-death? No, principally, in this book, it is Liebeskrankheit, love-sickness. For the idea and the point of a sanatorium is to get well, isn't it? This Berghof of Mann's imagination is the very abode of the will to live; simply fatuous and physical in some cases, hopeless in some, systematic and feasible in a few. It is as churning and writhing and jumping with life as a fishpond or a snake pit or a monkey house.

In this same chapter, Hans's second day in the place, he voluptuously smokes cigars named after one of the mistresses of one of the kings of France; and the constant coughing of an Austrian Herr Rittmeister arouses in him a sado-masochistic imaginativeness that he has not noticed in himself before: with his mind's eye he seems able to penetrate the cougher's body—he has never had a thought like that before—and that night he has a highly stylized dream in which he and his good and good-looking cousin are somewhere on a bobsled riding or sliding downhill, with the cavalier coughing gentleman sitting up front, steering.

The room next to Hans's is occupied by a low-class Russian couple whose intercourse is ardent and noisy, and it makes him nervous. He happens to be fretting about this when Frau Chauchat, the heroine —let me say rather, the hero's beloved (she scarcely deserves to be called a heroine) —makes her entrance. She too is Russian, and though not low-class, heralds herself by an unmannerly noisiness. Whenever she comes into the dining room she slams the door, which Hans has noticed and resented on previous occasions, without seeing who was doing it. Now he sees her: pale and freckled and redheaded, with seductive round arms but unattractive stubby fingers; a woman who looks like a schoolboy and makes him feel like one. These various initial hints of polymorphous sexuality notwithstanding, the part she plays in the novel is that of a sort of Goethean Helen to Hans's Faust; the furthest thing in the world from a Gretchen.

In Mann's representations of normal youthful passion there is often an odd effect of coldness or forgetfulness, a lack of empathy. The Faust-Helen pattern seems to come more naturally to him: peculiar, intense, imaginary intimacy of those who, as he phrases it in *Death in Venice,* "know each other only with their eyes"; a part of whose interest in each other is "unslaked curiosity," a part of whose mutual respect is simply not having a basis for disrespect. It is a pattern that turns up more regularly in homosexual behavior than in relations between males and females.

Before we have read twenty pages we realize that despite a Tolstoian gift for details of the human condition, for the texture and pattern of ordinary assorted everyday existence, this is not going to be anything like an eighteenth- or a nineteenth-century novel. In the "Lebensabriss," with reference to these preliminary chapters, Mann speaks of "the comfortable English key I began in." Comfortable? English? Sometimes in comments on his own work like this, whether in commendation or the opposite, he seems almost to be joking, enjoying the thought that his readers were apt to believe anything that happened to come into his head. But if this is a joke, it is one that he persisted in year after year; and he would always buttress and back himself up in any whimsicality about his writing by referring to his forerunners in fiction, the blessed hierarchy and peck order of his chosen old masters of novel writing.

Mann's joking on the whole was less effective than he seemed to think. He was a born worker; and even when in the nature of the given work the reader was bound to find it heavy going, the writing itself amused him. "My endeavor is to make the heavy light," he said in 1951 in an interview, perhaps ironically, "my idea is clarity; and if I write long sentences—a tendency inherent in the German tongue—I make it my business, not without success, to maintain the utmost transparency and spoken rhythm. . . . I feel myself to be primarily a humorist.".

Presumably he intended *The Magic Mountain* to satirize certain novels of the past, somewhat as Cervantes did in *Don Quixote;* Fielding and Jane Austen likewise, here and there. Mann's touch in the satirical way is delicate, almost too delicate. Some of his best pages are colored by sophistication and implicit bookishness. In so far as he gives himself English airs, he compensates for this soon enough, with deliberately, self-consciously German effects. When he has waxed lyrical or epical, he offsets it with a sentimental passage or a slight parody or a farcical turn. Though surely nothing in the entire great novel is exactly a laughing matter—with grief and disease ubiquitous, even morbidly glamorous in it—again and again, by the above means and other devices, he induces in us something in the nature of hilarity; a mood corresponding to his young hero's when he first arrives on the mountaintop and is influenced by the altitude: jocund, mystical, slightly hysterical.

In the way of a little further extension of his dualistic habit of mind, he was inclined to a kind of double entendre, but not in the ribald sense. The scene of the love-making of Hans and Frau Chauchat when they have had too much to drink is just a little ribald. Note that during it they converse in French, very Teutonic French.

As a rule the effect of Mann's dichotomousness in his way of writing was merely mockery showing through the earnestness, pathos and gruesomeness interspersed and blended with the pleasurable vitality; two tones at once, as in shot silk, or in certain fine composite minerals, which rather unifies the work, as to its mood and manner.

Its more important structural unity is just the portraiture, a constant comparison and contrast of the denizens of Berghof; cross-beams and cornerstones of the human nature there assembled. Of the mentality and character of his half dozen personages of greatest consequence in the sanatorium, Mann not only gives subtle and powerful, sometimes overpowering explanations, but lets us hear their own self-expression, explaining things to one another, haranguing one another, arguing.

Hofrat Behrens, the medical director of the sanatorium, is the type of scientist who has a playful mind, skeptical of all sorts of concepts, even those most germane and workable in the practice of medicine. To some extent he is a sick man himself. He is an artist in his spare time. He has had some amorous intimacy with Clavdia Chauchat, the hero's beloved. Dr. Krokowski, the staff psychoanalyst, theorizes extremely about amorous proclivity and the susceptibility to disease, to the effect that love makes one sick, and sickness makes one concupiscent; with the usual basic uncertainty as to which comes first, which is the easier to get at in treatment. He discovers that one of his patients has mediumistic powers and arranges séances with her for the very questionable benefit of other patients, including Hans. A good Italian named Settembrini, a political liberal and humanist in the nineteenth-century tradition, attaches himself to Hans as a substitute father and mentor, hoping to counteract the wrong ideas and morbid influences of the mountain.

The most astonishing and prophetic of the creatures of Mann's imagination in this novel is an Eastern European Jew named Naphta, orphaned in a pogrom, in which local avengers of Christ crucified his father; adopted, after that, by Jesuits, and given every advantage of worldly and theological education. Despite this, and somewhat in consequence of it, he has become a type of crypto-Communist and proto-Nazi. Catholicism and terrorism mixed, blood lust and dialectics mixed, have made a veritable witches' brew in this man's head, which issues in pages and pages of frightening and sickening talk. "Liberation and development of the individual are

not the key to our age," he declares. What it needs, what it is straining to bring about, what must happen to it in due course, is a "moral
chaos" and a "radical sepsis" and, in due course, an "anointed
Terror." Some such nasty combination of words issues every time he
opens his mouth; prescriptions of gangrene, applications of mag-
gots, lancings of things with a rusty knife.

He and Settembrini violently discuss all this for ten or fifteen
pages at a time, about a hundred pages, all in Volume II. Political
theory, history lessons biased in one way or the other, opposite
views of the future of European humankind: their debate raises the
tone of the work above the sensationalism and sometimes sordid
hypochondria inherent in the subject matter of the tuberculosis life;
but at the same time loads it down with what you might call editorializing, ideas that seemingly never develop, never move along with
the chronology of the fiction, and cumulatively constitute the great
fault of the novel as such, the work as a whole, the narrative per
se: its abstraction, volubility, voluminousness.

Very specifically in two chapters, this baptized Jew and this
idealistic agnostic Italian between them, conduct an important part
of Hans's adult education, the development and expansion of everyman's mind, which is *The Magic Mountain*'s main theme, refrain,
and gist: demoralizing devil on the one hand, guardian angel on
the other, contending for his soul.

In the characterization of those two, and in their fanatic debating, Mann certainly had an unfictitious and autobiographical
matter in mind. Settembrini bears a resemblance to Mann's elder
brother Heinrich, the author of *The Little Town* and of *Professor
Unrat* (popular in its motion picture version, *The Blue Angel*) with
whom Settembrini's creator had engaged in acrimonious controversy
during World War I. The question was, roughly speaking, whether
or not, in a time of national emergency, the creative man should
partake of the collective martial enthusiasm. In a sense, I think,
Thomas Mann wanted to partake of everything, always.

Heinrich Mann had objected bitterly to certain passages in the
essay entitled "Frederick the Great and the Grand Coalition"

(1915). This is said to consist in some measure of thoughts salvaged from an abandoned historical novel (to which, by the way, Mann refers in *Death in Venice* as a part of Aschenbach's lifework). For example, Mann notes that the brilliant, harmful eighteenth-century monarch was quite as capable of a tranquil career of flute playing and belles-lettres as he was of "the frightful stains and bloody horrors of war"; but instinctively and secretly, Mann goes on to say, he preferred the latter. Because he was a German, a typical German, he felt that "this secret instinct, this element of the daemonic and the super-personal," was a profounder thing in him than any personal idea or desire or principle. And, Mann concludes, it was destiny, urgent and irresistible in his mind and heart; it was the spirit of history incarnate in him. "He had to do wrong, in order that the great destiny of a great people might be fulfilled."

It is in flat, small pronouncements of this kind in his expository and hortatory work that Mann seems most foreign to us. When he aspires to be somewhat Latin-inspired in his prose style, at least Goethe-like, lapidary and lucid, he lets us see suddenly the rashness of his thinking, his sense of theoretical imperatives, feelings of predestination, and prophetic notions of what history has (so to speak) in *its* mind.

Heinrich Mann embodied his disapproval of all this in an essay on Zola, which evidently stung and challenged the younger brother deeply. During the further war years Thomas Mann produced a vast volume of musings and arguments, liberalism versus traditional authoritarianism, national Kultur versus the more civilized feeling of world citizenship, entitled *Betrachtungen eines Unpolitischen* (Reflections of a Nonpolitical Man) (1918); of which no English translation has as yet appeared.

A good many passages of Naphta's shocking discourse in *The Magic Mountain* doubtless echo that old disagreement between his brother and himself—more importantly perhaps, at the bottom of his heart, between himself and himself—and can be matched with passages in the *Betrachtungen*. By presenting one last version of it in the desperate colloquy of Settembrini and Naphta in such a way that the balance of the reader's sympathies cannot but be tipped toward the former, perhaps in proud sophisticated fashion Thomas intended a sort of apology to Heinrich.

It may be noted that Heinrich Mann apparently never budged from his liberal internationalism to the day of his death. Whereas the younger, profounder brother was to move through an entire spectrum of political convictions; and in the end, as an old man, he looked back calmly, complacently, upon all his thoughts, no matter how dichotomous—perhaps the more dichotomous the better—and referred somewhat proudly to the book that we in Anglo-Saxondom do not know. To such an extent was he born to be a fiction writer, with a sort of vocational deformation in the course of his lifetime of writing, that all he seemed to ask of life at the last was to round itself out, as a good story does; dark and nonsensical perhaps, but with shape!

Three quarters of the way through *The Magic Mountain,* Mann introduces a personage even more impressive than Settembrini or Naphta, though less intellectual, less inclined to serious conversation: Mynheer Peeperkorn, a "kingly, incoherent man," a giant and an immoderate drinker, almost an alcoholic. Both in and out of his cups, Peeperkorn personifies the love of life and the joy of living. Before long Frau Chauchat becomes his mistress; and after that he commits suicide, for a reason which Mann seems to find more respectable than the deathward urges of others of the Alpine society: a feeling of the onset of old age, which friendly frequentation of Hans along with their mutual beloved has intensified.

Peeperkorn, who has come to Berghof from the Orient, accompanied by a picturesque Malayan servant, advocating and taking the lead in convivialities of all sorts, as unbridled as may be in a serious Swiss sanatorium, is a type of aging Bacchus, to whom Frau Chauchat plays Ariadne. German readers of the twenties were reminded of Gerhart Hauptmann, the dramatist, also a pagan and bibulous personality.

More interesting to us now, in this character creation, are Mann's borrowings from that lovely small volume of Gorki's remembrances of Tolstoi which I have mentioned elsewhere: the trait of extreme

virility, with a corresponding horror of the physical debasement
of the decline of life; an anecdote of Tolstoi's rapturously watching the swoop of a hawk upon a barnyard fowl (with typical ag-
grandizement, half humorous, half Wagnerian, Mann assigns to
Peeperkorn an eagle instead of a hawk); and an image of the glorious old man of Yasnaya Polyana in the midst of his disciples "like an
orchestra leader playing at one and the same time on various instruments."

The Magic Mountain is what is (or was) known in German
critical writing and textbooks as a "Bildungsroman" or an "Ent-
wickelungsroman," a development novel. Hans does develop aston-
ishingly. Almost at the end of the vast novel—on the penultimate
page, to be exact—Mann refers to him as a *simple* soul. Simple,
perhaps, in the old primary dictionary meaning: honest and un-
cunning, but by that time certainly not uncomplicated, not innocent, not ordinary. Mann in his determined way, with almost
ostentatious skillfulness, has made him plausible, but hardly (as it
seems to me) probable, having conferred upon him an intellect too
far-ranging, spiritual interests too cosmic and esoteric. Is there any
other protagonist in world literature so well educated, at least well
informed, and indefatigably meditative and speculative? Mann's
suggestion is that his basic indecisiveness, his inability or disinclina-
tion to make up his mind, only adds to the extent and importance of
his intellectuality, verging on infinitude, or at any rate, constantly
broaching infinite matters. As we read the closing chapters, were it
not for the author's strong technique, somehow referring back to
the opening chapters every little while, echoing what he has already
said, jogging our memories, we might almost forget that this is the
same boy who first came to the Berghof: full-fleshed, clean and soft,
energetic though phlegmatic, rather sleepy when not excited, red-
faced with inhibition and fever.

Frau Chauchat points out to him that, whereas she lives for life's
sake, from moment to moment, impetuously and self-forgetfully,
what he wants from life is the educative effect, self-realization, self-
enrichment; and this difference between them rather vexes her.
Within Mann's intellectual frame of reference, as gradually disclosed

in the work as a whole, the reader finds this only natural: contrast between male and female, and between Teuton and Slav. Certainly, in the outcome of everything that happens to Hans during his sojourn at Berghof, the aggregate of everything that transpires about him, he gets what she has accused him of seeking.

Let me call your attention to the cultural sophistication of all this, not just a reviving and updating of old pagan religious traditions and myths, Prometheus, Orpheus, Theseus, Tiresias, Oedipus, which has gone on continually in European arts and letters since the Renaissance. In Germany, especially, this has been a more eclectically bookish and artistic epoch than the quattrocento or the cinquecento; also more theatrical and musical. The allusiveness and resonance in Mann's work derived from a whole shelfful of nineteenth-century writers as well as the ancients, and to half a lifetime of concerts and operas. Hans is a variant upon Wilhelm Meister, obviously; he is also Faust, with two Mephistos instead of just one; he is also Tannhäuser, as of Act I, in Venusberg; and once in a while, for a page or two, he is Parsifal. Does not the International Sanatorium Berghof also occasionally remind you of the *Decameron?* Except that the victims of Mann's plague are all up in the castle, not down below in the city; and they do very little of their storytelling themselves. Mann enjoyed his own copious aristocratic language, and would not have trusted any of his dramatis personae to bring out in a colloquial way the iridescent meaningfulness that he saw in them and in their various plights and crises. Settembrini is Socrates; indeed one of Naphta's insults to him is that evidently he has been corrupting poor undersexed, slightly homosexual Hans. Settembrini is also Sarastro, Hans is both Tamino and Pamino, and Frau Chauchat is the Queen of the Night.

❖

The Magic Mountain is an almost perfect example of its type of novel: the group portrait of a little world set apart. In form and structure it corresponds somewhat to Katherine Anne Porter's *Ship of Fools.* But naturally the German great man interprets his world in the philosophical way much more than the American woman of genius does, and sets his worldlings to philosophizing also, as in imitation of their creator. This results in the one notable imperfection of *The Magic Mountain:* its extreme length and looseness, in which one may see some self-indulgence on Mann's part, but which, for him, certainly, was a matter of aesthetic principle, creative innovation.

If I were teaching an advanced and leisurely course in novel writing, I should like to assign to a young would-be novelist, or to two or three of them, the exercise of drastically abridging it. Mann would not be so hard to handle in this way as some other discursive narrators, for example, Proust and Balzac, because the modes of his writing, historic, descriptive, expository, didactic, dialectic, ironic, are not, as a rule, closely combined or intermingled. He is apt to shift his mind from one to the other quite consciously and decidedly, taking pride in the gamut of his effects and assorted components of his narrative power.

The pace and scope of the first fifty pages of *The Magic Mountain* are exactly right, I think, with impact enough, and a definite indication of the general direction of the work, and a good ratio of items of fact to expressions of feeling. My young abridgers might try to keep that same movement and proportion throughout; and if they did so, I really believe that they would find it desirable, and certainly feasible, to eliminate two or three hundred pages of what follows; approximately a third! Most obviously curtailable are the several chapters in which his hero, Hans Castorp, with time on his hands on the mountaintop, gives himself a kind of adult education: scientific, historical, philosophical. Mann evidently was glad of the opportunity to educate his readers adultly along with his protagonist, and to display his own extraordinary erudition. And certainly a quantity of the political debating of Settembrini and Naphta could be removed, not to the wastebasket—for it is brilliant, and of prophetic interest even today—but to some separate book form or pamphlet form, as an essay in antithetical generalization, or perhaps a dialogue in the manner of Plato.

Also, every little way, from beginning to end, there are sentences

G

and paragraphs of Mann's running commentary on the issues and events of his fictitious world that could come away. Often we seem to be sitting in a large, darkened or dimmed auditorium, with scenes and characterizations shining and shifting, one after another, in the dark, like lantern slides, while the masterful narrator gives us a tremendous lecture along with his narrative, pointing out the fine points and the profundities in each bright picture, and arguing things back and forth. It makes a great impression, but of course it brings the narrative almost to a standstill now and then. I wonder whether it is worth while.

Precedent for it there certainly is. Nineteenth-century men and women of genius of the highest rank indulged in a vast amount of expository self-expression in their novels. Perhaps it was more important to Mann to feel that he was being a genius like them, to manifest genius in everything he wrote, than simply to master his form, and to be brief and evocative and expeditious. Indeed I know that there are worse faults than length and complexity. Mann's artistry never, never flagged or fell into ordinary stereotypes. In the totality of *The Magic Mountain,* nine hundred pages long, there are only a few slumps or anti-climaxes, a few pages of complicated violent action a little skimped, and some progressions and retrogressions just synopsized, not rendered; harmless little holes, inconspicuous little blemishes, in the massive construction. I complain of the too much, not the too little. The important lesson for my imaginary students of the art of the novel would be the mere subtraction and the negative benefit: how much more vividly and convincingly a great many matters of human interest and various dramatic or melodramatic passages would stand out if the pages and pages of expository writing leading up to them, descending away from them, could be scaled down, or if Mann had kept them under control in the first place.

What would *The Magic Mountain* be like, if it were edited by me or by imaginary disciples of mine? A less impressive, less imposing work, I dare say, not more than five or six hundred pages, but surely profound enough, with only as much biology and pathology and psychopathology and heredity as may be apparent in the problems and emotions of particular human beings; with just weather instead of meteorology, the changing seasons year after year instead of time in the abstract, and specific landscape, Alpine valleys and upland meadows and mountain tops, instead of geology; not intensely political, except in as much as it is a cross section of the society to which World War I was about to happen; not exactly philosophical, except in the way of the ordinary effects of love and truth and freedom and strength, and conversely, of animosity and falsehood and authority and weakness, and of a constant brooding awareness of ever-oncoming death. A work of heartbreaking humanity and macabre humor; a marvel, in its way!

Perhaps I ought to be ashamed of this hypothesis and fantasy of abridging a novel which I delight in, as is; which furthermore a million readers the world over have found to their satisfaction. Could not future readers be left to their own devices about it, to do their own skipping, without any prompting by fanatical advocates of simpler, purer narrative form? Yes, but let me make my point. If, at that stage of his development as a novelist, which was, in fact, the turning point of his art, Mann had been obliged or persuaded or inspired to reduce *The Magic Mountain* to one volume instead of two, he would have done just what I have been thinking of doing: sacrificed a vast mass of his marginal, interpretational writing, and a good deal of the abstract arguing of his characters also, and kept every bit of definite time and three-dimensional location and lifelike humanity and interesting action: narrative pure and simple! It could not be reduced in any other way. The superfluity is all in the expository prose. There is not the least fat or gristle or roughage or padding in the story line or the portraiture or the intimate conversation or the passages of poetical or emotional expression.

In fact, needless to say, there never was any question of Mann's reducing anything; quite the contrary. It is a point of some importance. He did not strive particularly to be a popular writer. As the author of *Buddenbrooks*, fame and fortune descended upon him so early in life that perhaps he scarcely had occasion to calculate his success in any way. But in this one respect, perhaps, the general cultural predilection of his time and place, the habit of mind of the cultivated reading public, influenced him more than he was aware. In Germany and Austria and in the several satellite Central European and Scandinavian cultures, during the half century prior to the publication of *The Magic Mountain,* there was a cult of the extensive, the massive, the overpowering, the colossal, not only in literature but in all the arts—as indeed in the United States also, at that same time, in architecture and machinery and other features of the new materialism.

By Mann's own account, later on, the impulse to be prolix and vast came from within. Even as a youngster, he declared, he had had "a willful love of mere largeness." Characteristically, whenever he became aware of any powerful predilection or peculiarity in himself or in his work, he would turn and consider the matter in its historic perspective, in terms of the creativity of the past, mirroring himself most willingly in studies of the nineteenth-century supermen, Wagner as well as the philosophers and poets and novelists. In 1933, in a long essay on the composer of *The Ring of the Niebelung,* he noted that a desire to have everything on the largest possible scale, "a taste for the monumental and the copious and the grandiose," characterized all or almost all of them. But at the same time they desired to have a great many things on a very small scale: factually, in the mise en scène of their lives, a quantity of bibelots and symbolic objects and scientific curios and, correspondingly, in their inner experience, minute subjectivities, fixations of intellect, and crises of conscience. But in every respect the detail only added to the monumentality. They heaped their pettinesses up in towering structures; organized them, always, with reference to some planned grandeur.

In another passage, referring to Tolstoi even more fondly than to Wagner, Mann called it a "democratic amplitude," and spoke of the strength of character and stubbornness that it took to pursue and cleave to an ideal of that kind, in a petty modern society and culture. The author of *War and Peace,* throughout his life, had been criticized for the relentlessness with which he carried through every bit of his tremendous concepts as planned, with "deliberate and splendid long-windedness." Hasty and weary modern readers resented this, Mann said. Only in the concluding chapters of *War and Peace,* if I remember rightly, is Tolstoi as theoretical and loquacious as Mann, and no doubt he was aware of this fact.

As I go on indicating and interpreting the oddities and extravagances in Mann's work, I hope that it does not seem simply humorous and disrespectful. Truly, I exaggerate only to clarify; I jest to arouse interest and to stir up differences of opinion. If *The Magic Mountain* seems satisfactory to you on all counts, if you defer to those important critical writers and professors who see in it the norm and the apogee of twentieth-century narrative art, well and good, more power to you, more power to it.

If, on the other hand, you feel as I do that it is far from perfect, never let my quibbling and theorizing lead you into any absolute disregard or disillusionment. Go back to it; reread it just cursorily this time; play my game of impertinent abridgment; skip all the tremendous thoughtfulness and the scientific lore of forty or fifty years back. Banish from your mind the small or middle-sized, lucid, evocative and symbolical modern masterpieces that (in principle) I prefer, and perhaps you do too: for example, Forster's *A Passage to India,* and Richard Hughes' *A High Wind in Jamaica,* and Colette's *Chéri,* and Virginia Woolf's *Between the Acts,* and to be sure, *Tonio Kroeger* and *Lotte in Weimar.* With a free mind, taking at face value, you will be surprised to find how much of *The Magic Mountain* is to be enjoyed and re-enjoyed, praised and prized.

The parts, indeed, are superior to the whole. It is what you might call a three-ring circus; whatever your point of view (wherever you sit, around the tremendous 900-page arena) you can never see it all in focus, in reasonable order; somehow there is dust in the atmosphere all through it, and glare in one part, obscurity in another; the tent poles do not stand straight; the vast canvas sags, the sawdust seems to pile up and pile up—but, all the while, on every page, in every square foot of the rings and around the track, there are wonderful little acts, magic and conjuring and sleight of hand and juggling and tumbling, and clowns and freaks.

◆

Some of Mann's best portraiture in *The Magic Mountain* is tiny; sometimes as many as half a dozen supernumeraries clustered in one small pattern, so clearly drawn and crystallinely lit that they practically detach themselves from the main creation. For example, a scene of young people on a terrace after their heavy sanatorium meal of meats and sweets, replete and idle and mischievous, with Mann's malicious intellect shining on them along with the Alpine daylight. I keep forgetting in what part of the two volumes to look for this; it has no very marked function in its chapter or in the unwinding of the work as a whole. There are a Balkan military man with an important mustache; a Dutch boy who collects stamps; a pair named Max and Moritz; and some devout person from Mannheim—is it a man or a woman?—who keeps lurking as close to the others as he or she can get, and persisting in an attitude of maximum melancholy and selfish desperation, which the others resent and are made a little melancholy by. The mere assorted liveness or livingness of these creatures is unforgettable; why? It is nothing, that is, it would be nothing, were it not the human race; it is Europe on the eve of one of its wars; and it is the purest fiction, in that aspect of the art which is even more fundamental than theme or message or form or plot: just getting to know people, people who doubtless have died long since, or perhaps never existed.

Then there is the opposite sort of small scene, not at all marginal or incidental; tensely composed, and vigorously intentional, with reference to the entirety of the work, endlessly worth thinking about. For example, an episode of almost blasphemous pathos, the rebellion of a little dying girl named Barbara Hujus against having to take the Last Sacrament; the hullabaloo she makes, and then "a gruesome sort of begging," suddenly muffled, as though the earth had already opened and swallowed her up. What has happened is that she has retreated from the priest under the covers, kicking with all her might. I am afraid that this impresses me as a truer representation of the love of life than all of Peeperkorn's personifying and attitudinizing.

No matter about the very hermetic, heavy, slow intellectual pages that happen to baffle me or bore me. Have I seemed to forget that it took a man of genius to compose them? Indeed not; it is unforgettable. Only these other lightweight pages, half-pages, paragraphs, which have a kind of naturalness and self-evidence that is like daylight, a feeling of close proximity that is like body heat, a little palpitation as of the breath of life, delight me so much that I cannot help wishing that he himself had been distracted from the full deployment of his genius more often, and given us an even larger amount of his fleeting and miserable and sublime humanity in miniature, thumbnail sketching of homunculi, for which he had a greater gift than anyone else on earth.

Reality, it occurs to me, is prolific in this type of weird little event, unique though unimportant humanity. Even journalism shows us a good deal of it. Literary writers neglect it as a rule, for the good and sufficient reason that it is difficult to organize it in any quantity in coherent book form. But Mann's organizing power and sense of construction were formidable. In his way, taking as much time and space as he liked, he could handle the slightest item about the least important of his supernumerary people just as strongly and importantly as the great social problems and the history lessons and the metaphysical matters, drifting clouds of the timeless and the useless, that in the end he preferred.

And despite his abstract preference, I must say, he never lost his more essential narrative ability having to do with human beings, even in the less naturalistic, more symbolical works of the autumn of his life. In *Dr. Faustus,* for example, not only are his principal personages as powerfully established in our minds as ever, with significances even more definite than in his early fiction, there is still a great quantity of miniature lives, little dramatic actions and expressions, characterizations for characterization's sake. Every so often he gives us slight glimpses of people who have no great raison d'être in the larger scheme of the work—like wild birds casting their shadows across windows now and then; like little animals more or less at home amid the expository tangles, in and out of vacant spaces in the deep, florid paragraphs.

It is the human bestiary that delights me. The dirty stable girl, Hanne, who teaches the infant composer Leverkuehn and other children to sing rounds, the alphabet of polyphony, is unforgettable. Privat-docent Eberhard Schleppfuss, Professor Dragfoot (another of the breed of Naphta), is unforgettable; would that one *could* forget him! The child Nepomuk, who took for himself the name of Echo, the only human being ever loved by Leverkuehn, screaming his miniature life away in spinal meningitis—akin to Hanno Budden-brook, and to the consumptive children of Berghof, and to one or another of the little Shakespearean princes—breaks my heart.

Even at that late date Mann (aged seventy and plus) obviously took an ecstatic interest in human nature—the finest thing in the *Entstehung* is an account of his transforming a little grandson of his into the ill-fated Echo, and trying not to frighten the little one's mother by the inauspicious creative act—and he still knew how to arouse the reader's corresponding interest. But in *Dr. Faustus,* as indeed in *Joseph and His Brothers,* absorbed in perceptions far-flung and timeless, and aesthetic and metaphysical issues of some difficulty, he found less room for the record of homo sapiens as such. Whereas in *The Magic Mountain* there is some slight hallucinating human beauty, sentiment or sensuality or enigma, on almost every page, with a brightness and emphasis, denoting (I think) pride in what he was able to do in that way.

For example, the funeral march of the Mexican lady who has two doomed handsome sons. "Tous les deux! tous les deux! both of them!" she says to everyone. It's the only thing she knows how to say. in French; she can't say anything at all in German. To the sound of music from a nearby hotel, Señora Tous-les-Deux paces around the garden with ceremonious woeful tread; Hans is watching her from his balcony. Then the music changes to a waltz, and his attention shifts to the lascivious Russians next door. Suddenly it occurs to him that there is some parallel between the two Mexican sons going to their death, as it were in double harness, and himself and his dear cousin Joachim; and he feels the strain of unenacted sex and the magnetism of old mortality.

For example, the gluttonous boy suddenly raging at the dwarf waitress Emerentia, stomping and pounding, shouting "I will" and "I won't"—it is something about the tea, not hot enough or not steeped enough. And his fury communicates itself to the others in the dining room, for no reason except the human contagiousness, mammalian contagiousness: "some of them sprang up and glared, fists doubled, teeth clenched; others sat white and trembling, their eyes cast down."

By that time, the historic chronology keeping pace with this fictive chronicle of the life in a health resort in a neutral country, World War I has begun to darken on the horizon of Europe, with intermittent but persistent flickers like summer lightning.

In that same chapter, almost at the end of the book, there are other symptoms of the basic recurrent illness of the Continent, evidently less curable than tuberculosis.—A female patient quarrels so strenuously with a woman who runs a lingerie shop in the village that it gives her a hemorrhage. A Jewish patient and an anti-Semitic patient come to blows in the hallway. The Polish patients all get to feuding, with tedious formalities, like diplomats. Hans's rival instructors, Settembrini the good European, and Naphta the totalitarian Jew, in the heat of an argument about political assassination —whether or not there is any justification for it in ethics—finally realize how irremediably they hate each other, and fight a duel. With a certain theatricality and magnanimity Settembrini shoots in the air; whereupon Naphta blows his brains out. Wishful plotting on Mann's part, I may say; for in fact the Naphtas of one stripe and another were to dominate German history for decades after that.

It was in 1912, we are told, that Mann began the composition of *The Magic Mountain,* and I have oftened wondered how he would have concluded it if World War I had not taken place. For that is all the denouement it has: the peculiar suicidal duel, then the historic thunderbolt. And by that time many of the dwellers on the mountain, the sick population of Berghof, have gone back down to the world at sea level, and many have died. Joachim's death especially has cast a desolation upon the latter chapters; because, surely, he was Dr. Behrens's most respectable and lovable patient. We realize at last that we have never quite loved Hans, perhaps because Mann, on the one hand, has made too singular a figure of him, and on the other hand, always somewhat made fun of him. Frau Chauchat has gone away somewhere, and Hans evidently has licked his wounds and more or less forgotten about her. For approximately a hundred pages everyone's story has been slowing down, like a huge top, with declining hum and little lurches. Then war is declared, and we see and hear Hans in the midst of it, just once: everyman, stumbling across a dull battlefield with three thousand other typical young Germans, singing to himself Schubert's "Lindenbaum."

Of all the incidents in *The Magic Mountain,* the one that most truly touches my imagination is Dr. Behrens's letting Hans look at his cousin Joachim's heart in the course of a fluoroscopic examination. (A doctor friend once let me look at my own, holding a mirror up to the fluoroscope.) While Behrens is calling attention to evidences of tuberculosis in Joachim's lungs, Hans independently notices something like a bag, a strange animal shape, darkly visible: "pulsating and expanding and contracting rather regularly, somewhat after the fashion of a jellyfish swimming."

"Good God, it is the heart, Joachim's honor-loving heart," Hans exclaims to himself. "I am looking at your heart," he says to his cousin in a repressed voice.

"Go ahead and look," Joachim answers, probably smiling back in the darkness.

After that, Behrens shows Hans his own hand, with the flesh dissolved from it in a mist; and on the translucent bone of one finger, his grandfather's signet ring, very black and seemingly loose, ready to be passed on to some successor and inheritor, some other temporary ring wearer. And "for the first time in his life," Mann specifies, Hans understands that he is predestined to die; and at the thought, there comes over his face "the expression it usually wore when he listened to music: a little dull, sleepy, and pious," his lips parted, his head inclined to one side.

The incident that I like least also has to do with the relationship of the cousins; Joachim this time posthumous and ghostly. It is the eighth section of the last chapter and is entitled "Highly Questionable." At the invitation of Krokowski, who has what I am inclined to call a decadent attitude toward such things, a girl named Elly Brand who has mediumistic powers raises Joachim from the dead for Hans to see and speak to. I imagine that, as Mann conceived this episode, it was to have been the climax of the book on one of its planes, that of the emotions and the private life. Surely he cannot have intended it to be anti-climactic, which it is in a way. In a short essay, *Okkulte Erlebnisse,* he gave us an account of his own experiences in this realm of spiritualism: "backstairs metaphysics," he calls it, with seemingly some disrespect but not entire incredulity. "May lightning strike me if I lie," he protests—and somehow it isn't an altogether reassuring protestation—and goes on to describe a handkerchief which levitated and hung in the air awhile, and a typewriter which typed itself, well out of the reach of anyone's fingers or other mere mundane percussiveness.

The occurrence in Krokowski's room is more romantic and meaningful than this, for better or worse. At the height of the trance, upon instructions from the psychoanalyst, Hans has to sit in front of frail maidenly Elly and clasp her hands and grip her legs between his knees. She tosses to and fro, as though in pain; it is a harrowing experience for Hans, lasting almost two hours. His struggle with her reminds him (or perhaps I should say, it reminds Mann, who reminds us) of the role of a midwife or it may be of a young husband and father-to-be, during a childbirth.

Meanwhile a recording of Valentine's aria from Gounod's *Faust* has been placed on the phonograph; the needle gets to the inside of the platter; the music ceases, and no one does anything about it; it scratches around and around and around. Whereupon, suddenly, there sits dear handsome Joachim, in his astral body. Hans, our somewhat simple soul, indefatigable experience seeker, dabbler in everything, whispers fondly to his cousin, "Forgive me, forgive me!"

What for? one wonders. It might well be, I should say, for disturbing Joachim's heavenly rest, only to provide an evening's dilettantism and sensation seeking.

The trouble with this scene, I feel, is not just a question of its healthy-mindedness or morbidity, or even of its validity in point of fact. In a work of imaginative literature it rarely seems to matter whether or not the writer believes everything that he writes. But reader reaction always matters. The fiction reader, particularly, wants the fiction writer to take a position, which may be fictitious or insincere, but which ought to be definite, so that the focus of the work as it refers to the lives of the narrated persons in whose reality we are asked to believe shall be clear and persuasive.

Apt to take both sides in every argument, addicted to antithesis, always longing for synthesis, and when synthesis was not forthcoming, often contenting himself with mere changeableness, flexibility, and ambivalence—Mann wasn't the writer to inspire confidence in a phenomenon such as Joachim's ghost. The very texture of his writing, his little effects of mockery and mimicry, and flights of rhetoric, make the reader dubious.

"Superstition is the poetry of life," Goethe said. Poets do frequently play around with themes of spiritualism and ghostliness, some of them in natural credulity, some only pretending to be credulous, vacillating between their truth and untruth; still others (Yeats, for example) making a mystery of the extent of their belief, the degree of their sincerity or insincerity, all their lives. Poetry readers do not mind. Novelists have to take somewhat more responsibility for their beliefs and disbeliefs, because of the length and breadth of the form of the novel; it requires consistency and consequentiality to hold it together. A certain candor about objectionable matters is a part of the novelist's constructive power; as you might say, tongues and grooves, nuts and bolts. If they are too loose, the work as a whole will somewhat sag and tilt. Decisiveness is more structural than suggestiveness.

Our word "superstition" is a somewhat less serviceable, less comprehensive vocable than the German equivalent, "Aberglaube." Goethe and Mann meant by it (I think) a setting aside of whatever objections one's critical faculties may make; a disregard of the counter-indications. Occultism is important indeed to a good many men: something primitive in them vestigial in that way, something neurotic thus manifesting itself. I do not suppose that it meant much to Mann personally.. It was a literary component, one of the accepted, expected devices of the romantic tradition, which he just used when it suited him. His use of it was mistaken and disappointing (I think); but it was not inspirational or compulsive.

His particular Aberglaube, excessive predilection, immoderate habit of mind, had to do with intellectuality and erudition. Except for the Devil in *Dr. Faustus* (provided by the medieval tradition and the previous great treatments of the legend), the supernatural provided him with only an interlude or a scherzo here and there; whereas in all his long novels, learnedness of some sort accounts for almost half the text.

An entire chapter of *The Magic Mountain* (Chapter V) is devoted to Hans's gluttony to know things, and the consequences of this: a sort of mental indigestion, an intensifying of his emotions, and perhaps, from the bourgeois point of view, a weakening of his character. In this respect it somewhat parodies Goethe's *Faust*, who also wanted knowledge rather than power or pleasure.

But this is realistic and didactic fiction, a cautionary tale as well as a modern myth and fantasy; and I think there is bound to be a question in the serious reader's mind, as to his agreement or disagreement with Mann's thesis or premise in it. Do we really believe that it is important for a rather ordinary, affluent young man in ill-health, like Hans, to stuff his mind with massive technicalities of anatomy and psychology and pathology and biology and biochemistry and pharmacology and radiology, as Hans does in Chapter V, just to be in the know and au courant, with no notion of merely professing a science or of doing laboratory work or otherwise making himself useful; to talk himself hoarse about political theory and sociology and theology and metaphysics, or to listen to various

fanatics talking themselves hoarse, in hopes of making all that auto-
didactic matter meaningful to himself somehow, of co-ordinating it
with his own vague awareness of his retarded psyche, presumably
psychosomatic pulmonary condition, and generally unfunctional,
unwilling, nonwilling way of life?

It expresses an idea of education entirely acquisitive and exhibitionistic; everything in mere concepts and verbal formulations, as it
might be for purposes of conversation, for showing off. All knowing-
ness; no training, no skills, no discipline! I do not think it either
commendable or important.

Despite Mann's techniques of shadings of humor and rather
poetical exaggerations, by which he (so to speak) kept hedging his
bet about some things, I think it safe to say that this entire matter
of educatedness was important to him. He must necessarily have
read all the treatises and textbooks that Hans read; and it is with
obvious enjoyment that he gave us the gist of them in a fantastic
sequence of epitomizing, synthesizing paragraphs and pages. The
great question arising out of all that reading matter was: what is
life? Repeatedly, more or less rhetorically, he asked it, or brought it
into Hans's conversation or his soliloquizing somehow. "It was the
existence of the actually impossible-to-exist, of a half-sweet, half-
painful, balancing or scarcely balancing, in this restricted and feverish process of decay and renewal, upon the point of existence . . ."

Perhaps I can make this sentence less obscure: it was the existence of a thing that in fact can scarcely be said to exist; a constrained
and feverish process of decay and renewal, with bitterness and sweetness in the balance, almost unbalanced, and always on the verge
of existing.

Of course, Mann's German is far finer than Mrs. Lowe-Porter's
English, and finer than my American; but no matter. It is a phenomenal, untranslatable way of writing at best, calling to mind the ·
bravura music that the castrati sopranos of the eighteenth century,
Farinelli and others, performed at the close of their concerts, daz-
zling both to the musical connoisseur and to rococo society at large.
I think that Mann meant, above all, to dazzle.

What was life? Hans echoes his creator's question. "It was a secret, ardent stirring in the frozen chastity of the universe; a clandestinely voluptuous and impure sucking and secreting; an exhalation of carbon-monoxide gas and various material impurities of mysterious origin and composition . . . a pullulation, something opening out and shaping up, something unstable and top-heavy (but with laws of growth inherent in it, controlling it), something brewed out of water, albumen, salt, and fats, which was called flesh and became form . . . nothing but the next step on the reckless path of the spirit dishonored . . ."

There are thirteen or fourteen pages of this, nonstop. Then Hans falls asleep and dreams of Frau Chauchat, a rather anatomical dream of "the fine-grained skin of her triceps," and "blue branchings of larger veins" around her elbows; and as he dreams, a heavy volume of embryology that he has been reading slips down and presses heavily on the pit of his stomach and obstructs his breathing. This takes only about half a page. But to my taste, as a novel reader, that half-page, the hero's sleepiness and slight eroticism, the heroine's round and pallid and freckled and blue-blooded arm— preferably leaving out some of the big words, such as "triceps" and "blastula" and "epithelia" and "rudimentary lanugo" and "organic plurality"—is more valuable and more instructive than all the vain passages of popularized science and eclectic philosophizing. It encompasses true facts of life, experience or (what is next best) vicariousness; it expresses sympathy and empathy; it reiterates a more or less universal ancient theme; it appertains to one of the established realms of narrative art.

Hans had never seen a dying man until he came to the Sanatorium Berghof. His father and his mother and his grandfather had all departed this life while he happened to be away from home or out of the room, and he felt somewhat defrauded of the experience. The great eyes of the first moribund man whom he visits in his sickroom, rolling toward the bright window, toward the open door, and toward Hans himself standing in the doorway, make a tremendous impression on him. Instinctively—it is Mann's adverb (Mrs. Lowe-Porter's adverb)—he tries to protrude and to roll his own eyes in the same manner, with slow significant gaze.

Then, as he comes away down the hall, he encounters Frau Chauchat, and finds himself more than ever responsive to her obscure affection and slight wiles of the flesh; something in him has been brought to life by the shock effect of the fatal event, the glimpse of the universal specter. Episodes of this kind (I think) truly reveal certain mechanisms of our poor human nature as it is in fact, connecting links not only between one human being and another (indeed every human being and every other) but between our psychology on its several levels and our experience. And all that is what young men and women, fiction readers, need to learn, and what the techniques of fiction, rightly conceived and skillfully exercised, are best suited to reveal and teach.

But even in *The Magic Mountain*—and, as I have already said, more and more disturbingly in the later novels—one feels that mere reality and humanity, psychology and physiology and motivation and coincidence, although Mann's supreme talent lay in that direction, were gradually ceasing to excite him and satisfy him. He developed a passion for ideas. On page after page his characters as he shows them to us just sit and think, or lie and think; and then little by little he begins to do more and more of their thinking for them, and to try to embody in the work as a whole a philosophy of some sort, coherent and integral.

What philosophy? As I confessed at the start of this essay, the abstract aspect of Mann's work is not for me to expound, in any depth or in detail. But in *The Magic Mountain* there is something simple about it still. It is a matter of antithesis, and it serves in the first place a rather formal, rhetorical purpose: elaborations of his figures of speech, first in one direction and then the opposite, deployments of his terms of reference in apposition or in alternation. But of course, once he got started in any dualistic train of thought, he was apt to follow it away loosely and truantly into the metaphysical darkness, where not only is everything the opposite of everything else, but perhaps everything is also the same as everything else; where of course his more serious interpreters have delighted to go along with him.

Unfortunately, spirit and nature, the two terms upon which

Mann dwelt oftenest, and most fervently longed to see synthesized
—in experience as well as in theory and art, at some future date if
not in our time—are the hardest for me to grasp, with my unabstract
mind. One thing that I do perceive is that Mann's frame of reference was always anthropocentric. By nature, he never meant just
the outdoors, the elements, flora and fauna. He meant human nature in so far as it can trust to its instincts and still succeed somehow, without too much inner conflict and sickening exhausting
effort; for example, Goethe's human nature. By spirit he meant self-
awareness and what we now call neurotic drives, and all that profundity and prophecy which so frequently appear to be connected
with sickness in some way; for example, Dostoevski's epilepsy,
Nietzsche's syphilis, Schiller's nose colds.

Indeed, it may be that Mann's feeling for dichotomies stemmed
in the first place from Schiller's famous essay, "On the Naïve and
the Sentimental." Goethe was naïve and he (Schiller) was sentimental; in other words, Goethe was classic and Schiller was romantic; to which Goethe replied that he (Goethe) was healthy and
Schiller was sick. See how I simplify things!

There is a rather apt or relevant aphorism about this in Holy
Writ: "the children of this world are wiser in their generation than
the children of light." Goethe was a child of this world; so was
Tolstoi. Schiller was a child of light. Mann, I think, was a child of
light who wanted to become (and did become, at last, for the most
part) a child of this world.

On the flyleaf of my worn old Volume II of *The Magic Mountain*
I find listed by me, years ago, some other paired-off or contrasting
values which Mann evidently saw exemplified in history or personified in his cast of characters, which he assigned to them as subjects
of their discussion, or discoursed upon himself, in interspersed solilo-
quies: Love and death (or, as I prefer to put it, love and disease),
impulse and intentional will power, science and the occult, music
and morality, progress and medievalism, liberal emancipatedness
and old Christian ideals, Freemasonry and Jesuitism; also, the
somewhat vague values that he ascribes to the contrasting nationali-
ties, German and French, Teuton and Slav, Nordic and Mediter-

ranean, and in the more remote historical perspective, European and Asiatic, and Hellenic and Judaic.

Of all these matters Mann solemnly discourses at times, and at other times makes rather a jest; and I note that he seems most apt to be facetious when he is reasoning in the abstract. His characteristic pathos and harshness, and his feeling of predestination and of bravery against fate, he expresses best in the simple narrative mode, in the way of individual instance and episode.

The several antitheses on my list having to do with progress pro and con, liberalism and religion, etc., obviously refer to Hans's rival instructors, kindly discursive Settembrini and cruel polemical Naphta; dichotomy incarnate. In Volume I, before Naphta's appearance on the mountaintop, Mann contrasts no less strikingly Settembrini's Latin leftishness and the old conservatism of Hans's Hanseatic family. But he does not dramatize or dialecticize this much; he simply shows it to us in an extended image. Settembrini tells Hans about his grandfather, who was a conspirator for liberty's sake. Which sets Hans to thinking of *his* grandfather, an extreme old Baltic grand bourgeois, somewhat victimized in his declining years by radicals; an entire lifetime and denouement of life at just about the farthest possible remove from what Settembrini has been telling him.

Then suddenly Hans remembers a late summer evening in Holstein, when he happened to be rowing on a lake as the sun went down; at the same time the moon rose across from it; and as he slowly propelled himself upon the water, the scene seemed to him more fantastic than any dream; daylight in the west, fixed and glassy, and the east all wreathed in the magic of moonbeams and mist, "equally convincing to his bewildered sense."

Oh, grandfather daylight versus grandfather moon! Which will win? Hans asks himself. Both seem invincible; each has his realm of lifetime, also presumably of universal time. He remembers how, in the rowboat, his eyes shifted from one scene to the other, until "the balance finally settled in favor of the night and the moon." I prefer to think that Mann meant: in favor of what was and is, in favor of what has happened and may be expected to happen again, the local and the timely, there and then; not just some more German nocturnalism and decadent death wish.

Let me give you one more example of Mann's fictional antithesis, meaningful in itself and of itself. When Settembrini comes calling on Hans in his sanatorium bedroom, he touches the light switch immediately inside the door as he enters, and at that same instant, starts one of his eloquent harangues; so that his rhetoric and idealism come to be associated in Hans's mind with a blaze of light; so to speak, epiphany!

Frau Chauchat, on the other hand, like a good many pale, freckled, Titian-haired persons, is light-shy; her blue eyes wince and redden; and one of Hans's gallantries when he is most in love with her is to rise from his table in the dining room and stride across and draw the western curtains to protect her from the violent rays of the Alpine sun.

It is in passages like this that to my taste Mann is at his finest. They are less reminiscent of the masters of the narrative art who meant most to him, Goethe, Tolstoi, Zola, than of Turgenev and Chekhov, or, come to think of it, contemporaries such as Colette and Forster.

◆

These finenesses, revelations of nature and human nature, each in terms of the other, by means of incident and symbol, have not been Mann's chief claim to fame. Nor did he principally aim at them in the latter half of his creative life. It took another couple of decades to bring his several innovations in the form of the novel to their full effect and to the point of maximum critical interest. His biblical tetralogy, *Joseph and His Brothers* (1933-1943), and his tremendous make-believe biography, *Dr. Faustus* (1947), are more original and profound works than *The Magic Mountain* (1924).

But if we look closely at the last-named, we can see that it was during the writing of it, not in the post-mature years, that his concept of the narrative art changed. The turning points are in it, betwixt and between pages, in arbitrary shiftings and reshapings in mid-chapter, and in a particular afflatus of the intellect, as it were of the strangest wind blowing through and through page after page of it, with consequences; in an enlargement of the dialectic, and a gradual and singular loosing and loosening of the ironic style, alternating between jest and preachment so rapidly that one loses track.

Even a superficial résumé of his career of writing prior to *The Magic Mountain* shows us something of what made it seem essential to him to turn and change. All his early fame and fortune had been based on one novel, *Buddenbrooks,* published in 1901. Throughout this essay (it now occurs to me) I have but vaguely referred to this brilliant and important work, and neglected to give a proper account of it. When Mann got the Nobel Prize, the Swedish Academy specified that it was for *Buddenbrooks,* although *The Magic Mountain* had been triumphantly published just before that. This may have been in deference to Gerhart Hauptmann, who perhaps minded seeing himself in the guise of Mynheer Peeperkorn; who nevertheless (Mann himself tells us) was chiefly instrumental in getting the prize for him. No matter; either work deserved it, both called for it.

Buddenbrooks is the most successful, the most thoughtful, the most depressing and uplifting of family chronicles. Perhaps a certain subjective embarrassment has made me stupid about it, or perspicuous only in one way, having written a family chronicle myself, differently conceived in every respect, and less successful. Though Mann certainly is one of the personifiers of the twentieth century, a part of my feeling about *Buddenbrooks* is that this first fruit of his genius is a nineteenth-century type of novel. As noted elsewhere, I have this same feeling about *Of Human Bondage,* which Maugham wrote in his forties. Mann wrote *Buddenbrooks* in his early twenties; nevertheless there is a strange maturity, even middle-agedness, about it also.

Though large and powerful, it is a relatively simple work. In construction and style, it probably did not call for much creative deliberation or decisiveness. As who should know better than I, a family chronicle is not a difficult type of narrative. In some measure the design of it can be made to follow a pattern of collective domestic reality as it has transpired in the author's own experience. Consanguinity and chronology will sufficiently connect things in it; the passage of time will keep them moving along in a sufficiently straight line. As obviously it was based on biographical and autobiographical fact, several generations of kith and kin in Luebeck, doubtless it entailed for Mann personally psychological hardship, stress of the spirit. But probably as soon as he applied the past tense to the material, the book more or less wrote itself. As a kind of borrowing from life and an inheritance from relatives, the effect of it in the mind of the young aesthete and prodigal son may well have been a feeling of good luck rather than mastery; a sense of commitment to further brilliant production in due course rather than of pride in his precocious achievement or confidence in himself.

At that time and, of course, continuously in the first decade of the century, he was storing up the detailed observations of multitudinous small-scale humanity which in due course crowded the scene of *The Magic Mountain;* but his environing, expectant reading public could not have realized this or foretold the glorious outcome. The young writer himself probably was not clearly conscious of it or certain of its worth. For the substance of any work of literary art, until artistry of some sort has begun to take effect, is but a clutter, a random and wearisome amassment, like the bundles of clippings and press releases in what is called the morgue in the offices of a great newspaper, but not sorted or alphabetized; like someone's hoarded accumulation of scrapbook material, untrimmed, unpasted, or fanatic accumulation of snapshot film, exposed but not developed.

What in the world was the development to be? What form of narrative could conceivably embrace and satisfactorily ennoble the poor odds and ends and bits and pieces of contemporaneity with which life was providing him? What theme with a will of its own, form-generating; or foolproof plot, which might enable him to dispense with form; or panacea-like way of writing, readable and admirable even without any new structure, without subject matter of importance or intrinsic interest? In his immature celebrity, and slowness to develop out of it and beyond it, Mann in his thirties must have suffered a great cumulative embarrassment and uneasiness.

It was not all in his imagination and in his swelled head. There was in fact a certain humility, if not humiliation, in that second stage of his career. In so far as the success of *Buddenbrooks* had been just lucky, his luck ran out. In so far as it derived from innate ability and a certain effortlessness, he didn't understand it, and couldn't summon it up in himself again. A decade passed, a decade and a half, and nothing that he produced sold so well as *Buddenbrooks;* nothing had so great a success of esteem either. He went on distinguishing himself by that production of short fiction which I personally admire so intensely; but, quantitatively, what did it amount to? Only about a dozen stories and tales; and *Fiorenza,* a sort of history lesson in the form of an unactable drama; and one novel, *Royal Highness,* somewhat unsuccessful and moderately admired but rather conventional. No other book-length work for almost a quarter of a century.

Along with his self-consciousness as to the relatively small amount of output of his fiction, perhaps he minded some of its qualitative shortcomings also, though they were less obvious: a reiteration of certain themes, a too constant concern with the Bohemian way of life and the neurotic or neurasthenic frame of mind; a narrow range of emotions, almost a specialization in regretfulness, modesty, mockery—the artist's temperament feeding on itself, the creative eyes staring into itself! Even his bourgeois subject matter of that time seems permeated with aestheticism; his children are all precocious and his young men somewhat childlike. Even his pet animals seem not quite at home in the houses of their owners, in a way that is suggestive of human parisitism, especially the parisitism of the arts.

In about 1912 evidently it occurred to him that objectivity, even in a calculated, methodical way, might help. He conceived and commenced an old-fashioned, Defoe-like novel, *Confessions of Felix*

Krull, a life story told by his protagonist in his own words; mimicry, almost parody, inspired by someone's memoirs that he had enjoyed reading. But that technique tired him; "a difficult feat of equilibrium," as he said of it years later. He was able to finish only the childhood portion, which he published in 1923, as a nouvelle-length fragment. (The rest of Krull's personality and exploits lay fallow in his mind until the very end of his life.)

His next production was *Death in Venice,* the most intense and least prosaic of his nouvelles, which (I suspect) expresses his own depression and sense of inadequacy as a fiction writer somewhat more importantly than its ostensible theme, the bewitchment and self-destructiveness of the elderly paederast, Aschenbach. He meant to follow this with another short narrative in similar vein, about a tuberculosis sanatorium, *Death in Davos* as it might have been called, or *Death in Arosa;* which project World War I interrupted.

Then in the war years he produced that essay which I have already mentioned, the *Betrachtungen,* and this more than anything else (I believe) happened to show him the way out of his rut of small form and limited theme as a fiction writer. For my present purpose, let me not attach too much importance to the nationalistic German themes of this noteworthy though little-known publication. It may interest you to compare it with Dostoevski's *Writer's Diary,* which also strikes jarring notes and suggests ethnic prejudices and other reprehensible attitudes.

In time of war especially, love of one's country and of one's combatant countrymen is apt to disturb one emotionally, and unless one has a really strong and cautious mind and a definite sense of intellectual direction this may lead to lamentable rationalizations; which in Mann's *Betrachtungen* it did. In a sense it is an unpretentious work. A part of his argument in it, with regard to the political and international issues at stake in 1914–1918, amounts only to this: that a creative man may be excused for not understanding such things very well. For obvious reasons it has not been published in English. Perhaps it should be now, Germany's situation in world affairs having been transformed and retransformed in the forty years that have elapsed.

In a study of Mann's lifework entitled *The Ironic German,* Erich Heller has pointed out that, in one of the impassioned anti-Nazi tracts, thundering away in exile in America—somewhat like Victor Hugo on the Isle of Guernsey—he borrowed and re-used, in quite close paraphrase but in reverse, certain extreme pro-German paragraphs of the *Betrachtungen.* Was this a trick that his aged memory played on him, or one of the extremes of his ironic spirit, endlessly protean, clever and fearless to the end?

The *Betrachtungen* has not been held against him as rigorously or as acrimoniously as you might expect, either in the Fatherland or abroad. After a war, a sort of amnesty applies to enemy ideas as well as enemy action. Mann, in his own mind, certainly invalidated all these ideas quite soon. Early in the twenties he found himself, if not perfectly reconciled to his countrymen's having lost their war, at least able to see that some good had come of their not having won it. He declared an honorable and helpful adherence to the Weimar government, whose policies of international liberalism were not far removed from those opinions of his brother Heinrich's that had irritated and inspired him in the first place. Presently, on the German horizon, he began to see dark signs of a nationalism more extreme than anything that he or Heinrich Mann had dreamed of, pro or con, which was to precipitate them into exile in due course. During World War II, Thomas Mann's foreign readers assumed that he bitterly deplored and regretted his German patriotism during World War I. But in so far as they did, it was an over-simplification. Toward the end of his life he reread and reinterpreted the *Betrachtungen* in a short essay, frankly expressing his sense of its crucial importance to himself and to others interested in understanding him and his creative work.

It was more important in its aesthetic influence on Mann (I think) than in its mistaken political orientation. Perhaps as a citizen he was always somewhat superficial, almost frivolous. It was as a novelist that the *Betrachtungen* shook him, enlightened him, changed him, sending him back to his lifework of novel writing with a changed sense of what he personally and uniquely had to contribute to the art of fiction; of all that might be included in a novel, for the first time, and how the inclusion was to be managed, as never before!

Suddenly he seems to have begun to realize the foolhardiness of his mind, the fitfulness of his convictions; and to have a warning sense of how rapidly, all his life, ideas of the kind that he had endeavored to express in the *Betrachtungen* would cease to mean anything, or perhaps, overnight, would mean the opposite of what he had first thought. But was that necessarily a shortcoming or a disadvantage for a novelist? Might it not be all to the good, enabling him to see both sides of every question, to make the best of both worlds, or the worst of both worlds, as the case might be; not in a confusion or a pusillanimity or a duplicity, which was the way of ordinary mortals, but for art's sake, fiction's sake? Was there not a virtue to be made of his many-faceted and kaleidoscopic nature, the multi-potentiality of his mind?

For a fiction writer, is it essential to come to a conclusion? In any case, if and when he does so, the greater the hurdle has been, the more impressive the leap of his intelligence and his fancy, as he clears it. The blacker the muddle, the brighter and more refreshing the elucidation! In any very thoughtful sort of writing, as in thinking itself, sometimes it may be just doing it that matters, more than the outcome. Obstacles to one's reasoning power, such as illogicality, obscurity, inexpressibility, may serve simply as a part of one's train of thought; a variation on the theme one started with. The main thing about narrative prose, Mann evidently thought or felt, was to keep it moving. His sense of the sequence of his ideas must not have worried him any more than his sense of proportion. He skillfully avoided outright repetition but indulged in any number of overlapping effects and résumés.

As to the political opinions that he had temporarily espoused and stated, overstated, in the *Betrachtungen,* I doubt very much (as I know literary men) whether he felt any great burning regret or point of pride. Only in the future, instead of committing himself personally, as he had done in the controversial war book, he would fictionalize everything of that kind, with far-ranging, almost universal identification of himself with first one hero or villain, then another, and with subsidiary personages as well, so as to have occasion, sooner or later, to utter whatever happened to come into his head.

Oh, now, perhaps, nothing in the entire scope of his profuse, excitable intellect would ever have to go to waste. As a novelist it would be his privilege, you might say his duty, to keep gyring up and down, circling right and left, apostasizing and changing sides. In the new novel of ideas with which his genius was burgeoning at last, every idea should have its reversal or rebuttal just as strong and perhaps as true, just as tragical or satirical—or, to use one of his favorite words, just as humoristic—as the original statement.

At that point surely he must have begun to see in his mind's eye Settembrini and Naphta shadowily alive, begun to hear their more and more meaningful, symbolical squabble, as though they were actors in the wings of a theatre waiting to be cued; and with reference to other propositions, political and philosophical and historical, other paired-off types of humanity as well, poised in anger, coupled in love, or dancing around one another in mere curiosity or mere frolic, antitheses incarnate: Behrens and Kropowski, Peeperkorn and Frau Chauchat, Hans and Joachim, followed by Joseph and Amenophis, and Potiphar and Potiphar's wife, followed by Leverkuehn and Zeitblom and Kretschmar and Schildknapp and the rest. The twenty years of Mann's almost unintentional watchfulness of the European species then roused up out of his mind, flocked on stage, went into action.

Taking (as you might say) tactical advantage of his idiosyncrasies and shortcomings, with his characteristic German sense of the Zeitgeist—perfect timing, as it proved!—he gave up a part of the natural skill and finesse with which he had begun a quarter of a century earlier, in order to assume a quite different position in world literature, more original, more modernistic, and by his own account of it more German, less French; deliberately, if not desperately, sacrificing certain beauties of his earlier work, shapeliness, pace, simplicity, lucidity, memorableness, symbolism, for the sake of grandeurs familiar to us now in the novels of his post-maturity and old age: panoramic effect, scope, and sweep, and maximum inclusiveness, especially including those generalities and didactic matters that can be transposed into fiction from philosophy, and transposed back in due course by university men in their theses and exegetical essays.

In my opinion he sacrificed too much. I am prejudiced. I love his talent of the beginning of the century, all that astonishing natural small-scale ability and entrancing technique, so precocious that one may be tempted to call it innate; whereas I only admire his genius of the thirties and forties and fifties. As long as his lifework is read and reread, and the first half of his production compared with the second half, some readers are going to regret and lament (as I do) his change of direction, the violent ambition of his middle age. How can I express my feeling about this, simply, humorously, so that it may be understood by Mann admirers who do not share it? It is (I imagine) what some contemporary of Franz Schubert's might have felt, if, having written perhaps a quarter or a third of his heavenly lieder, he had suffered a failure of nerve or a change of heart, and more or less ceased song writing, forcing himself forward in the century, amplifying and elaborating and somewhat coarsening his lyrical genius, in order to compose, as indeed Schubert might have done, two or three of the operas of Richard Wagner.

To the attentive, intensive student of literature, the text of *The Magic Mountain* itself provides internal evidence of the way this new aesthetic worked. After the first fifty pages or so, it began to swell and to go forward as with seven-league boots, but irregular boots, sometimes stumbling, and stopping for an analysis of what the stumble was about, circling and circling certain themes in the way of an explorer or a hunter, as it seemed uncontrollably. Some things evidently had to be written out in full before Mann could decide whether he meant them or not; sometimes he let things stand without really making up his mind about them. What price decisiveness? If he made up his mind too soon he might just have to unmake it over the page, in order to furnish this or that personage of fluctuating fiction with his characteristic truth or half-truth.

As the new way of writing hit its stride, surely he did not try very hard to control it. Non-sincerity and profusion, circumlocution and proliferation, humor and solemnity, intermingled and almost interchangeable: given literary genius, one may or may not approve of this non-responsible exercise of it, but surely it is bound to be enjoyable, inebriating, sportive; rather like the Asiatic concept of the dance of the god Siva, flaunting and revolving, flinging and stomping forever. Thus, about halfway through *The Magic Mountain,* the creative intellect of the post-mature but still youthful author found itself, eased itself; his genius approached its apogee; and he probably could see in great ranging outline all the rest of his life-work, to the very end.

As I have already remarked, he made a practice and lifelong intellectual exercise of comparing himself with his five or six favorite creative giants of the nineteenth century, Dostoevski and Zola and indeed Wagner, as well as Goethe and Tolstoi; and it was not just the gigantic dimensions of their principal works that excited and gratified, appealed to him and challenged him, it was the fact that they were epoch-making, reformers and revolutionizers of the novel (and in the case of Wagner, of course, of the opera). Several contemporaries of Mann's just then, in the twenties, were making bold attempts to alter the forms and fashions of twentieth-century creativity, transforming painting and sculpture and music and architecture as well as literature, lock, stock, and barrel. They were the modern men that he envied and longed to emulate.

Mann was in his fifties when he wrote *The Magic Mountain.* That is an age of profound inner changes, usually for the better if the corporeal and organic being has preserved itself well enough to withstand the disturbance of spirit, the change and intensification of working schedule. As Mann looked around the literary scene, and realized that in the twenty years gone by he had not matched *Buddenbrooks,* and that furthermore it was only a sort of German equivalent of *The Way of All Flesh* or *The Forsyte Saga,* I fancy that he minded it extremely. To be sure, Samuel Butler and Galsworthy had come along after him, and he was not really like them; but there they were, treading on his heels, breathing down the back of his neck; he did not want to be like them. *Death in Venice* might almost have been written by Maurice Barrès or by Colette; *Tristan* perhaps by Forster. He did not care to be in that class, or for that matter, in a class with Svevo or Romain Rolland or Sigrid Undset. Do or die, he wanted to be someone like, let us say, Joyce or Proust or Picasso or Kandinsky or Schoenberg.

Are these names all anachronistic? No matter. My point is not that Mann had particular modern creators in mind as his challengers and rivals; but that modernism was in the air, and that he quite consciously and willfully aspired to that kind of greatness. In the *Entstehung,* the memoir of his old age, he refers almost wistfully to James Joyce, whom he read then perhaps for the first time. He could not "have direct access to the linguistic structure erected by the Irish writer," he lamented, but the Joyce commentators, Levin and Robinson and Joseph Campbell, revealed to him "many an unexpected relationship and even affinity." Like *Ulysses* and *Finnegans Wake,* he thought (he hoped), *Dr. Faustus* was an anti-novel, destructive of many of the modes and creative premises of the past, forcefully engendering the future. And while it is his production of essays, short novels, and stories that is masterful, valuable, and delightful, the full-length and overextended novels doubtless are more important. They loom in the literature of the age like a mountain range.

Buddenbrooks is sheer and soaring as though thrust up by some young earthquake, cloud-capped and breezy. *The Magic Mountain* is a vast Andean plateau with environing abysses. *Joseph and His Brothers* is loftier than the foregoing, but distantly, as it is a historical novel, wall-like along the horizon. Amid the miscellaneous work of the years of exile, *Dr. Faustus* stands up highest of all, blackly wrapped in historic storm, flashing with superstition, avalanching down in its concluding chapters according to the old legendary plot. The *Confessions of Felix Krull,* sloping up from the abandoned work of earlier years, ends again in mid-narrative, breaks off like a shattered precipice.

Whereas the stories and essays that I have been reading and rereading all my life with so much more enjoyment, and now critically and didactically advocate, are mere foothills, upland pastures, vales with a vista, leading to no very sublime or pretentious conclusion; only, from time to time, to some contemplation of the same subject matter as that of the long novels, the same sublimities: health, affection, creation, revolution, destruction. Today, as in the eighteenth century, one may prefer the more comfortable and negotiable and human aspects of both nature and art to those absolute peaks which arouse the somewhat suicidal zeal and courage and competitive sense of born mountain climbers.

When we gaze too far up over our heads, instead of the challenge, the flirtation with death, and possible vainglory that mountaineers are dazzled by, we observe the hopeless and broken aspects of the huge pieces of rock gnawing at the heavens, the effects of infinite wind blowing from all sides at once, the clouds swirling like insanity, and dirty glaciers dully perishing of their snail's pace downward, and murderous avalanches upon occasion, with fanatic carrion birds obsessively perched and patient and waiting around. Is there anything on earth so disorderly as a mountaintop?

The culture of small England and perhaps backward France is still current and fervent, even in the undereducated United States, despite the inventions of the metaphysicians. An altitudinous valley rather than a mountain—an aspiring hillside or a flowery hay-meadow with well-nourished and nourishing flocks, with habitations of beloved and loving fellow men not too far apart, with easy voices and small bells and musical instruments in the leisure hours, with whitely veiling cascades flourishing down amid the trees, rather than an earthquake or a landslide—constitute for us an image of heaven on earth. Furthermore, it is from these more modest standpoints, looking up, looking ahead, that the peaks themselves appear most godlike. Divinity and beauty both derive in some measure from distance and perspective.

❖

"The master of German prose!" was Hermann Hesse's salute to Mann at his funeral. I have read only a small part of Mann's life-work in the original, years ago; and my knowledge of German is not exact enough or comprehensive enough to qualify me to praise his manner of writing in detail, the texture and temper of his prose as such. No doubt it is praiseworthy. The vocabulary is large and also choice, well matched in its several tonalities according to mode and purpose. The formation of his sentences gives pleasure, an almost dreamlike pleasure, as though one were watching a puzzle solving itself, putting itself together, or a knot tying and untying itself. This masterful syntax, with an effect of sinuous movement down the page, a seemingly tireless continuity—in so far as it is proper to reach across language barriers for comparisons of this kind—has sometimes made me think of André Gide, though Mann never has the Frenchman's sharp focus and earnestness. Gerhart Hauptmann, when Mann read a chapter of *The Magic Mountain* aloud to him, was reminded of George Meredith: Mann tells us this with a nuance of some gratification in the *Entstehung*. Whereas literary German has a dark tonality, density, ruggedness—at least it seems so to an Anglo-Saxon reader—Mann gave it a unique pearly light and satiny sheen. Unfortunately, in Mrs. Lowe-Porter's translation it comes out woolly, tweedy.

Perhaps one ought not to generalize about style, as to the orientation of the writer's mind indicated by it; but in Mann's case one is almost irresistibly tempted to do so.—He has a way of seeming to joke when he is in dead earnest, or vice versa; a somewhat self-conscious, almost self-satisfied manner whenever certain subjects come up, not at all the manner of a man remembering or revealing or explaining things, but rather of one putting on a performance; a certain detachment or disengagement even in passionate advocacy or in indignation about something. He is a little impersonal, lawyer-like, no matter how passionate his argument may be, as though warning us that presently he may find himself arguing on the other side. In a word (and it is one of his key words), irony is his predominant mode.

Do you remember Emerson's great saying about insincerity?—"I am always insincere, as always knowing that there are other moods." It expresses a major part of the ironic disposition; and it would seem to have a more direct applicability to the art of the novelist than to any other intellectual endeavor or spiritual condition, though presumably that did not occur to Emerson.

In Mann's case, certainly, the multifarious and ever-alternating habit of mind pertained to his aesthetic rather than to his real life. His temperament was better regulated than his diction and imagery, his conduct more orderly than what he had to say or tell. But in ironic thinking and writing, there must always be an element of egotism, at least egocentricity and self-concern, whether or not this meets the eye. For it is a matter of overexactness, of too many nuances and qualifications with some quintessential opinion at the back of one's mind at all times, presumably inexpressible but to be hinted at. In a way it is more personal and introspective than the other self-dramatizations of writers, such as righteous indignation, impropriety, rebelliousness, devoutness.

Referring to irony in general, not Mann's particular practice of it, Jacques Barzun has called it "the least democratic of the modes of literature." It must also be the least translatable. Even in the original language it interposes itself, it intervenes like a veil, or like a shimmer or a glitter, between the author's mind and the reader's mind. According to Erich Heller, one of the most interesting and persuasive of the Mann experts, it is a peculiarly or at least pre-eminently German style. In both vocabulary and syntax the German language itself, he says, "is better suited to expressing the mobile confusions and dynamic exasperations of the mind than its stability and equipoise."

We must not try to simplify the ironic concept. Heller says that it would be "unkind to ask for a satisfying definition"; and indeed the three or four meanings supplied by the dictionaries I have on hand are incommensurate with recent literary and philosophical usage, even non-German usage. Mann made almost a trademark of it, especially in the autumnal production, and it signified many things to him, lifelong preoccupations, inspirational and even esoteric. In the essay on Goethe and Tolstoi he speaks of it as a kind of simultaneous glancing at both sides of every question, "slyly and irresponsibly." Confronted with an array of opposites, what it likes to do is to play back and forth between one and another; it is never in a hurry to adhere to a particular creed or platform, or to come to a conclusion. Behind it, or antecedent to it in the mind of anyone ironically inclined, seems to lie a surmise that, in matters of the utmost human interest, simplification almost always turns out to have been small-minded and immature. The goal to strive toward, Mann concludes this passage by saying, is not decisiveness but harmony, synthesis.

"Irony must be brief," Jules Renard said. "Sincerity can spin itself out." Obviously Mann never felt bound by any such rule or regulation, and out of his leisureliness, every now and then, something hasty and extravagant sprang. In the space of a paragraph, even in a single sentence, we find him suddenly slipping into high gear; tyrannousness of mind somehow comes over him for no particular reason; he can't help it or stop it. In no time, almost before we have taken notice, he has gone too far, made nonsense of his thought.

In its very nature, in the tension that it represents and the many-sidedness that it enunciates, irony cannot sustain itself very long in any one key. Note the sudden great swoop of Mann's mind, up and away from one or another of its wise, humorous attitudes into indiscretion or dogmatism about something, at times just for the enlivening rhetorical effect, the change of pace, but at other times (one senses) under a strain, perhaps weary of his reasonable and superior role. Something in him liked to be swept off his feet.

There is a tradition of this kind of headstrong, pell-mell thinking in German literature. Mann gives us an example of it in his important late essay on Schiller. He begins by reminding us that the artist is a child, "to whom nothing seems nobler than play." This appealing and pertinent observation he carries to extremes in the next sentence: "Man alone of all creatures knows how to play." But what about dolphins? what about raccoons? Then in a rush, from bad to worse, enjoying his thoughtlessness, he adds a foolish third sentence, perhaps mainly because the two previous sentences seemed to predicate it or something like it: "Man is wholly man only when he plays."

One could just as aptly say the opposite: man is wholly man

H

only when he *works*. As this stands in Mann's text it is a little uncertain how much of it he derived from Schiller, how much he himself made up out of whole cloth. As of that date, Mann had worked
harder than almost anyone on earth for about six decades; and you
would have expected him to spot any such nonsense.

Alas, I am afraid that if one had challenged him about it, his
answer might have been simply that literature is never work, always
play; or worse still, with the ultimate German sophistry, that in a
profound sense work and play are alike, identical, interchangeable.
An important rule of really German thinking (I guess) is that one
cannot win.

Even in his work of obviously tragic concept, this most ironic
man of letters, ineradicable son of the Fatherland, amazes us by
the shiftiness of his mind, slipping from conviction to conviction,
veering like a weather vane from idea to idea, turning from things
in the absolute to mere showing off, from the law and the prophets
to facetiousness and paradox. It is but a detail in the midst of greatness, an effect of sentences and paragraphs here and there. I mention it because it is more recurrent than any other of his failings;
also I suspect that it has discouraged and deterred more readers
than anything else that he did or left undone.

In his youth Mann was more Schiller-like than anything else, or
so regarded himself; and turned to Goethe (as Schiller had often
turned) as an alleviation of the dreariness of his immaturity, a
medicament for his psychic embarrassment and conflict. But in
due course, as the Goethean wisdom and his own native power and
obstinacy took effect and bore fruit, I think he must have wondered
whether he was not, even innately, Goethe-like. Perhaps he taught
himself to pretend to be, for the auto-suggestive effect, and in the
end felt quite comfortable with that hypothesis, in that posture. A
great part of his public surely liked having a Goethe-like image of
him, fatherly, Olympian.

As the identification of himself with Goethe developed, in mature and post-mature years—when he was more preoccupied with
the superman of Weimar than ever, and wrote several essays on him,
as well as the pleasing short biographical novel, *Lotte in Weimar*

—here and there his eulogy and euphoric analysis gave way to vigorous faultfinding. Doubtless this relieved him of some inner pressure of his self-criticism. Goethe the greatest of scapegoats!

"He had an ambiguous impishness, an element of equivocation, negation, and all-embracing doubt, which led him to self-contradictory pronouncements." I think that this was as true of Mann himself as it was of Goethe, perhaps truer, and I think that he meant this to be understood by those of us whom it fascinates to detect his judgment of himself, and who think him worthy to be judged by the highest standards. Upon occasion, he said, it amused the superman "to abandon and betray his followers; to confound the partisan of this or that principle by carrying it first to one extreme, then to the other extreme." This way of playing fast and loose with his disciples and hangers-on perhaps was to counteract their flattering, softening influence on him; perhaps it was to force them to stand on their own feet and to think for themselves; or perhaps it signified, more simply, boredom and contempt.

It enabled him to extend his dominion over almost everyone around him, and to play as great a part at the court of Weimar and in Germany at large as, in due course, in the realm of timeless civilization to which his genius entitled him. This procedure in society and this attitude toward his fellow men were treasonable and nihilistic in a way, Mann thought; and this, too, he called by the dear name, the dread name of irony.

It is perhaps what Americans (and some Englishmen and Frenchmen) find most worrisome about Germans, or I should say, about the German nation as a force in modern history, a continuing force with ups and downs: the immense old sophistry and fatalism forever ebbing and flowing in their heads, one effect of which is seemingly to authorize and justify for them any sort of national happening whatever, any combination of willfulness and fantasy that they may undertake. At the back of their minds they have a certain ever-ready irresponsibility and all-round exculpation. As in the librettos of Wagner—surely one of the most influential forms of folklore ever to beguile a gifted and hard-working people—there is always some love philter or mind-changing headgear or self-propelling sword lying about; up in the trees there are articulate occult birds forever singing and melodiously rationalizing things for them, giving them misinformation. Whatever the passionateness or the barbarity in the plot, they have something to attribute it to.

Again and again, in historic crises, that same great irony which Mann exemplified as well as explained, both denounced and defended, has taken, in the collective German mind, the form of a really harmful changeableness and extreme educability. It has made them the least reliable nation on earth. In 1914, in 1933, in 1939, as you might say intoxicated by it, somewhat enjoying it, with the wildest energy on record in the modern world, their eyes tight shut to world-wide probability and other rational considerations, they responded absolutely to the Zeitgeist, however it happened to blow in them and upon them, with destructive results abroad, suicidal results at home.

❖

Probably as Mann first conceived *Dr. Faustus,* and made initial decisions about its form and technique, he was concerned to give it a more objective tone than he had found for *The Magic Mountain* or for the Joseph tetralogy. The subtitle is: "The Life of the German Composer, Adrian Leverkuehn, as Told by a Friend"; the narrating to be done, therefore, neither confidentially by the protagonist, as in the unfinished make-believe autobiography of the swindler Krull, nor in Mann's own unmistakable though unspecific voice, but by the composer's schoolmate and lifelong confidant, Zeitblom; as you might say, Hamlet narrated by Horatio.

The effect of this, as it worked out, was not really objective, only bifocal or bipartite: Mann's opinion of his own character divided in half, and exaggerated in the two directions. Zeitblom is the bourgeois intellectual, haunted by tradition and dreaming of posterity, indefatigably observing and recording everything, sternly passing judgment on his friend, and at the same time finding excuses for him. Leverkuehn is the absolute genius-type, in eternal conflict both within himself, and between himself and the rest of mankind, incapable of loving anyone, incapable even of self-love, immolating himself as thoroughly as possible, making a kind of compost heap of his life for the nourishment of his lifelong production of masterpieces of music. What tormented him above all was his rivalry with the great geniuses of the past, and that itch of modernism from which so many contemporary minds suffer, which seemingly nothing but absolute originality, innovation, invention, ever really alleviates or counter-irritates. Mann himself was both a Zeitblom and a Leverkuehn.

Leverkuehn, as I have said, is a triply composite character: he is Faust reborn, he contracts Nietzsche's sickness and succumbs to Nietzsche's madness, he writes Schoenberg's music—quadruply composite, if you count Mann's identification with him. Thus he goes to his death aglitter with multiple genius, doomed over and over, charged also with Mann's own preoccupation with the incomparable misdeeds and further guilty potential of the Fatherland, in its two-fold aspects of creative energy and destructiveness, morbidity and power.

From beginning to end of the volume we seem to hear that all-important dualistic nation at the heart of Europe imploring the other nations for forgiveness, as indeed it always has done, between wars, and somewhat simultaneously asking to be admired and feared. Mea culpa, for the most part, in affecting low tones; and in the same breath, Achtung! From beginning to end, with what might be called reverse patriotism, with cruel touches that only genius could devise, weighty implications of blame and regret on every page, Mann drives his protagonist to his apotheosis as a musician of genius, and then over the edge, in entire deterioration of his nervous system, general paralysis and death, due to the neglected venereal disease.

However it may have been in Nietzsche's case, Mann gives us to understand that Leverkuehn chose to have syphilis, because of its supposed glorious effect upon the brain, a heightening of the creative faculties as in an Indian summer; glorious autumn colors before the stormy madness and the ice-cold terminal deterioration set in. It is strongly implied throughout the volume that in the case of other great men also, scientists and statesmen and soldiers as well as creators, the extremes of cerebration and of idealism, revolutionary or reactionary as the case may be, are all a part of a corresponding and connecting psychopathology; the greatness aggravating the sickness, and vice versa, in a truly vicious circle.

All this, furthermore, as conceived and handled by Mann, is an image or symbol of political history as well. To borrow one of his phrases from a very early essay on Nietzsche, it stands for "the overweening self-dramatization of the German world," which also comes to a climax every so often, in extreme stimulation of the romantic imagination and tremendous intellectual effort, then subsides in disorder and craziness—discipline and overwork leading to self-destruction; breakthrough followed by breakdown; the mind devouring itself and excreting itself. In this early text Mann extends his grievous metaphor beyond the reference to the mere dangerous fatherland, to a view of the entire continent. Gluttony of the intellect, succeeded by retching and colic of the soul, he says, is "the immortal *European* drama."

We Americans do not often frankly express our feeling about that continent of our origin, as to its immortal drama. Humbly and appreciatively, we admit that not only has it the greatest concentration of masterpieces of the arts on earth, and at the top, higher standards of living than anything enjoyed by even the richest of our compatriots, but that it is almost fabulously inhabited by intellectual giants. Stupendous developments in Asia and Africa notwithstanding, little Europe is still the crucial area, the fecundation place, the world womb. Marx (about whom I feel as Martin Luther felt about Aristotle) was a refugee German, like Mann, like Schoenberg; and the next intellectual savior of the world, or deadly tempter and destroyer as the case may be, is likely to come from somewhere in Europe once more.

It has been at peace for fifteen years, but with some blackness and whirlwind still going on in it. Its host of intellectuals notwithstanding, presumably at regular intervals in the future (as in the past) it is going to run mad; to find itself spellbound by this or that obviously evil and cheap spell; to go reeling along in history as though it had no head, or as though it had half a dozen heads, with concussion or aberration in every one. Despite the examples set by its great artists and various saints, what especially characterizes it is a competitiveness unparalleled elsewhere in the world; pride of race; luxury and gluttony and avarice (peculiarly European sins); reckless defiance of the poor; insufficient belief in the future, and consequent reckless exploitation of the present moment—après nous le déluge!

As we read *Dr. Faustus* and other texts of the conclusion of Mann's life, it is disheartening indeed to find that almost sublimely calm man, uninterruptedly fortunate, powerful, and famous even in reduced circumstances in exile, taking so dark a view. But surely this disheartenment was what his genius was peculiarly, if not uniquely, suited and oriented to bring about. I have complained at length, perhaps churlishly—and from what you might call a parochially transatlantic standpoint—of his immoderation of form, of his sometimes pretentious metaphysical language, of the affectation and artfulness in the detail of his work here and there. Let me conclude with a more positive statement, worthier of him. He had the courage and the prowess to tackle really self-transcending themes (rare in the modern world), and for better or worse, he made them a matter of his self-concern. Whatever your pleasure may be, as to the subject matter that you come upon in books, certainly there has not been anything in the century of greater consequence than the German paroxysm—almost an entire national mind in a Faust-like, Nietzsche-like, Leverkuehn-like condition, wrapped round and glimmering with hell-fire; its incomparable collective energy exploding in open sores as in dehydration of some sort, proliferating and puffing itself out like malignancy, foaming at the mouth like rabies, drooling like paresis, dooming itself in every way at once.

Certainly it took fantastic bravery and strength for the historic storyteller to involve himself in this diagnosis and indictment, to give authority and intimacy to what he had to prescribe and recommend. Better than anyone in our time he knew how to hate, as well as to sympathize with, various decisive and timely types of human beings, and to corroborate a vision of the evil of humanity at large with a pitiless and highly dramatic self-examination, casting himself into the crucible along with whatever other fuel he could lay hands on, so that his bronze and gold should be molten in the right way.

❖

Dr. Faustus is Mann's only truly tragic work, remorseful and punitive, and yet it has strange childish aspects. His superstitiousness is not just a blemish here, as it was in *The Magic Mountain;* it is featured throughout the work, whether to induce in us an unwholesome half-sincere anxiety, or to make us laugh, or both. The turning point of the entire tale, the shift in Leverkuehn's life toward his absolute originality as a composer and his damnation as a mortal man, occurs during a long talk with the Devil (who, by the way, quotes a bit from Nietzsche's *Ecce Homo*). This of course is a part of the old Faust folk legend, but to my way of thinking, an unassimilable, indigestible part.

We are not actually present, that is to say, Zeitblom is not present, at the dialogue or parley in which the glory, the privilege, the pleasure of revolutionizing music is accorded to Leverkuehn. The doomed man himself notes down on sheets of his music paper what the Devil has said to him; which his biographer transcribes without editorial alteration and without quite deciding what he thinks. Throughout the second half of the novel Zeitblom keeps recalling this, blowing hot and cold, turning the possibilities and connotations over in his mind. Was it all a lie, fabricated by Leverkuehn? Or as the bedeviled composer is non compos mentis, or soon will be, was he already hallucinating at that point? To the reader, in the last analysis, it seems quite possible that Zeitblom is merely pretending to be skeptical because he is really credulous by nature and is ashamed of it: or conversely, that he is pretending to be credulous as this may seem to palliate the implausibility of the biography of his friend in some particulars.

To my way of thinking, the introduction of an incarnate, articulate Devil among the personages of so realistic and up-to-date a tale was a mistake. The Devil also appears in *Death in Venice,* does he not? but in 1913 Mann still had a light touch. The reader is allowed to question whether the figure who makes a devilish appearance in the tale of Aschenbach really is the Devil, in successive avatars: someone wandering in the cemetery at Munich, a guitarist in the hotel in Venice who keeps making an ugly face, a gondolier without a license.

In Gide's autobiography, *Si le Grain ne Meurt,* when he leaves his corrupting friends, Wilde and Douglas, in North Africa, and returns to Normandy to get married, he too complicates the tale by bringing the Devil (le Malin) into it, and having him whisper this and that; which lamentably lowers the tone and tension of that important book. If one has any sort of belief in a harmful demigod or antigod, the mere stock figure that one has seen in a thousand cartoons and posters, the bogeyman encountered at a hundred fancy-dress balls in rented red garb with an arrow-tipped tail, is bound to seem inadequate, impious, and irritating. On the other hand, if one is a disbeliever and what one is reading is otherwise plausible and serious, then the satanic majesty must strike one as a kind of joke, not in the best of taste, and a distraction from whatever the actual wickedness or sickness may be, enthroned in the protagonist's mind or coiled around his heart.

The old scarecrow of our race having been brought down out of the attic and stationed in the midst of things, and this having been made the decisive event in Leverkuehn's life, the pivot on which the form of the novel chiefly turns, he ought to have been taken seriously by someone, to deepen the impression, to stabilize the tale. The reader would like to be able to follow some straight or at least definite line about it, at least as a convention, for his reading purposes. Zeitblom's attitude really is too timid and infatuated. We peer and probe into the dense, darkling pages, through the provincialism and the medieval pastiche, amid the theology and musicology and the editorializing of all sorts, hoping to discover and partake of Mann's own view to some extent. Is he inculcating something or advocating something? Or is he fooling us, making fun of the miserable world? Is it conceivable that he himself believed in the evil personification or deification, to the extent of at least having a horror of it? This part of the text seems not to convey any very definite emotion, certainly not horror. On the one hand, as to any moot point or riddlesome matter, our sense of the forceful mind of the author keeps us from taking his stand-in narrator seriously. Mann, on the other hand, seems to be hiding behind Zeitblom. They mask each other.

All this relates closely to the inartistic effect that I complained of in the episode of *The Magic Mountain* entitled "Highly Questionable"; the séance in the psychoanalyst's room at which the spirit of Joachim is made to materialize. Here, once more, Mann makes rather an issue of a matter of belief: perhaps believing himself, perhaps not; perhaps assuming that the reader is a believer; or simply wishing to delude and beguile, but going about his craftiness with a somewhat heavy hand.

I repeat: Mann did not have the style of a man who believes in things. Despite his occasional archaism and skillful mimicry, he always seems well educated or over-educated, with a tone and an implication of the ungullible present time. How much more easily material of this kind is handled by the Nordic tale writers, Isak Dinesen and Pär Lagerkvist and others, without unseemly levity or old-timiness! Their short forms help them, whisking their supernatural and improbable personages up and away before the reader gets into his logical vein or his captious mood. Also, they do not interlard the supernatural with current events, or vice versa. The reader concentrates on what they themselves are chiefly concerned with, the storytelling per se. When they come to their ghostliness or devilishness or other anomaly, it is not against a background of their having set themselves up for hundreds of pages as serious thinkers, digesters of the sciences, explainers of the wisdom of the day and age.

As originally published in German, the colloquy of Leverkuehn and the Devil ends on page 386, which is the exact center of the volume. Think what fanatic insistence and unrelenting hard work that must have taken, on both the author's part and the printer's part! I have neglected to inquire whether the Fischer Verlag has reproduced this effect in subsequent editions. Understandably, Mrs. Lowe-Porter and the firm of Alfred E. Knopf, Inc., gave it up. Can you imagine a writer of Mann's mighty and essential gifts, a thinker with his far-ranging and crucial interests, devoting himself to a contrivance so minute and arbitrary? It does notify the reader that the author wants him to pay particular attention to the passage thus fussed over, but at the same time (I think) it diminishes the seriousness of what page 386 has to say.

Fritz Kaufmann, in an intensive study entitled *Thomas Mann: the World as Will and Representation,* which pleased Mann—he said that it was like a mirror, and that he enjoyed looking at himself in it—has called our attention to another bit of symbolic virtuosity: the chapter arrangement, hocus-pocus! I must admit that, reading in my amateur way, comfortable and contemplative, I might never have noticed it for myself. It is this: twenty-one chapters in the middle, that is, three times seven; flanked by thirteen chapters on either side, which is to give an impression of unluckiness, if you are impressionable in that way (I am not); forty-seven chapters in all. And, most magically and impressively, the beginning plus the middle amounts to thirty-four chapters, and the middle plus the end also amounts to thirty-four chapters.

Spellbound by this, temporarily spellbound, turning from Kaufmann's authorized exegesis to the portentous fictive biography itself, I discovered that in fact there are forty-nine chapters; not forty-seven. In order to arrive at the desired superstitious computation—thirteen plus thrice seven plus another thirteen equals forty-seven—three chapters had to be given the same number. Was the numerically minded author cheating a little? Not exactly. For the thrice-used number is thirty-four; the two extra chapters are thirty-four continued and thirty-four concluded.

Thirty-four, let me tell you—Kaufmann having told me—is the most prestige-ful number in all arithmetic. Do you remember the old magic square that is in the background of Dürer's famous engraving "Melancholia," with digits arranged on it in such a way as to add up to thirty-four, however you go about the addition, up and down, or from side to side, or crossways? In *The Magic Mountain* it hangs over Hans Castorp's hypochondriacal sickbed in the International Sanatorium Berghof. Here in *Dr. Faustus* it hangs again, in the room in which poor Leverkuehn, in spite of (or because of) his accursedness and his syphilis, revolutionizes music.

The themes of the misnumbered chapters are the heart and core of the meaning of Leverkuehn's story; Mann's message throughout the book, a two-part message, perhaps less ironic and duplicitous than any corresponding formal pronouncement in his fiction. First: the close connection between an immoderate love of the arts (especially music) and a barbarous collective immorality, to be observed in Germany at its worst, that is, Nazi Germany. Second: the deadly peril of those mysteries and mystifications which are a form of calculatedness gone wrong, the ill effect of those exercises of willful intellect which are a preliminary to a loosing and loosening of instinct, wild and self-indulgent.

This second principle may have been in Goethe's mind when he said: "General ideas and great conceit have a way of always causing terrible trouble." Note Goethe's small and seemingly almost ingenuous way of wording things; absolutely unlike Mann's way.

Let me try to restate the lesson of *Dr. Faustus* as it applies (I think) to Mann's own case: A farfetched and revolutionary aestheticism when it coincides with a regression into, or a revival of, medieval interests and doctrines, is evil, does harm. This great cautionary novel is an example of what it portrays and excoriates. I say this with no sense of wronging the noble old didactic novelist, though I realize that I may be provoking his admirers grievously. He himself specifies in the *Entstehung*, "I felt clearly that my book itself would have to become the thing it dealt with: namely a musical composition." That particular nameliness is but a modicum of what happened, a superficiality and a trifle.

Dr. Faustus is a work of "sham conservatism," as Mann described Schoenberg's *Harmonielehre*. More than any other creative work that I can think of, it combines up-to-date extremities of style and structure with an idealism of olden time, a headlong willfulness with an abandonment to whim and mystery. I believe that Mann intended us to observe this, and to give him credit for it, and to blame him as well. In this respect as in other more general German traits of intellect and temperament he was willing if not eager to be compared to Faust and Nietzsche, to be confused and indeed identified with his doomed, antipathetic composer.

◊

Fritz Kaufmann has called our attention to the recurrence of the word "Durchbruch," breakthrough, here and there in Leverkuehn's life story. In the early part of World War II, the so-called Blitzkrieg, it was in frequent use by military men, or at least by war correspondents, to describe the breaching of enemy lines by tanks and other vehicles of aggression, and their entry into an important undefended or unsufficiently defended area, as it were virgin territory. More recently it has been reapplied by scientists, physicians and physicists and others, to the sort of basic research that opens up great sequences of new therapies, new destructions, new utilities, such as cancer treatment and missile deterrents and weather control.

In *Dr. Faustus* it distinctly refers to Leverkuehn's (and Schoenberg's) creative innovation, dodecaphony. Away from Wagner! down with Beethoven! back to Bach, or still further back, into the Middle Ages; then a rebound and a reconquest of the musical world in a new way, with little or no competition of other contemporary composers, and with an audience all one's own in due course. And according to Kaufmann, breaking through like this in some way is an innate spiritual craving, at least in Central Europe; "a watchword of German life." He goes on to say that "each new work of Mann's has been a fresh attempt to break down the walls that separate being from being."

What being from what other being? I wonder. Does he mean to suggest that the principal purpose of Mann's mighty evolvements of fictitious form and style, late in life, was to speak more directly and intimately to his readers; that, likewise, Schoenberg's innovations in musical harmony and polyphony were for the sake of his audiences, to facilitate their listening?

Champions and interpreters of modern art and literature often make claims of this kind; and I almost always find them unacceptable or incomprehensible. Certainly, the reading public and music lovers and art lovers in our time—with a sense of the importance and the uniqueness of modernistic masterpieces such as *Dr. Faustus,* and Joyce's *Finnegans Wake,* and Schoenberg's *Moss and Aaron,* and Kandinsky's colorful, amorphous decorative paintings, and the coarse and cruel images of Picasso's old age—have been gradually taking down or wearing down what Kaufmann calls "walls," stone by stone, stake by stake, strand after strand of barbed wire, accustoming themselves to every kind of abstruseness, cacophony, and deformation. In terms of extent of fame and amassment of wealth, Picasso must be accounted the most popular painter who ever lived. The name of Joyce is more glorious than any other in the prose literature of the modern world. But surely it is a sophistry to argue that these modernists intended to make their several categories of creative work more popular, more democratic; to communicate more generally or more exactly or more movingly, by easement of language, simplification of idiom, focusing of imagery; to facilitate and sweeten the sights and sounds of art for everyone's or anyone's benefit.

What has principally preoccupied and excited them has been to withstand and shake off and defy the dwarfing influences of their perhaps greater predecessors. Picasso has kept looking back at Cézanne, Schoenberg at Wagner, Joyce at Ibsen and Dickens. And, certainly, the walls and separations and restraints that Mann was heroic against, especially in the latter half of his lifework, were those that differentiated the novel writing of the past—and the productions of academicians and commercial writers of his own day who went on working in the old modes—and that ever-hypothetical, ever-expanding, exalted and uneasy artistry which was (or was to be) peculiar to himself; between the epoch-making novels of his giant predecessors, Goethe and Balzac and Zola and Dostoevski and Tolstoi, and whatever manuscript he happened to have in progress, or perhaps at a standstill, on his desk.

❖

Now to recapitulate, simplifying my thesis as best I can: Mann's breakthrough (to use Kaufmann's word for it), his specialty and innovation, was the philosophical novel. Even early in his life, when he was a facile young genius, the author of only *Buddenbrooks* and *Tonio Kroeger,* one could tell that he was not going to be content to have his future protagonists simply reading Schopenhauer and Nietzsche, submitting to old influences, unhelped by him. Surely, for an intellect as proud and swelling as his, there must be more serious employment in works of fiction; some way of keeping all the significances of the given work in mind at all times, so that the component parts would combine to say one thing, and to say it as profoundly as possible.

In certain essays and critical studies, and here and there in short works of fiction that were in fact preliminary sketches for novels that he had in mind (or hoped to have in mind presently) his more ambitious and independent interests began to appear and to develop: a kind of overarching zenith and encircling horizon and all-embracing climatic condition and constant well-focused bird's-eye view and summarizing spectrum. In his future novels, perhaps, the mere moralizing and rationalizing about everyday activities and excitements of the human species, all-important in ordinary novels, could be relegated to the lower half of the picture, even less than half, as in one of those painted landscapes of the seventeenth-century Dutch masters or the impressionists in France that are almost all sky: small patchwork of fields, faint tracery of roads, little buildings crouching in the distance in the midst of indistinct foliage, and almost perfunctory, scarcely recognizable little human figures: their only purpose in the work, or their chief purpose, to give scale and contrast to the vague immensity of the air overhead, the firmament, the world prospect or Weltanschauung, the metaphysics!

The metaphysical or philosophical novel is an old, even old-fashioned category of the narrative art, but few practitioners of the large forms of fiction have ever buckled down and actually produced any such thing. The eighteenth century gave us delectable contes, hybrids of the parable and the fairy tale, inculcating or combating this or that principle of outstanding thinkers of the age: Voltaire's *Candide,* for example. Goethe's *Elective Affinities* certainly meant to be philosophical, but it too is a fairy tale rather than a novel, despite its giant size. In its mere narrative aspects, characterization, motivation, plot, it is incoherent. Wherever talent or genius may lead, German talent or genius, Goethe is sure to have been there before one.

There is a voluble echoing of Swedenborg and Saint-Martin and Lavater in Balzac, is there not? and of Bergson in Proust; principally as a means of emotion and impressionistic ambience. But in the work of both these Frenchmen, who are true novelists, how marginal and optional the abstract ideas seem, amid their agglomeration of data of human nature; how much more fervent their consideration of social stratifications and tensions, the classes and the masses, and matters legal and ecclesiastical!

Modern fiction has scarcely been characterized by abstract intellectual interests. There are some recent novels *about* philosophers that are worth reading, but they are biographical, historical, with hardly a metaphysical word. A few bona fide philosophers have written novels, mainly as an outlet for the autobiographical impulse; Santayana's *The Last Puritan,* for example. *The Root and the Flower* by L. H. Myers used to have enthusiastic readers, perhaps still has. Aldous Huxley is brilliantly thoughtful, but the thinking in his novels is never very thorough, because of his eagerness to satirize. The flourishing though not very successful existentialist school of French fiction writers did not develop until after

The Magic Mountain. I understand that in Germany, despite the absolute interruption of German mental life for twenty years, philosophical novelists are springing up; some of them under Mann's influence, others counteracting him.

Perhaps *The Magic Mountain* and *Dr. Faustus* are the most specifically and authentically philosophical novels ever written. (Page for page, the greater part of *Joseph and His Brothers* also is cogitation rather than mythology or anthropology or other scholarship.) But I make this assertion less happily than I do Mann's other claims to fame. For, alas, the philosophical novel is an unfortunate form, with inherent defects. Almost by definition it is not apt to mean as much to the reading public as the other classifications of narrative that have been in use for centuries, in and out of fashion—the fable, the allegory, the cautionary tale, the reminiscence, the adventure, the chronicle, the short story, the nouvelle, and the true novel, with its account of everyman's manners and morals, of sociological conditioning and divine coincidence.

The very thesis and premise of novel writing is that the human condition and situation, existence, subsistence, actuality, all hang together and can be imaginarily encompassed in one general view, simultaneously microscopic and telescopic; as it were one universal substance, with little differentiation of body and soul, of reason and feeling, of the momentary and the immortal.

Philosophizing in a novel always seems idiosyncratic and one-sided. It pertains to the mind of the author rather than to the mind of any reader that he may think of himself as writing for, or the minds of the characters that he is writing about. Human beings, as they manifest themselves in those sequences of infatuation and intrigue and competition and aggression and counterattack and reconciliation that we call plots, do not think alike. Even a small novel contains a good many characters; by definition it is a long and elaborate and multifarious and troublesome structure, hard enough to put together and to keep clear in the creative mind. If, in addition to identifying all and sundry in it and providing them with a background of previous life, and establishing their contacts and mutual influences, and displaying them in lifelike action, the novelist undertakes (to some extent) to make intellectuals of them all, it must enormously increase his responsibility and his labor.

If he is not to bore the comparatively unintelligent or anti-intellectual type of reader, all his thoughtfulness will have to be kept light and clear. Furthermore, he will want to show some impartiality among his dramatis personae, to let them all have their say, that is, to say it for them, fairly and squarely. The type of reader who happens to be philosophical in his own right may be vexed by this, as a kind of promiscuity of intellect; all things to all heroes and heroines, even all villains and villainesses.

Speaking for the ordinary reader, neither highbrow nor lowbrow, somewhat roughly speaking: if you provide him with a convincing record of someone's existence or of something that has happened, an equivalent to experience, he can reason for himself about it. Whereas, if it is the other way round—if the reading matter that he has in hand is theoretical, ideological, impersonal—he cannot reverse the process; he cannot predicate the experience with which presumably the philosophical writer began; he cannot personify the abstraction, incarnate the thesis. It is a dead end for him.

And in moral and political philosophy, nowadays, there are issues so desperate on the one hand, so blissful and glorious on the other hand, that one scarcely wants them raised by the shifting and shifty population of a book of fiction, dualistically or pluralistically argued by puppets, each in his way, with the author just looming behind them, unwilling or unable to take sides, ironically smiling, ambiguously sad!

For my part, if an idea is of that caliber and consequence, a matter of life and death to me—or to other people in worse circumstances than mine are at present—I look for it in the tersest, clearest aphoristic form, memorizable, so that in a pinch, or at a turning point someday, I may be able to utter it in my own behalf: password or watchword or open sesame, motto or creed or prayer—not in questionable dialectic, page after page, leisurely and discursive, a tournament of braininess. Indeed, if a given author is a great man, I like him to do his thinking for me in his own words, signed and sealed; in his own tone of voice, not ventriloquously, parceled out to all sorts of mouthpieces; and in earnest, not just for the loose exercise of his excess of intellectual energy, and vain prolongation of his book. As Goethe said, "If I am to listen to another man's opinion, he must express it positively. I have enough of the problematical in myself."

I often wish that Mann in his later life had had an Eckermann, to keep him from expending his wisdom in a wearisome dialectic and a massive playfulness, pouring his mind all topsy-turvy into the great gaping last manuscripts. Let me cite two or three instances of what I think of as philosophical frivolity, coming from him; obscure and therefore objectionable matters.

Almost at the end of *The Magic Mountain,* when World War I begins, and Hans rouses from his long hypochondria and sad leisurely self-development and descends into the grim valley of Europe and enlists in the German army, Mann refers to it as "a personal mercy and grace" for his young everyman, "a manifestation of divine goodness and justice." I want to know—indeed, as a national of one of the nations that, twice in the century, have been involved in war due to Germany, I *desperately* want to know— whether Mann really means this. He contrives to end the sentence— also, come to think of it, the book's final sentence, which is about the renascence of love after the sickness and necrophily of the battle—with a question mark. At that point in Hans's life story, he says, "rodomontade is out of place." At mid-point in the twentieth century, I say, contrived or evasive expressions of opinion about some things are out of place. Some questions come to mind as naturally, as physically, as tears to our eyes; and to all intents and purposes, irony is a refusal to answer.

Earlier chapters of *The Magic Mountain,* of course, raise less painful but no less important issues with the same extreme alternativeness, so that it is a torment not to know which side Mann himself is on. Lecturing to an excited and sighing audience of the patients at Berghof, Krokowski, the antipathetic psychoanalyst, says, "Symptoms of disease are nothing but disguised manifestations of the power of love; and all disease is only love transformed."

A couple of hundred pages further on, Hans's good mentor, Settembrini, declares to him that the body is to be honored only when it is beautiful and free, desirable and joyous, but despised "in so far as its specific essence is perversity, decay, sensuality, and death." Isn't this a false dichotomy? Can the flesh by itself be un-innocent? Is it evil of the body to have to die? Are not senescence and mortality a part of nature, even as natural as the flower of youth and the prime of life? Throughout *The Magic Mountain,* as we have seen, Settembrini personifies liberal Mediterranean humanism; but here surely Mann has him on his knee and is ventriloquizing with him, perpetuating the old Judeo-Christian inner conflict and arbitrary sense of sin.

Surely Krokowski's thesis of psychosomaticism is not just a characterizing expression of his individual mentality and emotional prejudice. All these are themes of the novel as a whole, and as one's reading of it draws to a close, as one gazes back on it in its entirety, surely these main dichotomies seem unresolved; question marks loom over it all, as high as mountain peaks, as dim and swirling and disheartening as clouds. They are matters of Mann's personal lifelong meditation, and he has expressed them in various essays even more plainly and responsibly than in fiction.

In *Dr. Faustus* the questions are more complex. Whether Leverkuehn's music is good or bad, beautiful or ugly, is unanswerable; indeed it is not asked. What we want to know is something about the health or ill-health of his mind in the early chapters of the book, before his syphilitic insanity manifests itself. Was it not a little insane of him to contract syphilis in the first place? Is it true that syphilis is conducive to great explosive spiritual states, to transports of intellect, heightenings of creative power? Does Mann expect us to believe that the Devil as such exists? Does he or does he not mean to suggest that he himself believes in an evil demigod or antigod? Or is Leverkuehn's interlocutor at the turning point of the work just a metaphoric man, a mouthpiece, a figure of fun? The great strength of the Devil (devout Catholics and devout Protestants both say) is our not taking him seriously. Leverkuehn certainly is intended by Mann to personify Nazi Germany; but does not Mann also identify him, here and there, with pre-Nazi and post-Nazi Germany, and with general German psychology and creative power?

These are shocking uncertainties. However, the very central subject of *Dr. Faustus* is mental wrongdoing, Manichaeanism, questionableness. Thus perhaps, although it has none of the youthfulness or the narrative bewitchment or the human profusion of *The Magic Mountain*, it seems a more perfect work of art. It is absolutely unified; it is long, but at no point simply for lengthiness' sake; it never meanders or trails away to nothing; and although it depresses and confounds and overburdens and baffles the mind of the reader, it does not contradict itself.

There is one other objection to the philosophical novel that I shall make superficially, lightly. If any qualified philosopher reads this, he may want to chide me or castigate me for touching upon it at all, for certainly it is beyond my competence and beyond the intended scope of this essay. In philosophy, to a great extent, words themselves, in their grammatical relationship and syntactical arrangements, are the subject matter. Even more than in the obscurest and most modern poetry, they designate and connote themselves.

Now, as I shall be hanged for a lamb, why not for a sheep? A good deal of the obscurity of modern philosophy from the eighteenth century on, especially the German and the German-derived schools of thought and their contemporary by-products, such as Marxism and existentialism, is due to what in other categories of literature would be called bad writing. Philosophical style has been rendered doubly difficult in our time by the necessity for incorporating into almost every treatise or discourse certain terms and concepts that have originated in the realm of mathematics and the sciences. The Germans of course have greatly specialized in all these disciplines. In so far as we blame them for their writing in a confused way, one other excuse for them ought to be mentioned (Heller does mention it): the German language itself is somewhat more primitive and unfinished, less lucid in detail and less expeditious than English or the several languages based on Latin. But in so mysterious an area, can we tell what is cause and what is effect? In the eighteenth century a number of German thinkers and writers tried to be as clear and brief as the French; Goethe succeeded in great measure, even Schopenhauer succeeded. In his philosophical vein Mann, the greatest German writer of the twentieth century, did not succeed.

Here let me set down something that I have often expressed in casual conversation, anxiously now, as Mann devotees may resent my light epigrammatic expression even more than the idea I have to express.—Mann was not a great thinker, though he felt that he was. Certainly his feelings were great, and his greatness in general developed itself by means of the initial error of attaching too much importance to his abstract thoughts. His ideas were not powerful; surely a host of German postgraduate university men could have out-argued him, re-educated him, led him perhaps on still another grim German divagation and sanguinary wild-goose chase. But his confusion of intellect and inspiration resulted in literary power. It gave him—as a simple creative man of good will—a general mental athleticism unusual in belles-lettres, incomparable in fiction. And he gives wonderful exercise to the mind of any young reader. Even to overvalue him and to be disillusioned by him in due course is educational. In this regard he may be compared to Gide; another sort of hero of the intellect, even less satisfactory as a novelist.

◆

The writing of *Dr. Faustus* was tiring to the aged author; and no wonder. He had to interrupt it just before the end to undergo a serious surgical operation, and returned to his desk with a great scar halfway around his chest. But then evidently he felt indomitable, capable of no matter what, not to be baffled or frustrated by any sort of creative hardship. At least he pretended that this was the case, in order to go on hopefully working until the end. If one can manage it, a constant industriousness doubtless is the best way of shutting one's eyes to the approach of death.

In the spring of 1947, resident in Europe again—in German-speaking Switzerland, not in Germany proper—he produced a little historical novel, *The Holy Sinner,* cunning and erudite and meaningful, and after that *The Black Swan,* the postmature love story of a sort of female counterpart to Aschenbach, his least successful nouvelle; and then he resumed work on that fictitious autobiography of a swindler, *Confessions of Felix Krull,* which he had left unfinished in 1912. I cannot think of any instance in literary history of an enterprise so obstinate and long drawn out. Finally, in 1955, his daughter Erika has informed us, he conceived a sort of poetical drama to be entitled *Martin Luther's Wedding,* for which he piled up a quantity of notes and a rough draft.

Goethe said, "He is the most fortunate of mortals who can bring the end of his life around to its beginning again." In more ways than one, Mann was fortunate, and did so, most surprisingly, perhaps, in a short and simple essay on Chekhov. That and another work of criticism, an essay on Schiller first delivered as an oration in Stuttgart upon the one hundred and fiftieth anniversary of his birth, taken together, impart to us in strange contrast and melancholy harmony some of his important final thinking about himself. Hail and farewell! Hail to Schiller, the great neurotic prototype and inspirer of his youth, "universe-intoxicated, and toward his fellow men, didactic!"

The Chekhov essay is a more confidential piece of writing, not characteristic of him at all, humble and fervent, uncomplaining and unexplaining. Farewell to Chekhov in a way, but mainly farewell to himself, and to his immense lifework, and to certain of his lifelong intentions and illusions about the narrative art.

It begins with his confessing that the death of Chekhov, in 1904, only fifteen years his senior, meant very little to him because he was not familiar with the short stories and romantic comedies of the beloved Russian. What was the cause of this ignorance? he asks, and answers with a reiteration of his old interest in expansiveness and bulk, but, this time, in a rueful rather than a boastful tone. It was "probably because I was under the spell of the *magnum opus,* fascinated by those monumental epics, which are the fruit of sustained inspiration and are brought to completion by the power of indomitable patience; for I worshiped the great achievers like Balzac, Tolstoi, and Wagner, and it was my dream to emulate them if I could."

This was published in East Germany in 1954, then broadcast in English in a somewhat abridged form in the spring of 1955. I quote from the anonymous BBC translation, smoother and more idiomatic than that afterward published in book form. "Whereas Chekhov (like Maupassant, whom by the way I knew much better) confined himself to the modest dimensions of the short story; this did not call for heroic endurance throughout years and decades, but could be tossed off by some happy-go-lucky artist in a day or two or a week or two, at most. I felt a certain disdain for this, hardly realizing then that genius can be bounded in a nutshell and yet embrace the whole fullness of life by virtue of a brevity and terseness deserving of the highest admiration. Such works attain to full epic stature and can even surpass in intensity the great towering novels which inevitably flag at times and subside into noble boredom."

I believe that these paragraphs justify, in so far as criticism needs justifying, what I have had to say about the somewhat overextended and self-abandoned form of his principal novels. Here, too, he seems to be informing us, implicitly, of the work that he would have liked to do, perhaps after another volume of the wild and facetious life of Krull, and perhaps *Martin Luther's Wedding,* if still longer life had been vouchsafed him. Another change for the changeable one: Bildung and Entwicklung for the all too educable German!

It is a kind of information that, in spite of science and my better judgment, inclines me to believe in immortality: the instance and good example of a dying soul still so limber, and free from vanity, and eager to be (and capable of being) original all over again, with mighty acknowledged immortals of the arts going before, showing the way to his originality.

In a scientific age, it is hard to conceive of the body as *not* dying, but easy for the mind to conceive of itself as continuing to live. In any event—survive what may! perish what must!—in the whiling away of our various existences on earth, we have to die a good many secondary deaths, as in a ritual or a simulacrum; and as Mann's fictitious Schiller reminds himself, in the early story entitled *A Weary Hour*, in which so much of Mann's genius does appear "bounded in a nutshell," there is a certain virtue in just bringing things to a conclusion, even a life, even an essay. "For then some new work can begin to struggle into being and into shape, giving out light and sound, ringing and shimmering, hinting at its infinite origin, as in a seashell we hear the sighing of the sea."

One or another of Mann's editors having had the bright idea of republishing this miniature early story as an appendix to the ponderous Schiller essay, *Versuch über Schiller*—fifty years having elapsed between the two texts—this lovely sentence appears on the last page of his *Last Essays*.

Chapter Eight

Talks with Thornton Wilder

Whatever we succeed in doing is a transformation of something we have failed to do. Thus, when we fail, it is only because we have given up.

—PAUL VALÉRY

Did you happen to see, on the front page of the *New York Times* dated November 6, 1961, a two-column article announcing the production in the near future of three one-act plays by Thornton Wilder, part of a double cycle of fourteen, *The Seven Ages of Man* and *The Seven Deadly Sins,* long rumored and hoped for? It was an important piece of journalism, the work of a good writer named Arthur Gelb, illustrated by a flash photograph of the famed novelist and playwright, based in large part on an interview with him, full of the ethos of his art, and of those technicalities of staging which count for so much in the aesthetics of the theatre. "We have to kick the proscenium down," he told the *Times.*

It was also stated in the *Times* that the announced triple bill at the Circle in the Square was to be Wilder's "first new stage work in nearly twenty years." To express this situation more precisely, it was his first *entirely* new stage work to be produced *in this country* since 1942. *The Matchmaker,* first given at the Edinburgh Festival in 1954 and brought here the following year, was a revision of *The Merchant of Yonkers,* a comedy somewhat unsuccessfully put on stage in the late thirties. In 1955 another play entitled *A Life in the Sun* was produced in Edinburgh, and subsequently, in a German translation, in Zurich and elsewhere on the continent of Europe, with success. This has been regarded by the pundits and potentates of our theatre as not good enough for Broadway. For the past three years, according to the *Times*—longer than that, friends of Wilder's tell me—he has been at work on the double cycle of one-acters.

Of greater significance—at any rate, of livelier interest to me, a book reader more than a theatre-goer—is the fact that he has not published a novel since 1948. In 1952 he spoke of a novel in progress, which he has not published, presumably has not finished. However, Arthur Gelb and I are not entitled to speak sadly of an actual lapse in his creative life, certainly not of any idleness or indifference.

What happened was a mysterious lull, or a number of lulls, delays, hesitancies, changes of plan. And I have ideas about this, all in chiaroscuro, as in portraits by Rembrandt; golden in the center and either very profound or strangely empty in corners of the canvas. The literary creativity of the day and age—it has been a good long day, a glorious enough age—is a shadowy theme, and it gets harder and harder to expound and diagnose, especially American creativity, with our culture basically changing in some ways; but let me try.

❖

Wilder and I first met in 1928 in the South of France, in Villefranche-sur-Mer. I was in my late twenties, he in his early thirties, both of us flourishing and promising, neck and neck in literature at that point. *The Bridge of San Luis Rey,* his second novel, had just won the Pulitzer Prize, and my publishers had given their prize to my second novel the previous year. Though, in his case, allowance always has to be made for an ebullient good nature and sometimes an inclination to flatter those he makes friends with, I think it can be said that he took a real and lively interest in me and in what might be expected of me as a writer. It thrilled me to make his acquaintance.

For two or three hours on successive days we strolled here and there in and around Villefranche, looking down upon its famous harbor scooped out by Hercules on his way from one of his more famous labors to another, with anchorage deep enough for ocean liners and battleships, including our battleships; visiting the ceme-

tery where some nineteenth-century U.S. Navy personnel lie eternally sleeping; descending into the Rue Obscure which is a sort of
elongated open-ended cellar under the tenement houses on the quay,
coming back up into the Riviera sunshine, gladly exhaling the sour
old crypt-like atmosphere, and inhaling the fragrance of the commercial flower beds, carnations and stock, distributed upon the
shelving foothills, and strolling along elsewhere, I have forgotten
where. Perhaps I ought not to say strolling: we went so vigorously,
and at intervals stopped and stood face to face, in a rapture of
articulateness, with gestures.

Perhaps at that time Wilder himself, as a man of literary genius
just beginning, and possibly a new friend, appealed to me more
than the work he had published. Certainly my admiration of *The
Bridge of San Luis Rey* fell somewhat short of the consensus. To
this day, with my over-all appreciation of him at its peak, *The
Bridge* satisfies me less than his other novels. To be sure, it is well
written, with a soft and regular brightness like a string of matched
pearls. It has another quality of his style, which, since then, he has
developed and perfected in all the forms of his writing, in drama as
well as narration and exposition: an effect of energy, but with no
nervousness, no hurry; and constant enthusiasm, though always
stopping short of hyperbole and fatuity. Is all this somewhat self-
conscious and proud? Yes, but are those not favorable characteristics
in a young or youngish writer?

The imperfection in *The Bridge of San Luis Rey,* I thought (and
still think), is the subject matter; more specifically, the plot, which
is tight, intentional, functional, with the function above all of
bringing out the significance and the importance of what happens.
Every inch of the way, the parts keep proving and reinforcing the
theme of the whole. The theme is, roughly speaking, the old enigma
of how hard it is to understand the will of God, that is, the ill will
of God; and perhaps one cannot take a great interest in this without
some simple religious belief.

Also (I find) the atmospheres of two or three different cultures
and national backgrounds in it somewhat neutralize or nullify one
another. It is a tale of South America, but in design and mode and

manner it is quite French; and with the author's imagination reaching, almost straining, in those two directions at once, his own North American temperament seems somewhat muted, neglected. You might think it the work of a much older man, and a more professional type of writer, than the extraordinary young schoolmaster who did write it.

In that first encounter of ours in Villefranche, I remember venturing to tell him that I personally rather favored his earlier work of fiction, *The Cabala*, a sort of intimate portrait gallery of various cosmopolitan contemporary Romans who presumably had been hospitable to him during a sojourn in Rome, with a glamorous light of his youth freshly shining on them, and with dark touches of a worldly wisdom that presumably they had taught him.

But no, he protested, to my surprise, none of them were persons that he had known. Just as in *The Bridge of San Luis Rey* one could discern the lovely seventeenth-century phantom of Mme. de Sévigné, and relearn a lesson from Mérimée, and rehear a lilt of Offenbach, *The Cabala* was bookworm's work.

He blushed to tell me this, he said, but then corrected himself for blushing: one should never be ashamed of any method one may have found for oneself, if it works. For each and every sophisticated up-to-date Roman, he had had in mind some hero or heroine of bygone fiction or drama, or haunting figure out of someone's correspondence or memoirs.

"In any case, surely," he said, "it can't have fooled you, least of all you, penetratingly intelligent as you are, with the added advantage of expatriation. You must have recognized my little derivations, my transparencies; seen right through them!"

It was my turn to blush, somewhat in self-pity, having had only about half a college education, less than half. In his lovely fantasia of the Eternal City I had not recognized any of the historical prototypes or the timeless themes borrowed from the past reservoir of culture, the world library. Come to think of it, just one of his points of departure had struck me: the death of Keats, which he had obviously taken and modernized.

One major difficulty of all human endeavor, especially of literary endeavor, he reminded me that day, is our almost invariably getting started with our lifework before we have achieved maturity in any of the essentials. What fitfulness and zigzag would result from our having to begin all over again, from scratch, each of us individually, or for that matter each successive generation! But we do *not* have to. Preceding and underlying our fragmentary notions and ephemeral feelings are the effects of the eternal thoughtfulness, the emotions of everyman, the ever-cumulative encyclopedic general experience.

Inspiration is something like a sap, declared Wilder, which, in its season, riseth as it listeth from the deep old roots up and up into the twigs of today, causing the budding of one's limitedly individual mind, the blooming and fruit-bearing of the particular talent one happens to have.

Of course it surprised and enchanted me to hear this, especially to think that characters as lively as those cabalists of his—the sex-stricken teen-age boy, the Wilder-like youngish American with a puritanical eagerness to be spiritually helpful to the boy (which turns almost to rage when the boy is not helped), the extremely romantic and foolish little French princess, the demoralizing Socratic old Cardinal—could be derived just from reading matter and from creative daydreaming; not necessarily freebooted out of the society in which the writer has to live, the company he keeps and wants to go on keeping, the family he is anxious not to hurt. How this would simplify the novelist's life! Even in our self-disciplines, our concentration on the blessed necessary daily grindstone, our resistance to the temptations of society and other gregarious involvements, it would strengthen us to be deprived of the excuse of having to pursue subject matter. At least temporarily, as I listened to my brilliant confrere, I had a vision of a really liberated and self-sufficient literary production. It reminded me of that seventeenth-century biologist who believed, at least persuaded others to believe, that he had originated life; generated a mouse, in fact, out of an accumulation of bits and pieces of old clothing.

❖

One's memory of the appearance of one's friends operates strangely as a rule, almost akin to caprice or mischief. When I happen not to see this or that friend for a few months, images of bygone existence and outlived physique often recur in my mind, just as the first outline of an oil painting will sometimes work up out of the underpaint, through the glazes, into the final version; and when I remeet him or her, or when I encounter an up-to-date photograph in a newspaper or a periodical, it startles me.

Nothing like that in the case of Wilder. His physical aspect has been extraordinarily constant, perhaps I should say continuous. Photographers do not metamorphose him much; almost every photograph is a good enough likeness. The years have not made a great difference. By the time he reached man's estate he had ceased to look boyish, and he still is rather youthful. Life has only roughened his features, etched his expressions deeper. A certain stoutness in the last few years has saved him from the bleak, intense look that comes over a good many American men in their sixties.

The three of his physical characteristics that especially please me and amuse me are of today and of the past alike.—A singular way of laughing, forcible but not loud, expressing as a rule (I think) a general joy of living rather than a sense of fun at the time and in the circumstances. A flashing of his eyes once in a while; the occasion perhaps suddenly seeming to him a great occasion, or an emergency in some way. Certain emphatic manual, digital gestures when he talks, somewhat in the manner of clergymen of a past generation or of old-time political campaigners.

Believe me, it was exciting to talk to him, to be talked to by him; an excitement not really easy, not exactly recreational, especially when it came to his telling any sort of story, which often, suddenly, would be fraught with tenseness, responsibility, restraint. Much of our conversation in Villefranche was only gossip, great gossip! main natural ingredient of the art of fiction, to my way of thinking. My way of thinking was simpler than his.

I would have sworn that all the incidents and overheard conversations and synopsized lives with which he regaled me in Villefranche were things that he intended to write about, in the not-distant future. His mind, I thought, had already got its range, taken aim. Every so often in a word or a phrase I was able to discern his creative processing, even vague outlines of the forms of fiction to come. But this was almost always followed by a word or phrase indicative of his feeling that things might have to be kept in confidence, or changed beyond recognition, or postponed, until this or that disadvantage or danger in someone's everyday existence had passed. A kind of conscientiousness along this line evidently kept warring against his impulsive young aspiration and inspiration to write fiction. It concerned him always painfully not to be, or not even to appear to be, invasive of anyone's privacy; not to amuse himself (or, for that matter, *me*) at anyone's expense; and not to take either a moralistic attitude or an antisocial attitude about anything.

At times he made me think of a boy climbing a tree, carefully placing his feet on limb above limb, finally peering into a bird's nest containing eggs or little birds, and holding his breath, in order not to sully anything with his human odor, not to disillusion or disincline the parent birds when they got back.

I remember his telling me the story of the self-destruction of a beautiful girl who had been born to some prominence in New York society and at an early age was successful on the stage. The man whom she fatally loved was a friend of Wilder's; therefore he had some knowledge of the miserable event, and perhaps, he thought, it was wrong of him to inform me of it. "But perhaps not," he said. "As literary men, I think we must feel free to tell one another everything that has interested us profoundly, or helped us or hindered us in the work we have in progress or in mind. Even things that have harmed or destroyed people; even things that may still prove harmful!"

I think that, except for the discourtesy, he would have liked to admonish me or to implore me not to retell it to anyone *not* literary. He told it superbly, in a nervous and dramatic way, accelerating his telling from point to point. The faster the words came, the

more exactly he was able to select them—sharpshooting words!—
and the more he lowered and softened his voice. At the conclusion
he held his forefinger up straight and briefly pressed it to his lips.
(A good photographer named Rollie McKenna has photographed
him doing this.) It is the gesture of the patron saint of Czechoslo-
vakia, St. John of Nepomuk, who was martyred for refusing to
divulge secrets of the confessional, and who protects pious Roman
Catholics from libel and slander.

On the fatal day the poor compulsively loving girl talked and
talked on the telephone to her poor beloved man, threatening to
commit suicide unless he requited her love more satisfactorily. She
had made rather a habit of telephoning him, in an overwrought,
unbelievable way, and perhaps his disbelief colored the tone of his
voice so that she noticed it. "No, dear. No, I'm sorry. Yes, I promise.
Darling, now take it easy, please take it easy."

Lamentable universal phrases! Sometimes the suicidal state of
mind is above all an absolute determination to be believed, to be
taken seriously, to be worried about. His calmness, meant to be reassuring, may have been more injurious to her just then than anything else that he had done or left undone. Even to be reassured may
seem insulting. Sometimes it is a matter of our suddenly seeing ourselves as others must see us, hearing ourselves as others are hearing
us: histrionic, redundant, boring!

Suddenly she ceased to harangue him and put the receiver back
on the hook—it was a pay telephone in a hotel lobby or a drug-
store or a railroad station—and later that evening did what she had
been threatening to do, I forget by what means: soporific medicine
of some sort or perhaps defenestration.

My impression, as I remember it, was that Wilder sympathized
with the presumably destructive man more than with the destroyed
girl. This puzzled me. Years later it seemed to me that I came upon
the secret of it in his superb historical novel, *The Ides of March*,
wherein Caesar explains his having lost patience with Clodia
Pulcher, who persistently loved him for years, while trailing a
wrecked life around behind her, compensating for a tragic misfortune in her childhood by nonstop mischievousness and cruelty ever

I

since, acquitting herself of every charge but never ceasing to feel guilty, exhibiting herself as the victim, the victim, whatever has happened, re-erecting a sacrificial altar at every turn and exhibiting herself on it, striking attitudes on it, victimizing herself if no one else is available to do it for her. It is the harshest page Wilder has ever written, and one of the profoundest. I can think of only one other outburst or outcry as passionate: in the last act of *The Skin of Our Teeth*, when, immediately after one war, stirrings and sproutings of another begin, and the Adam-like father reproves his Cain-like son, eternal incorrigible war instigator.

❖

I also told him a love story, one with (so to speak) a happier ending: matrimony instead of self-murder. It involved my next-door neighbor there on the Riviera, a young woman from New Orleans somewhat childish of mind but physically perfect, like an antique Venus, in and out of the water all day long, and a well-to-do young man also from the South, who had been a classmate of Scott Fitzgerald's at Princeton. They had grown up together, and at an early age she had resolved to marry him and had persisted in this dream.

He seemed not to care much for women, and kept sailing around the Mediterranean in a luxurious little sailing vessel with two or three young employees to help him navigate. But he was fond of her in his way, and at intervals he would drop anchor in our harbor; whereupon she would always propose and repropose marriage and he would decline in a friendly way.

One day she grew impatient, and as he was putting out to sea and she stood on the sea wall waving bon voyage, she suddenly dove off and swam out after him. As the wind, to start with, was blowing fitfully and not in his direction, she caught up, and noticing a rope of some sort hanging overboard, grasped it and hung on and let herself be towed along in the wake of the boat, like a hooked mermaid. They were well out past the lighthouse, in dark active water, before he or one of his sailors noticed and rescued her.

Not long after that he married her; and, oh, how it appealed to people's imaginations there on the Riviera; to some sentimentally, to others in the way of a sense of humor. A marriage definitely not made in heaven; only in the sea, which brought forth Venus in the first place!

His idea, as she confided to me some time after, was that the reality of marriage to him would rid her of her foolish fixation of love, but it had no such effect. Their marriage lasted quite a few years. They were scarcely happy; he drank, and she tagged along after him on his rounds of dissipation, unwisely. However, for a few years, marriage preserved them from worse unhappiness to which they were probably, separately, prone.

In response to this, what do you suppose my great young confrere said? "Isn't it a pity that we can't write stories like that?"

That surprised me even more than what he had confided to me about the bookish, impersonal origins of *The Cabala*. The point of the story of my Venus-like neighbor, I should have thought, was its obvious writability. I believed indeed that she wanted it written and had pursued me a little and furnished me with certain gratuitous details, to inspire me. There often apparently is a certain magnetism about literary men for girls with breaking hearts, as also for soldiers between battles, and presumably for Adonis-like men in luxury sloops: with certain emotions at their height, or in intermissions of emotion, a sort of longing to be somewhat immortalized. Why not? What harm?

But I well understood what it was that troubled my conscientious fellow writer: the thought flashed from him to me like a spark or, alas, the opposite of a spark: the great moot matter of the invasion of privacy by the use of people's idiosyncrasies and misfortunes in our fiction writing. Many of us shrink extremely from the risk of hurting or irresponsibly influencing people with whom our lives are cast. It gives us the best excuse in the world for avoiding certain difficult subjects; an excuse most welcome to any of us who happen to find ourselves in disagreement or in conflict or in maladjustment with present majority morals or mores.

Thus Wilder and I in 1931, even when we failed to see eye to eye, were contemplating the same or similar problems; and at that age we were both optimistic. What bliss to be young, especially to be a young novelist—what price glory in any other arena, we thought—to know stories of suicidal girls telephoning, of child-minded girls towed out to sea by men they loved, and to see no earthly reason why one should not write them as they deserve to be written, fancying that one understands everything, and that if there are difficulties in the narrative art, one can learn to surmount them; if one lacks innate ability in any way, it can be compensated for by hard work.

◈

Have I given the impression that Wilder came down to Villefranche just to see me? Of course he did not. Even at the time I didn't think it, but I felt it; and something of the excitement of his visit has continued for thirty-three years, blotting from my remembrance whatever other engagements or interests drew him to the Riviera.

I have never known anyone to give his friends so much satisfaction of pride, even of vanity. He has continually excelled in the important though slight and improvisatory expressions of friendship, at least in his relations with his fellow writers. He is conscious of this and perhaps occasionally sorry for himself about it. A news weekly once quoted him as having said, "On my grave they will write: Here lies a man who tried to be obliging." Doubtless all this manifestation of his good will has been beneficial, ego-enhancing, especially in the cold, uneasy, touchy literary life. In so far as he has given us swelled heads, he himself has counteracted it by taking himself away every time, before long. Before you get used to it you have to undergo a kind of disintoxication, withdrawal symptoms.

Not long before his visit to me, he had been traveling all around Europe, by motor and on foot, down through France and Italy, accompanied by the then world's champion heavyweight prize-fighter, Gene Tunney, who was passing the time until his marriage in Rome. I remember Wilder's saying that whenever he happened to mention good books, the aspiring young athlete bought them, as soon as they came to a city with an English-language bookshop, until he had a great rucksackful, Atlas-like. And the more heavily he burdened himself with a world of reading matter all the day long, the drowsier he felt in the evening when it came time to read.

In England the two friends had called on Bernard Shaw, who had also boxed in his young manhood and written a novel about boxing. This sociability must have been fraught with funniness, I imagined; but my confrere seemed not to have found it so. From his account of it I got a somewhat stylized impression of the mighty youngster coming up in the world at a great rate, and of the aged popular playwright rather affected and smug in his patriarchal role. (A little later Robert Benchley wrote an excellent take-off on this encounter, with the pugilist talking highbrow, the dramatist, Madison Square Garden jargon.)

My amusement at things that Wilder told me sometimes embarrassed him, I'm afraid. He did not want me to think that he was making fun of his friends. If it ever sounded so, would I excuse it and forget it, please? "To the laity," he said, "we writers must often seem malicious. No harm in it, when it is just between ourselves, in a whisper!"

Sense of humor, I think, may be defined as the fun that we refrain from making. I think Wilder often refrains, with tactfulness in the subconscious as well as on the intentional surface of his mind. With reference to something else that we had laughed in unison about, without an exact identity of view, he said, "Our humor is a primary color, a primary color! We mix it even into our convictions, and into our sorrows."

We have always differed, significantly, I suppose, as to what amusement we find in the life around us. I have a certain feeling for slapstick and surrealism, and for the equivalent in behavior, even the behavior of fond friends. When things strike my funny bone, darker emotions perhaps somewhat underlie my glee: sensuality, superstitiousness, even retribution or revenge in some way. People's oddities and extravagances charm Wilder, but he never seems to long for their frustration or their downfall; no great sense of roughhouse or of booby trap.

He is a prouder man than I, and takes into account, perhaps overestimates, others' pride, and even in his conversation behind their backs, is careful not to disgrace any of them. Irony, furthermore, is habitual and delightful to my mind, but is not his habit, at least not his forte.

◆

I have remembered one very foolish detail of our conversation in Villefranche. Come to think of it, what he said was not foolish; the folly was all in my reaction, overreaction. It has stayed in my mind as it were a feather of my young life, wafted up by both his breath and mine, and never wafted down again, amusing and symbolical in the prevailing air for years, for decades. Memorableness is a kind of significance in itself, I think.

It was a matter of his sense of his own early celebrity and of his belief in fame. Having expressed his generous and favorable opinion of my two novels, he wanted to influence me, for my part also, to get to be more successful and famous in the near future. As I had been awarded a prize and seen the title of that prize novel on the best-seller list, I seemed to myself quite successful; all was well, wasn't it? I tried to convey this thought or feeling to my wellwisher. Oh, the fatuousness of that time of life, when one considers oneself a made man, a self-made man!

My new friend, my thrilling fellow writer, brushed my complacency aside, and went on to explain the facts of the American literary situation to me. Earlier in the year he had gone lecturing in Texas and thereabouts. The Texans and others, he was saddened and irked to find, had never heard of me. Indeed he realized that my excellent second novel had made a reputation for me, but what I did not realize was that it was scarcely a national reputation. Harper & Brothers with their blessed prize doubtless had sold thousands and thousands of copies, but all that sale must have been in the two or three metropolitan areas, New York, Boston, Chicago. Which, in a vast democracy, wasn't good enough.

With a little modesty and realism beginning to dawn on me as he went on with this theme, I finally asked, in a voice perhaps peevish or wistful, what was to be done about it? Did he really think that Albert & Charles Boni, his publishers, were a more powerful outfit than Harper & Brothers, my publishers? The reviews of my book, I reminded him, had been nationwide and wonderfully laudatory.

"Wonderful, wonderful," he agreed, but went on to say that, as to the development of real reputation and as to the marketability of one's books, book reviews never do much for one. Front-page publicity is the desirable, the needful thing; some mention, at least, on a page mainly devoted to news, not just literary criticism and paid publishers' advertisements.

At that point, for my part, the balance of this conversation shifted. My mind seemed to strain, to quiver, to dip, like a dowsing rod. I could not be sure what the underlying emotion had become: was it laughter? was it anger? With a little exertion of courtesy and circumspection I changed the subject.

I had seen some front-page reports of his hiking around Europe with the book-loving boxer, and I realized suddenly the dissimilarity of my destiny, incommensurability of my problems. For the life of me I could not think of anyone that I could have gone hiking with in any noticeable or publicizable way, or of any other such newsworthiness. I did not suppose that the author of *The Bridge of San Luis Rey*, my new friend, who amused me more than anyone else I had ever met, had gone hiking on purpose. Having somewhat observed him in the decades that have elapsed, I know that every sort of publicity vexes him and seems a constant inconvenience and waste. But, with or without self-consciousness, I think that literary genius, impulses of friendship and other such informal self-expressions, and literary renown, all hang together; and this is as it should be. Perhaps we have come full circle.—I now believe in a kind of cultural patriotism and a greater degree of involvement and exposure in the literary life than I ever dreamed of as a young man. Whereas doubtless Wilder has wearied of all that; longs for modest circumstances, remoteness from the Rialto, rustication.

Now in retrospect I see something else as well.—Though the newsworthy novelist may not have been aware of everything that went on in his immense young intellect, to some extent surely that hiking companion of 1928 served as a model for the protagonist of the novel that he published in 1934, *Heaven's My Destination*, his only work of fiction situated in present-day America, corresponding to his great indigenous comedies, *Our Town* and *The Matchmaker.* One fourth of George Brush, his knowledgeable sister Isabel tells me, portrays their father; one fourth, presumably, is Wilder himself; one fourth is the champion boxer (I think); and one fourth is Voltaire's Candide.

It was that surprising front-page story in the *New York Times*, above-mentioned, which reminded me of our absurd talk about publicity and reputation and success, so long ago. Think of being able to command that kind of attention, with a cheerful flash photograph and headlines: "Thornton Wilder, 64, Sums up Life and Art. Sees Hope for Man's Survival!"

Still more recently, when he wrote to a high school junior about an amateur production of *The Skin of Our Teeth*, "a two-page hand-written letter," he got two half-columns entitled "Wilder Advises Long Island School Cast." Can you beat that?

Perhaps I have been envious of him all these years without an entire awareness of the fact, and therefore without quite the philosophy and the humor that as a rule I pride myself on.

◈

What I certainly envy now is his having written *The Ides of March*, a novel more appealing to my imagination, more relevant to my intellectual interests, than any other novel by a fellow American of my generation. I shall never forget the pleasure, the emotions more and more mingled, the increasing seriousness, almost solemn nity, with which I first read it, hastening on from page to page. A part of my excitement was just selfishness; I kept thinking that I would give five years of my life to have written it myself.

No one, no one with any literary inclination or aptitude for reading, could fail to enjoy it, I felt sure. But in fact a number of the book reviewers to whom it was assigned did somewhat fail, misreading its political philosophy, perhaps disliking its morality, and fussing over little issues of its factual accuracy, eagerly displaying erudition or counter-erudition of their own. Wilder had facilitated this last function for them by specifying in a foreword certain of his independent conceptions, alterations of the historic record, especially some dates, so as to bring the lives of his two important secondary characters into focus with the final fatalities in the life of his protagonist.

In his foreword Wilder calls *The Ides of March* a fantasia, but that word does not (I think) exactly suit it. It is composed of what appear to be, but are not, actual materials of biography and history: simulated letters and journals and commonplace books, confidential police reports, and other assorted memoranda; all verisimilitudinous to the point of forgery. No descriptions of anything or anyone; no overt interpretation or commentary by the author—his principal personages and important bystanders comment incessantly, according to their several levels and degrees of intelligence, and always in character. All that the author is assumed to have done is to arrange and annotate the pseudo-documents as to points of fact, dates and identifications and cross references.

That arrangement, which establishes the design or pattern of the work, is hard to describe; it is most original and even arbitrary, but not at all hard for the reader to follow. It is in four parts, or "books," covering the same main events four times over, starting a little earlier in each part and ending a little later. By means of this odd recurring and expanding chronology, centered upon the month of September 45 B.C., turning back one month and going forward six months, concluding with March 15, 44 B.C., the ides—on which date fanatic lovers of the old Roman liberties finally stab the Dictator, Julius Caesar, to death—the reader is given an extraordinary impression of a fate running its course; a sort of bird's-eye view, constantly on the wing, back and forth, and higher and higher; and the passing of the historic time corresponds to the gradual increase of our understanding of the great matters at issue.

With the exception of *Heaven's My Destination*—which is a cautionary tale, entirely timely, as of its publication date and the phase or stage of American life that it pictures: roughly speaking, the depression—all of Wilder's works of fiction have been in some way historical novels. The balance of past and present in them, the interplay of the tenses of the narrated lives and of the narrator's mind and the reader's mind, differ considerably. In *The Cabala* everything derives from the past, as he informed me upon our first meeting, but is disguised as the present. In *The Bridge of San Luis Rey* and *The Woman of Andros* he gives us the past per se, the past for the past's sake; a matter of beauty and recreation and educative effect. In *The Ides of March* the basic themes are of today, or so timeless that as we read we think modernly; the characters in it are important types of humanity alive now, recognizable by every reader (I suppose), though in the guise and habitat and behavior patterns of ancient Romans, noble and otherwise.

The following Romans, principally.—Caesar. His silly young wife Pompeia. His invalided and absent friend Turrinus, to whom he addresses a continuous account of his life and his thoughts in a journal-letter (the bulkiest and most important of the component parts of the book). The glorious poet Catullus, who is a weak, unlucky, and angry man. Clodia Pulcher, who vainly loves Caesar, and whom Catullus desperately loves. The aging great actress Cytheris; and Cleopatra, the Egyptian queen, who takes Mark Anthony away from Cytheris. Also, of course, a quantity of less individualized, subsidiary humanity, serving and influencing these principals and witnessing what they are and what they do.

The main part of the plot is the thing not at all invented or imaginary, indicated by the title: the conspiracy and the propaganda leading to Caesar's assassination; the swift, almost simple transition in Roman politics which was to affect all of humanity, at least in the Western world, for centuries to come. Therefore, necessarily, the main theme is the matter of political philosophy: mysterious dictatorship, and sorrowful shortcomings of the more democratic forms of government; noble intentions of the Dictator, as it happened indeed paradoxically in that olden time in Rome, and mixed motives of his opponents and assassinators, who were an oligarchy pretending to be a republic, an oligarchy bringing on an empire.

The other themes are as follows.—Religion, both pro and con. Love, both beneficial and harmful. Two kinds of great friendship, that which is built upon intimacies of childhood and early life, exemplified by Caesar and Turrinus, and that which, with good luck and good management, may develop along with sexual attraction and may outlast it when it is spent, exemplified by Caesar and Cleopatra. Extraordinary unilateral friendliness, on Caesar's part, toward Catullus, who hates him. Evil, almost in the absolute, done to Clodia in her childhood—an uncle violated her—and visited by her upon other people all the rest of her life. Heroism, Caesar's heroism, open-eyed and not hopeful, but unprotesting and unfaltering, on his way to his historic end.

Wilder's Caesar is a more comprehensible and more profound human being than any other portrayal of the supreme Roman known to me. Furthermore, he has an intellectual power and a superiority of cultural interests somewhat rarer in fiction than it has been in fact at one time and another in history. He takes an almost modern interest in what we call the psyche, but as the determining factor in morality and in civic and creative activity rather than as a matter of mental health and mental illness. He keeps dreaming of moral perfection as it might be, as it ought to be; hails and kindly cherishes various instances of genuine though imperfect virtue in the society around him; but is not fatuously optimistic or sentimental. On the other hand, although he never shuts his eyes to wrongdoing, his realism has not made him cynical. In his every utterance, in every word of his writing that we read over his shoulder, he testifies somehow to his conviction that goodness is infinite but not absolute, not invariable; whereas evil is eternal but not omnipotent.

A part of the secret of his deep, peaceful, humorous nature, and of the clarity of his expression of what he thinks and feels, is simply courage. While his life seems all of a piece, he always has a duality in his mind: his desires on the one hand, things he dreads on the other hand; and he never renounces the best that might happen or forgets the worst. He keeps imagining things up ahead, so as to make provision of understanding and pride for this turn of events or that; he is not going to be surprised by anything. This gives him his stature; a certain superiority to everything that happens, whether it is a necessity or an accident or a punishment, even impossible love, even violent death. As Beethoven queried in the margin of his late quartet: Muss es sein? must things be as they are? The answer, of course, for the creative artist, is the work of art. But no man, as a man—not even the sublime genius, not even the ruler of the world —has a choice of answers; the only thing he can say is yes.

What an array of the glorious though often sorrowful variations of love there is in this novel! how instructive and helpful to any lover, and to any friend or relative of lovers! In Caesar's case a spiritual and Platonic feeling predominates. Though we see him in a fond and sensual relationship with Cleopatra, Wilder represents him as a healthy-minded, healthily lustful man, not particularly subject to the amorous passion in the romantic, sex-linked way. Two things he feels passionately: his devotion to Turrinus, a matter of remembrance and gratitude and never-sated mutuality of mind, and an inconsolable tenderness toward his dead daughter. With reference to the latter, but perhaps alluding at the same time to the more secret, earlier affection, he says of himself, "At the memory of one whisper, one pair of eyes, the pen falls from my hand, the interview in which I am engaged turns to stone. Rome and her business become a clerk's task, arid and tedious, with which I fill my days until death relieves me of it."

Love also at its worst: for example, the rape of Clodia at the age of twelve, "in an orchard, at noon, in the blazing sun," as she tells Catullus, with some suggestion of her having responded not quite innocently even to that misfortune. In any case she is both damaged in spirit and perverted in intellect after that, leading a life of revenge, obviously enjoying her misbehavior intensely, though pretending to be motivated by self-pity. She loves Caesar, because he seems to her sufficiently free from old moral prejudice to understand her wickedness and to join in her self-directed pathos. Perhaps he has yielded to her a little in the past, but never an inch within the span of the book. Meanwhile she torments the life out of Catullus, partaking of sexual ecstasy with him one minute, putting him to shame next minute, and doubtless constantly goading him to hate Caesar.

Various secondary instances of the many-definitioned thing also, such as the almost incestuous closeness of Clodia and her brother, a twinship in mischief, on the whole less harmful than any of her other relationships; and the absurd matrimony of Caesar and Pompeia; and the absolute sadness of great-hearted Cytheris, letting her darling go without a whimper, without even disapprobation, because she truly loves him, and chooses therefore to look upon his passionate defection as just a part of the general incontrovertible process and prospect of old age.

Perhaps in these synopsizing paragraphs I have intellectualized Wilder's work too much. In fact it not only depicts maximum emotion at several points in the entangled tale, but imparts to the reader great sympathy and deep natural sentiment. The death of Catullus, especially, only half a page—Caesar, the greatest of his admirers despite his virulent opposition, seated at his bedside, consoling him for the long folly of his love of fiendish Clodia, talking to him about Sophocles, reciting one of the choruses from *Oedipus at Colonnus*—I find heartbreaking, perhaps because of someone whom I love, or on my own account, or both.

In Richard Goldstone's *Paris Review* interview with him in 1957, the subject of which was the art of fiction, Wilder gave it as his opinion that no "self-effacement" on the part of the fiction writer can keep us from hearing "his voice recounting, recalling events that are past and over." I say that this is not true of *The Ides of March*. I hear in it the very tone and the warm breath of life of everyone concerned *except* the narrator. What this invaluable colloquy with the young university man records most impressively is one of Wilder's fits of longing to be back in the theatre, not at the novelist's lonely, uncertain, haunted desk.

And in this connection let me point out something about this novel that may not occur to you as you read it. More than any other work of fiction that I can think of, its singularity of structure and power of execution derive from Wilder's experience as a playwright. Everyone in it is characterized primarily by his own self-expression, secondarily by others' report and comment. To be sure, all this takes the form of written records and exchanges instead of dialogue, but all the narrating in it is like that of characters in a play; none of it is in the author's voice, speaking to us directly.

Even Cornelius Nepos, the panegyrical Roman biographer, extracts from whose commonplace book (simulated) figure importantly through the volume, little by little becomes a person in his own right, dim but idiosyncratic in the background, messengering and chorusing. The believability and the differentiation of the entire cast of characters, the servants, the police spies, ill-natured but exquisitely intelligent Cicero, the old Roman ladies, the Egyptian queen, are uncanny; each and every one with his or her general frame of mind, momentary state of mind, and peculiar, non-negotiable style of communication.

◆

Harper & Brothers, his publishers (from *Heaven's My Destination* on) as well as mine, asked me for a written opinion of *The Ides of March*, and used this in an advertisement. (Not having the least understanding of what sells books, I guess, I asserted that it was the finest novel in the language since Maugham's *Christmas Holiday;* a decade.) I also wrote to Wilder personally at some length, which pleased him, and led in the course of 1948 and 1949 to an exchange of letters, four or five each; happy and earnest communications.

This mysterious era of ours, the general impression notwithstanding, has been blessed with a good many important and abundant letter writers: among others, E. M. Forster, Katherine Anne Porter,

Raymond Mortimer, Lewis Mumford (Van Wyck Brooks tells me), and others. Wilder is one of the best. Naturally his correspondence is more impulsive in style than anything else he writes (or anything else that he lets us see). Its brilliance is in detail, and in the animation of his ideas, kaleidoscopic, often wth several kinds of writing in the same envelope, even on the same page: sometimes concise and intense, particularly when it has reference to some piece of work that he has in hand; sometimes just fluent and indulgent, friendship-enhancing; sometimes with an explosive brightness, squandering energy in every phrase, as it were bits and pieces of aphorism and epigram and even oracle.

I was reminded to look up one of those letters of 1948°by a point that he made about his new one-act plays in the *New York Times* article in November, 1961. The note of happy portentousness, even jubilation, in his replies to Arthur Gelb's questioning, chiefly referred to their having a great over-all theme, or I should say, two great parallel and connecting themes: the seven stages or phases of the physical life, babyhood and childhood and immaturity and maturity and postmaturity and senescence and ripeness for death, and the seven key weaknesses and errors that in due course bring about a corresponding decadence and breakdown of the spirit—"things that repeat and repeat and repeat in the lives of the millions." Pride and avarice and envy, lust and anger and gluttony and sloth, are in every home, he told Gelb; and with universal subject matter of that magnitude, the creative man, by realizing and exteriorizing the public consciousness and conscience, can help everyone. The creative playwright especially; for in the theatre, as Victor Hugo said, "the mob becomes a people."

Century after century, Wilder said to Arthur Gelb, every mature literary artist has tried to forge or to crystallize some definite statement of his philosophy; and he went on to cite various instances of summarizing, culminating, consummating art, the lifelong cerebration and passion all in focus and in one structure: Ibsen's *Peer Gynt,* Eugene O'Neill's vast chronicle play (not terminated because his health failed), Beethoven's opuses 130, 131, 132, and 135.

In his letter to me dated May 23, 1948, he said that for some time he had been seeking or at least desiring a large and fundamental concept and project to work on, and asked me to think about it, so that presently he could come and discuss it with me. "A writer spends his time hunting for his real right subject; that subject which Meredith never found, which Cervantes almost missed, which Henry James caught three times, and so on—and where is mine?"

Can one, he wondered, arrive at one's principal and final theme by contemplation or calculation, or must it be heaven-sent? Can one even, by taking thought, preserve oneself from this or that erroneous undertaking or hollow, infertile concept? All this was what he wanted us to have a good long talk about.

◆

Needless to say, the prospect of that talk pleased me. As it happened, we did not have it that year. One of his sisters succumbed to a painful illness, arthritis or perhaps a displaced vertebral disk. After that he and she traveled to Dublin, and then he went up into the Engadine on what he called "a Nietzsche pilgrimage." Also he had to give a seminar at the American-financed post-war emergency university in Frankfurt am Main. German, he told me, was his most proficient, lifelong foreign language, and he had never before had a chance to use it.

Finally he asked me to dine alone with him at the Hotel Gotham in New York in April, 1949, which of course I accepted with alacrity and immense expectation. During dinner, served to us on a wheeled-in table in his sitting room, we did not broach any of our premeditated professional or vocational subject matter. We have a slight family connection: one of his cousins is married to one of my brother's wife's half-sisters. One of my sisters is an upper-echelon employee at Harper's and from time to time concerns herself with his published work. Another of my sisters was then in psychoanalysis, with complications of marriage and employment and place of residence. Of this assortment of kith and kin we gossiped in the mildest and most ordinary way, moralizing or philosophizing just a little, with perhaps one shared prejudice running through it all: the feeling, in which almost all creative persons indulge occasionally, that our keeping in a good frame of mind for our work's sake is more important than any of the aspirations, the anxieties, or the tribulations of the bourgeois, even the bourgeois to whom we belong, whom we love.

Then the room-service waiter wheeled his table back out of the room. With a somewhat stepped-up or keyed-up hospitality at that point, my host pushed two armchairs into a sort of debating position, catty-corner. The waiter returned with two bucketfuls of ice, and Wilder brought out of his bedroom two bottles of good whiskey, to each of us his own bottle, and we got down to brass tacks—"burning questions of métier," as he put it.

I think it must be characteristic of him to express a considerable humility about what he has written, especially his novels, but to rouse himself up in a very different temper, courteous, but not at all submissive, when he has occasion to play the part of a critic or a teacher. As to the theme of the evening, proposed by him almost a year in advance: the mature artist's having to discover and decide upon a major subject matter for the latter part of his working life, it was connected in my mind, in the way that I wanted to expound it, with my enthusiasm about *The Ides of March*.

He had no patience with that approach whatsoever. Wilder the proud critic wanted not to have to hear about Wilder the modest creator. Oh, to be commended generously by me, he said, was bound to set off in his mind "a hurly-burly of self-examination, self-reproach, mixed with delight, yes, delight!"

Not entire delight! He could not help lamenting the negligences and the short cuts that he observed in the novel of Julius Caesar's Rome, and that surely, with my eagle eye, I too must have observed. "How I go through life," he exclaimed, "postponing the book that I shall find worthy of being really worked at, someday!"

I too take pride in my criticism; but if I have an eagle eye, it is to see merit somewhat more clearly than demerit; and it seemed to me that I could vouch for the immense merit of *The Ides of March*. In my almost gluttonous interest and enjoyment I had put it to the test. Having read it to my heart's content in the ordinary way, I had immediately reread it aloud to one friend, and afterward read important passages to a number of friends on various occasions.

When one praises Wilder, he takes it very alertly and earnestly, as though he mistrusted one about it. Thus my stating that I had discovered great beauty and significance in his novel by reading and rereading it aloud seemed to worry him more than it pleased him. "Indeed you could do what a good actor does for a weak play: subtly right the balances, tactfully fill the hiatuses, to keep it from seeming what it must seem to any inattentive reader: a sedulous array of erudition, a painstakingly assembled mosaic!"

During this self-deprecatory talk, gradually, by his own eloquence, he cheered himself up; and he gave me credit for his pleasanter feeling. "Heartwarming it is to know that, when it fell into place in your mind, you could see its shortcomings, and yet, as you say, love it. Because with all its incompleteness it asks to be loved. A good many of its critics have denied that. It has been called frigid, when it is all for fun and all about the passions. It has been called calculated, when it is recklessly spontaneous. It has been called hard, when it is all atremble."

Now let me interrupt Wilder's discourse for a moment to say to you that I am well aware of the improbability of my having remembered the things he said to me twelve years ago, word for word, with his very punctuation, his pauses for breath, and the cadences of his light and virile voice. Especially in case of a literary conversation, touching upon the creative insecurity and ambition, hope and bad conscience, a writer's memory is less reliable than it is retentive. I should not have had the courage to put in quotation marks so important a part of his hypotheses and beliefs about his writing as of that date, save for the fact that in one of his letters preliminary to our dining together he had dealt with some of those same thoughts. I have let my memory and my pen be guided by certain of those written sentences, honorably endeavoring to make this a truthful record, but with perhaps a fiction writer's truthfulness rather than that of a journalist or a scholar.

What a talker he was, and still is! What a performer! It amuses me to find that in this evocation of him I cannot exactly recall how he sits or takes a chair. In my mind's eye he is always springing to his feet. Every time I opened my mouth, or almost every time, he would advance upon me and talk me down, using the stiffest forefinger in the world for emphasis, beating time for his ideas, Toscanini-like!

Sometimes, perhaps when a part of his argument seemed to him crucial or difficult, he would pause briefly, and his upper lip would descend rather firmly upon his lower lip, which made his minimum mustache bristle. His eyes brightened amazingly, like those of certain small animals, such as shrewmice and porcupines, which have a high metabolism and consequently extreme appetite, hunger pains, morning noon and night.

Principally, he thought of the novelist as what the Germans call a "Menschenkenner," an instinctive understander of the workings of the mind and the mysteries of emotion of all sorts of humanity; and he believed that he ought to be omniscient, or to feel omniscient, or at least, for the form's sake, to pretend to be. Tolstoi, for example, as I remember his eloquently declaring some years later, when the National Institute of Arts and Letters awarded him its Gold Medal for Fiction, "was like a great eye, above the roof, above the town, above the planet, from which nothing was hid"—comprehensive, steady, blinking at nothing, with (so to speak) twenty-twenty vision.

The idea most vigorously expounded by him at the Gotham was that the development of introspective psychology and other such explorations by scientists and sociologists of our human causes and effects, motivations and miscarriages and violences—all that strong sequence of ideas which Balzac suggested to Charcot, and which Freud derived from Charcot and developed in his revolutionizing world-wide way, followed of course by Watson and Kinsey and other American researchers—have profoundly disturbed and overthrown that omniscience. The creative writer is no longer regarded as the humanity expert, and often ceases to seem authoritative even to himself.

With slight amendments or emendations I could adhere to this theory. Not even Tolstoi (I thought), certainly not Balzac or Dostoevski or Dickens, could actually know and understand and, in the godlike way, rightly evaluate human nature in its entire extent and inner profundity, but they *felt* able to do so. And, buoyed up by that feeling, they never hesitated to invent and to present and to set in motion, in the midst of life, all types of men, women, and children; to reveal and expound their inarticulate thoughts and inexpressible emotions, putting words in their mouths, ventriloquizing for them; and thus to give a universal or at least general eloquence to their crowded scenes and complex plots.

Whereas, in fact, since the turn of the century, novelists for the most part have been retreating from this kind of maximum and multifarious enterprise, evading the issues of the all-round creative power and all-embracing characterization and universal spokesmanship, by means of various modernizations of form, complexities of style, concentrating more and more on their own autobiographical substance, as to which they can be as authoritative and godlike as they please—who is to gainsay them? And thus the narrative art has been weakened, disembodied, and scaled down; self-consciousness prevailing over both universality and popularity.

It was superb. We were like a couple of baritones or bassos in one of those rather brawling duets of conspiracy and challenge which enrich the operas of Bellini and of Verdi in his youth; and as it must be also (I suppose) in the confraternity of vocalists, there arose a feeling of perfect friendship between us, not attentuated or embarrassed in the least by our differences of opinion about those mysteries of the literary art: authority and self-confidence, characterization and analysis, psychology and morals.

I remember voicing a few objections to his thesis as somewhat too eloquently and too simply stated that night, but I cannot recall whether he accepted or refuted them. Toward midnight, perhaps we both began talking at once, in fugue rather than antiphon, and more or less nonstop. The evasion of the responsibility of omniscient understanding, I said, first became crucial in the novels of Henry James; that novelist in the important autumnal part of his colossal lifework situating himself always at a remove or two from his dramatis personae, mostly just overhearing them as they gossip with and about one another, in indefatigable supposition and subjunctiveness, in a guessing game. Which was before the influence of Freud took effect, wasn't it?

A great deal of twentieth-century novel writing, it occurred to me —Henry James in his great late phase as aforesaid, and Joyce, and Gertrude Stein, and Kafka—fell somewhat farther short of my expectations and requirements than of Wilder's. *The Golden Bowl* and *Finnegans Wake* and *The Making of Americans* and *The Trial* and *The Castle* were arch-examples of the withering away or frittering away of the novelist's old authoritativeness, and general and objective knowledge, and firm grasp of human nature. As the author of *The Ides of March* admired these modernistic masterpieces, what made him complain so fervently of the decline of the traditional forms of fiction?

We both were complaining of ourselves, in self-defense and for self-discipline, mustering up courage and whistling in the wind, the immense dark eclectic self-conscious argumentative modern wind. In this connection let me note an odd thing about Wilder's literary taste. Surely a classicist as a writer, rational and liberal in meaning and message, lucid and moderate and almost popular in style, he has always been something of a romantic as a reader. Year in and year out, I remember, he has been in an all-out enthusiasm about, and more or less actively campaigning to promote, this or that extreme genius: all the above-mentioned, and even Sartre, and in nineteenth-century literature, Kierkegaard and even the Marquis de Sade.

That year of our great debate was his Kafka year; or was that 1948? "The great Jew returning to the realm of international literature," as he wrote to me, "fiercely honest but with a featherlight subtlety, splitting hairs but never trivial." Indeed he proposed to incorporate some of the influence of the author of *The Trial* and *The Castle* in a play to be entitled *The Emporium*, which I think he did not finish, in any case has not produced. "I am never ashamed of my imitations," he said. "I reel from intoxication to intoxication."

We kept up our two-man symposium until about 2:30 A.M.; and

then my blessed friend, inspirer, tormentor, followed me down out of the hotel, explaining that he was too overstimulated to go to bed; he would have to take a long walk; and away he went, down Fifth Avenue, in the dimness of the April night, under the glaring and lonely street lights. Unlike him in this respect (as in other respects) I was stumbling with fatigue, and my head had begun to ache. But I too felt some euphoria in my way, at least optimism, as to the infinitudes of artistic and literary form—is there anything more cheering to a man of the arts or a man of letters than that?—and as to the eternal interestingness of human nature; no one more interesting than Wilder.

◆

Looking backward upon that night at the Gotham, mocking my great fellow writer a little, mocking myself quite a lot, I have sometimes said to myself, and perhaps to one or two friends with a particular interest in the literary life and a sense of humor about it, that the gist of our conversation was simply, on my part, as a novel reader, an ardent desire to have another historical novel by him at his earliest convenience, or sooner; and on his part, somewhat less simply, a challenge and a directive to me to try to write objectively, extravertedly, in the great tradition somehow, and perhaps a vague wish to counteract influences that Freud and Kinsey and other such might be having on me, as to the possible use of my private life as raw material for fiction up ahead.

Allowing fully for my somewhat extravagant humorousness and ironic sense, this particular backward glance has troubled me, because neither of us, in fact, has produced a novel since then.

I wonder if my very personal reader-appetite and my program for him vexed him in his pride a little. For historical fiction, even the romantic and meaningful kind, which is the nearest thing we have to the poetical chronicle plays of the Greeks and the Elizabethans, has declined in prestige in recent years, although we have distinguished exponents of the form, and although they (and the host of undistinguished producers of what may be called costume novels) cater to a very large reading public. In the hierarchy of the old masters of fiction, Walter Scott himself now has to sit well below the salt. Everyone loves *Madame Bovary,* while no one cares for *Salammbô.* There is no denying the sublime general power and lovely evocativeness of *War and Peace,* but the chapters about Napoleon, his invasion of Russian and defeat by the climate and the Russian people and historic bad luck, bore us now. Mann's tetralogy of ancient Israel and Egypt is less rewarding to the common reader than *The Magic Mountain,* less impressive to up-to-date intellectuals than *Dr. Faustus.*

In so far as Wilder vaguely imagined my embarking on an indiscreet, inauspicious kind of fiction writing, and was opposed to it, I will vouch for his having intended this opposition kindly, constructively. Just as he had keenly felt my fatuity about the extent of my success when I was a young prize-novelist, perhaps now it seemed to him that I had no idea of the trouble I might make for myself and others by my pen; and perhaps he thought me braver in that way than I have ever been in fact.

With these several wonderments in mind, and all the while, diligently though not effectively, endeavoring to produce first one novel, then another, naturally I gave great thought to our Gotham subject matter: what has deterred or delayed or abashed or confused or enfeebled novelists in recent years. The more I thought of it, the more closely I found myself agreeing with him about the anti-creative side effects of Freudian psychotherapy and of various other social sciences.

But I also developed some ideas of my own, which let me mention with as little elaboration as I can manage.—

First, journalism, wonderful modern journalism, has had a worse impact on the art of the novel than any of the sciences. Not only has it lured away a great personnel of talented narrators, it has moved into, if not taken over, important areas of subject matter. In Balzac's time, when an ambitious and serious youngster arrived in the national metropolis and capital, needing to know what made the wheels go round, the interworkings of love-life and fashion and finance and politics and religion, he read Balzac. The corresponding twentieth-century youngster in New York or Washington reads mainly newspapers and magazines. Balzac put a good many journalists in the *Comédie Humaine,* with a vision of their future magnitude, but they gave him little competition.

Second, Flaubert has haunted literature and literary criticism for a century (somewhat as Aristotle haunted the philosophy and theology of the Middle Ages), and his example and cult have made novel writing harder for the serious, self-respecting writer. It had not occurred to anyone before him to try to apply the perfectionism of the poets to the vastest form of fiction—even a small novel is longer than any epic.

Balzac, as his indefatigably corrected proofs attest, wrote as well as he knew how, but he had no conception of the tightness of construction, the fine focus, the mastery of language—the unique and exact word for everything, exactly in place everywhere—and the absolute euphony, as it were someone singing in a dream, that Flaubert attempted. Fiction was Balzac's livelihood, in an extravagant, heroic way. Flaubert was a man of means. He was as strong as an ox and he dedicated himself, consecrated himself, to his work, like a mystic or a saint; but produced relatively few novels.

The great fiction writing of the nineteenth century went on rather in Balzac's footsteps or Scott's than in his, but meanwhile his concept of the art gestated or incubated in the minds of the molders of opinion, the arbiters of taste, for the twentieth century. Some of the Flaubertian fiction writers, those who descended from the master of Coppet through Maupassant, have systematized their novel writing and narrowed it down, in order to combine a measure of craftsmanship and fine finish with a desired expeditiousness and productivity: Maugham for example; Colette for example, in another way. Others have engaged in herculean minutiae of form and style, and broken their hearts, broken their backs: Virginia Woolf for example, whose swift and copious Balzac-like journal, when it can be published, will surely outweigh *Mrs. Dalloway* and *The Waves.*

Third, the economics of writing and publishing at present are unfavorable to the art of the novel. Indeed more than any other classification of free-lance literature (except the drama), it lures one with the possibility of making a good living. But because of the lengthiness and laboriousness and slowness of the form, and the concentration of mind that one must bring to bear on it, novel writing is a full-time occupation. Talented youngsters, with the dynamism of youth—their minds still rather uncluttered, their hearts not too full, their subject matter still simple—can demonstrate their talent well enough, while at the same time gainfully employed in some other way. But often this kind of initial success is a mixed blessing, because the successful ones expect themselves to continue the double working life, and others expect it of them. But in the long run, as a rule, if one makes an avocation of the narrative art, giving it only evenings, weekends, vacations, sabbaticals, the product weakens or worsens. It is advisable not to undertake full-length fiction writing unless one is sure of being able to produce a great quantity of it in a popular vein, or unless one has an independent income.

Fourth, cosmopolitanism and social mobility have complicated the problem of narrative realism. To be sure, writers travel around more than they could do in the past, and they are not likely nowadays to be excluded from any society (unless they prefer and provoke exclusion). But, still, the best plots of this day and age are farther flung and more comprehensive and heterogeneous than their experience and competence as a rule. The old novelists wrote about a rather compact society of which they themselves were a part, born and bred, for a reading public which was homogeneous and which they knew well. The contemporary writer almost never achieves that degree of "saturation" with his material (to use Van Wyck Brooks's fine word), or that degree of familiarity with his public.

But this is a challenge, not an impediment; a problem of form and technique, soluble surely. Presently someone will find a way of writing these characteristically modern stories—far-flung as they are, fascinating and meaningful as they are (though only half comprehensible)—more or less as we tell them, viva voce; not buttressed with expertness about business matters and legal matters and local conditions and politics and economics, not verisimilitudinous with effects of diversified conversation, foreign ways of talking, dialects, and mannerisms of the classes and the professions and the proletariats, or otherwise developed in the artful nineteenth-century way; but simply and swiftly, in broad outline, in neo-epic fashion, or as it were another *Thousand and One Nights.*

Fifth, the improvement of the social status of writers in our time, while certainly pleasant and salubrious for us as human beings, has not been entirely to our advantage in the particular enterprise of recording the environing contemporary life. Respectability has been conferred upon us, indeed wished upon us. Our families almost never thrust us out; the communities in which we reside do not snub us or mistrust us. A great many people to whom, at first glance, or at a distance, we would have assigned villains' parts or clowns' parts, turn out to be quite friendly and ordinary and amiable. We develop merits and moderations that are irrelevant to our calling.

Sixth, the multifarious anxiety and inhibition having to do with the use of details of the personality and the experience of real men and women of the writer's acquaintance, for the characterization of the creatures of his fictive world, trouble us profoundly.

If one is to understand this as it is in reality, and as the writer's inspiration and frame of mind are affected by it, one must distinguish between libel and the less specific, less actionable invasions of privacy. Libel, in so far as it may be within the competence of a man of letters (without legal training) to define it, is a representation of something in a man's character and/or circumstances which his friends, his neighbors, his business associates, and other such, will recognize; which therefore will be of assessable damage or disadvantage to him, in the way of impairment of physical or mental health, the diminishment of earning power, the devaluation of property, etc. It is opening a window into a man's life, exposing him to disapprobation and interference. As a rule, with advice of counsel and a modicum of literary aptitude and practice, one can remove from a given work, or sufficiently attenuate in it, grounds for legal action along this line.

The mind of man is a mirror holding up a mirror, looking

at itself. Now and again the mind of the fiction writer, especially, turns the mirror around and holds it up before this or that fellow man, obliging him to look at himself whether he wishes to do so or not; at least flashing in his face the literary brightness and pride and qualitative and evaluative power. Often this seems more invasive of his private life, more shocking to his human, all too human nature than any of the other functions of literature. Most people have no objection to being portrayed in books—ask their permission, they will say yes—but they want the portrayal to correspond to their own view of themselves and to their code of morality and respectability and good taste.

In the nineteenth century, I fancy, one frequented novelists (Balzac, Dickens, even Tolstoi) at one's own risk and peril. And perhaps a good many of those who did so fearlessly, and whom novelists took to be representative of their several social classifications and castes, typical and normal, were in fact exhibitionistic in some way, eager to be fictionalized, immortalized. Others were rather bohemian and disclassed, and had nothing to lose or did not care.

Likewise, today, it may be observed that the concentration and the brunt of our strong, serious, realistic fiction writing falls upon the weak, unfortunate, marginal, and even criminal segments of our society; those who cannot strike back at the writer. Secrets of his own, if he has any, may also entail some self-intimidation—what in depth psychology is called "schamfurcht," shame-fright—but as a rule, novelists' good qualities are more incapacitating than their fears.

A number of the great novelists have seen eye to eye with the majority of their contemporaries and fellow countrymen about moral matters and social problems, which has simplified their relationship to society. Jane Austen, for example, doted on the little world that was hers to portray. Trollope believed in the rise of the great nineteenth-century British middle class, and gladly, helpfully, whitewashed it from top to bottom. Even Proust passionately cared about society, the fierce and cynical and snobbish aristocratic society of Paris, and in the composition of his masterpiece prevaricated to some extent, to protect his own worldly position. This disfigured the work slightly here and there, but his self-respect was not at all undermined or his creativity enfeebled by his having done it. For he believed in the collective living myth that he did it for.

The difference between Proust and Gide in this respect marks another important change in the ethos and the art of fiction. In the order of beliefs in Gide's mind, truth took precedence over everything; nothing in the world was worth a lie. When he had to bypass the reality in any respect, it cost him his self-esteem. He devised some rather abstract, devious, diagonal forms of fiction, so that his truth-telling would not disgrace persons near or dear to him, or break the heart of Mme. Gide, whom he quixotically loved. I believe that he deserved the Nobel Prize, but his novels are not first-rate.

I sometimes say to myself: Ora pro nobis, David Graham Phillips! That most gifted narrator of his generation (certainly more gifted than Dreiser) wrote a story of a poor dishonored girl in a small town, and a poor foolish young man in a small town read it, and jumped to the conclusion that it referred to a misfortune of his own sister's, and in a turmoil of family feeling and morbidity came to New York, discovered where Phillips lived, rented a room in that same street, watched and waited, with a crazier and crazier mind, and finally shot and killed the author. As it appeared afterward, it was an error. Phillips's story either referred to some other girl in some other place or it was a figment, I forget which.

I have a realistic mind; the chances of being murdered seem to me not worth considering. (Automobile accidents and infectious hepatitis are my bugbears.) The thought of hurting any man enough to make him murderous horrifies me.

I sometimes say to myself: Ora pro nobis, Vesalius! At the close of his career, the epoch-making first great anatomist performed an autopsy upon the body of one of his patients whose disease and death had baffled him, and came upon a living, beating heart, and thus accidentally stopped its beating forever.

Now, to recapitulate.—The inspiration of a work of fiction and its primary and principal content are the easy part. Subject matter is apt to be in every man's mind as much as in one's own; it comes to us out of the soul of the world. Polymorphous love, and the universal disasters, tyranny and anarchy and the chaos within, and the irresistible laughing matters, and the fantasies and romanticisms that most effectively ravish one away, despite one's stupors and fatigues and the ruts in one's life—those great themes are common knowledge. Narcissus knows them by heart; are you not he, to some extent, some of the time? Yes, certainly, if you are a writer. The great plots are on every shelf of the library; borrow them (as indeed Wilder advised me to do, decades ago).

However, as Mann noted in his diary at an early stage of the work on *Dr. Faustus,* when you have the concept and plot of a novel well in mind, you come to the difficult matter of "stuffing the book with characters." For which purpose, he said, "much full-bodied reality is needed"; one suffers, and the work of narrative art suffers, from "a deficiency of concrete observation."

Plot in itself and by itself is never (or almost never) a very strong or convincing aspect of a novel. Even things that we see reported in the newspapers every day of our lives, and accept at their face value without a second thought, will not be believable in fiction unless you have substantiated them with minute particulars, "thefts from reality" (Mann's phrase), imprints of living flesh.

As I have noted elsewhere, Balzac himself, who wound up his plots like an Elizabethan or a Jacobean dramatist—now like Shakespeare, now like Ben Jonson, now like Webster or Ford—said that what interests one in a novel, in the last analysis, is the quantity of glimpsed detail, the asides and the incidents along the way; not the over-all turn of events or the holocaust at the close or the happy ending.

Somehow the modern creative mind, though inarticulate, though inhibited, seems more in love with the creations (so to speak) of the Creator than great writers have been in the past. Perhaps this is because the concept of a supernatural author of the world is no longer very convincing or clear to us. We fall back on the particulars. Only the whole seems able to invent a detail, we think. Only the almighty, the inexorable, the arch-creator, can come up with a face, an outcry, a body odor, a footprint, and other minutiae that give life to a universal theme. Gide used to say that, even to change the color of the iris of someone's eye, in the transposition from human actuality to the fictitious form of it or substitute for it, falsified the record. Nothing that could ever be invented or fabricated, he thought—and many of us also think—could compare with what we have seen, heard, touched, enjoyed, embraced or been embraced by, hurt or been hurt by. This does not make novel writing easier for us. It seems, sometimes, to make it impossible.

Blessed or sacrosanct uninventible detail! When it is human detail, by virtue of its uninventibility, verging on uniqueness or at least great idiosyncrasy, it points to the source, the model, the individual prototype. And the trouble with the old true form of the novel, in this as in other respects, is its length and breadth. It covers so much ground, it eats up so vast an amount of raw material.

The drama does not require this high degree of plausibility and closely knit sequence of motivations. The physical presence of the actor, for one thing, has a unifying effect; it binds up implausibilities and non sequiturs that in a mere narration would break the spell. Furthermore, a play is a short work—only a little longer than a short story, a little less long than a nouvelle—and it requires far less of the precious and perishable human substance.

The crux of the matter of the novel is character, characterization, portraiture. The very significant point made by Wilder that night at the Gotham was the undermining of the authority and self-assurance of the novelist, even that questionable opinionatedness which once served him well. If you feel authoritative enough, you can start with a theme, a hypothesis, a passage of history, or an item of the day's news, and concoct or formulate (true or false) the persons involved, that is, to be involved, as the work progresses. If you do *not* feel authoritative, and you want your portraits to be verisimilitudinous, your plot to be plausible—the causes and effects in your cross section of human nature to work, to convince, and to edify—you probably will have to start with characteristics of actual humanity, flesh and blood.

But must characters in a novel always be convincing? The human comedians of Balzac really never fooled anyone, except Balzac. The essential appears to be the entrancement and the hallucination of the novelist himself. Balzac carried around in his head some two thousand men, women, and children, and seems never to have made any listing of their names, their dates, their various shifting residences and other vital statistics, and scarcely ever made a mistake. On his deathbed he cried out, "Bianchon! Send for Bianchon! He alone can cure me!" Bianchon was the fictitious great doctor in the *Comédie Humaine.*

The great and grave questions for the novelist are: What persons can you get to pose for your portraits? Can you paint them as you see them, or do they look over your shoulder, and protest and lament, and flee away? To what extent does your anxiety about portraying people reflect and disguise a fear of self-portraiture, self-betrayal? Do you feel free to use the human material that appeals most strongly to your imagination? Or have you had to give a lien or a mortgage on it to those who provided it in the first place? Must you work only with your second-string experience, second-hand knowledge of the world?

◆

This has no great bearing on *The Ides of March* because there is a minimum of portraiture à clef in it. I have spoken of that beautiful lovelorn girl, self-destroyed so many years ago, of whom Wilder at the time seemed to disapprove, perhaps finding it difficult, as his Caesar coldly explains to Clodia, "to be indulgent to those who despise and condemn themselves." A female friend of mine believes that the character of the wise and tender aging actress, Cytheris, was modeled upon a certain friend of hers and of Wilder's. Her reasons for believing it are not convincing to me. But if I were Wilder I should have no objection to the lady's thinking of herself as Cytheris to some extent, if it seemed to her a happy thought.

There is almost always some derivation of that sort in novels. When someone questioned Proust about the sources of certain characterizations in *À la Recherche du Temps Perdu,* the supreme masterpiece of modern fiction, he said, "A book is a great cemetery in which, on most of the gravestones, the names have worn smooth and are indecipherable." And, as a rule, I may add, the novelist buries a number of his dead in the same grave.

The political resemblances in *The Ides of March* are of obvious interest. Even as late as 1948, one could not read any account of the life and death of Caesar without being reminded of Mussolini. Wilder must have intended to allude to some of the recent history of our transatlantic democracy as well, perhaps to point a moral to well-meaning men in politics and in the government service. With scarcely an incongruity, Cicero's criticism of Caesar, perspicuously bracketing the private personality and the public exercise of power, might have been applied to Franklin D. Roosevelt by Senator Taft or some other respectable conservative of that generation.

The dedication page of *The Ides of March* reads as follows: "To two friends: Lauro de Bosis, Roman poet, who lost his life marshaling a resistance against the absolute power of Mussolini: his aircraft pursued by those of the Duce plunged into the Tyrrhenian Sea; and to Edward Sheldon, who though immobile and blind for over twenty years was the dispenser of wisdom, courage, and gaiety to a large number of people."

Thus avowedly the novelist's admiration of those two modern personages entered into his portrayals of the poet Catullus and of Caesar's invalid friend Turrinus. Which enables me, for what little light it may shed on the processes of fiction, to compare and contrast Wilder's characters with a few superficial remembrances of my own, legendry of a society in which I too have moved slightly, as it were a juxtaposition of two painted or sculptured figures, nobly posed and costumed, toga-clad and sandal-shod, richly framed or loftily pedestaled, with a handful of snapshot photographs.

Lauro de Bosis translated some plays by Sophocles and Frazer's *The Golden Bough,* and wrote the prize poem for the Olympic Games in 1928, the subject of which was the fall of Icarus. After that he came to New York in the employ of an Italian-American cultural organization, and a little later taught at Columbia University. In New York he met and was loved by an older woman, the greatly gifted and successful monologuist, Ruth Draper.

In 1930 he revisited his native land, by which time the Fascist regime had bitterly disappointed him; and he wrote a diatribe against Mussolini, to be mimeographed and mailed to hundreds of sympathetic persons all over Italy, all of whom presumably would forward copies to their friends, snowballing in every direction with perhaps devastating effect. Reportedly, it was Bernard Shaw who suggested to Ruth Draper's young friend that this be done.

He himself returned to New York, leaving the further handling of the campaign to two associates. Someone tipped off the Fascist police. The mimeograph machine having been discovered in the apartment of Signora Adolfo de Bosis, the poet's American-born mother, she and the associates were arrested and brought to trial. She made a personal appeal to the Duce and escaped punishment. The associates were given long prison sentences.

I never heard Ruth Draper tell any part of this story. R. L. Cottenet, an old friend of hers and mine, used to say that in all probability Signora Adolfo de Bosis gave some information prejudicial to her son's associates, perhaps unwittingly; that in any case Lauro de Bosis believed that this had happened, and felt dishonored by it and bitterly undeserving of his own good fortune, safe and sound in exile. He considered returning to Italy in defiance of the dictatorship, but Ruth Draper and other friends persuaded him not to. It would have meant immediate arrest and imprisonment, while serving no particular purpose; and doubtless it would have reinvolved his mother and other sympathetic and blameless persons.

Then, at his wit's end, he decided to manifest his convictions and emotions from the air over Rome, somewhat as d'Annunzio had done over Vienna toward the end of World War I. He composed another subversive text and had it printed in great quantity on featherweight paper. Ruth Draper made him a present of a small airplane. He took flying lessons in England, and with a minimum number of hours of solo flying to his credit, started toward his native land. That first flight was unsuccessful. He came down in

K

Corsica, doing himself no injury, but smashing his plane and strewing his manifesto around the wild irrelevant Corsican countryside. This mishap only intensified his feelings, both patriotic and personal.

Therefore he had a second edition of his manifesto printed, and persuaded his famous friend to buy him another airplane, and on a Saturday afternoon in October, 1933, did reach the Eternal City and showered it with the provocative slips of paper. It was rumored that some slips descended upon the Duce personally, irritating him so that he broke an armchair. Planes of the Fascist air force were alerted and pursued the poet out to sea, and in due course came back to their bases, presumably licking their chops, but declaring that he had outdistanced them. No trace of him or of the second plane was ever found.

Now that he is dead and gone, one is aware of a dark or at least cloudy aspect of his character and fate, with his great distress like a lightning-flash at the heart of it, and the flashing seems almost aimless; at any rate he never aimed it very well. Perhaps ambiguity was a part of his charm: as a man of literary temperament bravely but ineffectually engaged in the life of action; as an expatriate (to some extent) even before it became necessary for him to think of himself as an exile; as the Italian son of an American mother, bitterly resentful of her helpfulness but also profoundly appreciative of it, with another mature American woman close to him, willing and able to help him vindicate himself, though probably not seeing eye to eye with him about his situation. In Italy and in England there have been some controversial magazine articles about all this. I am inclined to think that the moral of his story is a matter of cosmopolitanism rather than patriotism and political idealism.

Now that we have seen what it took in fact to dislodge Mussolini: a huge and desperate and extremely harmful war, Lauro de Bosis' Icarus-like, Catullus-like, d'Annunzio-like deed—and likewise the masterminding of Bernard Shaw, in this as in other connections during his long lifetime—may strike us as foolish and unreal. The whole of his life, climaxed by that, would serve as the plot of a

Balzac type of novel, if any modern novelist happened to have international journalistic experience enough to handle its foreign scenes and the several heterogeneous societies involved in it, and at the same time sufficiently understood the odd combination of political principle and problematical psychology.

Certainly I do not altogether understand it. Perhaps it is not even exactly true, as I have heard it told and have now retold it. Both Signora de Bosis and Ruth Draper are dead; whom else could an ambitious but scrupulous novelist question? whose exact knowledge of their secrets would put a stop to one's speculation and fantasy? Tales that everyone has respectfully refrained from telling, during the lifetime of those concerned, sometimes go on forever, with a kind of ashamed half-life, unverified, but at the same time unrefuted, unscotched.

It pleases me to recall that I was just lightly brushed by one feather of the wing of the twentieth-century Icarus, the first time he fell, in Corsica. In those days Barbara Harrison, my brother's wife, had a little house in Paris, in the Rue de Vaugirard, across the street from the Senate; and an English friend of hers and of Lauro de Bosis' brought the first edition of his manifesto there, and he picked it up there. When it all came down as though out of a celestial wastebasket over Corsica, a piece of the wrapping paper was still plainly labeled: 32 Rue de Vaugirard, which the Corsican gendarmes spotted and reported to the Sûreté in Paris. She and Monroe Wheeler had been publishing their little series of de luxe books at that address, and in due course they were summoned and lengthily and tediously interrogated. The French notion was that possibly 'Harrison of Paris" was a front for undesirable international propaganda. Bureaucracy in France is a vast pack-rat, my French friends tell me; so perhaps in a cellar or an attic in Paris my dear ones' names are still on file, annotated with the official suspicion and disapproval, as of that date.

During World War II our Federal Bureau of Inquiry sometimes categorized people as having been "prematurely anti-Fascist." Thus, half concealed and half revealed by petty and picturesque details of

one's own life, one can glimpse the vast understandings and mis-
understandings of the nations going on in the century, bringing
about war and peace.

◆

I am a portrait lover, that is, a believer in what one can learn about
people by giving attention to their physiognomy, indeed their entire
physical being. The beauty of Ruth Draper meant a great deal to
me; a gypsy sort of beauty, but with a soft kindly expression and
laughing eyes. You could see that she took the greatest pleasure in
her perceptions of people, but that she was not sure enough of
herself to criticize them or judge them severely. As a performer she
had very proud and commanding postures and movements, but her
manner in private was modest, almost ordinary. It is because I have
her fond, keen face in my mind's eye that I understand her
affection and loyalty and (in the end) absolute sadness better than
anything else in the romantic story of de Bosis.

There is a bust of him in Rome, up on the Janiculum, near the
American Academy; it is said not to be a good likeness. I might have
caught sight of him in New York or in London; I never did.

The other extraordinary personage praised by Wilder on the
dedication page of *The Ides of March* I did see during the winter
of 1941-42 and remember vividly. Somerset Maugham, as an old
friend, suggested his inviting me to lunch, and urged or com-
manded me to accept the invitation. As a young man of romantic
appearance and lovable character, so described by Maugham, he
had written two triumphantly successful plays, *Romance,* played by
Doris Keane, and *Salvation Nell,* played by Mrs. Fiske. When
scarcely middle-aged, he suffered a sudden appalling breakdown of
his health, and for many years after that, bedridden and blind, he
lived on in a rather grand though tragic way, with his devoted
mother near at hand, and with competent and devoted employees
caring for him and enabling him to extend hospitality to an elite
of the theatre and to other friends, whom (as Wilder's dedication
attests) he inspired, advised, and influenced. Playwrights read suc-

cessive versions of their plays aloud to him; actors and actresses performed important scenes at the foot of his bed, on a make-believe stage, forever dark, but doubtless illumined for him by his past experience of the theatre and his subtle intelligence.

His knowledge of literature and the arts and whatever else was going on in the metropolis, with a natural emphasis on the performing arts, was extensive and definite. One could scarcely imagine his deriving so much just from friends visiting him, secretaries reading aloud; and a New Yorker of my acquaintance believed, or pretended to believe, to make a good story and a point, that his blindness and paralysis were in some measure an artifice; that occasionally in the middle of the night he would arise and disguise himself and slip out into the city. What for? not in any case to make mischief or simply to pursue pleasure—according to everyone he was a saint as well as a martyr, an ascetic as well as an aesthete—but conceivably to find out about things and to make himself useful to people he cared for, at rehearsals, first nights, vernissages, and publishers' parties, or perhaps to visit, inspirationally or consolingly, someone else's sickbed even crueler than his own.

Lunching with him was an odd and uneasy experience. He lived in a penthouse apartment, and as I remember, a separate elevator deposited me up there in a small square foyer, where I was asked to wait, surrounded by doors and by voices beyond the doors; perhaps a secretary's voice, a nurse's voice, a cook's voice. Presently one of them summoned me through one of the doors and left me standing in the center of a large room, facing a richly draped bed; and there lay Sheldon's handsome head on a small black pillow, wearing a black half-mask; and his sweet, strong voice told me to approach and to sit in an armchair exactly placed, near him.

The way the bed was draped contributed to the uncanny, I am tempted to say occult, impression that Edward Sheldon made on the unaccustomed visitor. A Persian rug, or it may have been just a heavy brocade, was drawn quite smooth and flat across it, and hung foursquare to the floor, with not the least mound or hump or other indication of the crippled body stretched out under it. In fact it must not have been stretched out, but curled up in a hollow space

contrived for it by the upholsterer's art, as it were a precious bibe-
lot in a jeweler's box or a delicate scientific or surgical instrument
in a fitted case.

It was like a dream; or like something in a surrealist painting,
or in an existentialist play or in one of Isak Dinesen's Gothic
tales. I was struck by the fine healthy texture of his cheeks and
mouth beneath the half-mask, by the rosiness of his complexion.
He told me that in clement weather, even in winter, he had his bed
wheeled out on the penthouse terrace, which kept him agreeably
sunburned. Just then a manservant happened to be out there,
feeding pigeons. Presently the vast banshee sound of the air-raid
siren arose over the city, and it was either the first test of it, or the
first time that I happened to be in town to hear it tested. As we
spoke of this I was impressed by Sheldon's lack of interest; certainly
the oncoming of the war did not frighten him or worry him.

Some weeks after that I called on him again, and then the contact
between us lapsed. As one of his familiar friends explained, he
never wanted anyone to visit him out of a sense of duty or sympathy,
and perhaps I had not sufficiently pressed for another invitation. In
fact, I had not enjoyed my two visits.

Mrs. Flint, the great-lady professor at the University of Chicago
who, in 1917 or 1918, first told me that I had literary ability—in
fact she went a little further than that, in the over-enthusiastic style
of the higher education of those days—was a cousin of Sheldon's. I
remember his asking me why I had left the university without even
a B.A., what had motivated my long sojourn in France, what was
the ratio of fact and fiction in *The Grandmothers,* and what had
caused me to become interested in falconry. I guessed that he had
done a little homework about me, aided by a secretary.

The intensity of my interest in him, perhaps I should say curiosity about him, made me shy. For some reason I often feel disinclined
to ask direct questions; it is easier for me to *be* questioned. But I
take very little pleasure in hearing myself talk about myself, unless
the theme is something that has just occurred to me or just happened to me.

When I reported back to Somerset Maugham that I had failed to make friends with his strange, wonderful fellow playwright, he expressed disappointment but not astonishment. He was never a man easy to astonish. The next time I saw him he confided to me a theory that he had hit upon, as to the cause and nature of Sheldon's ill-health.

I remember that we were sitting in his sitting room at the Hotel Ritz-Carlton, and just as he broached this topic, the room waiter came in with a martini or perhaps a gimlet; he gave an emphatic discreet look and waited until we were alone; then he heard the chambermaid in the adjacent bedroom, and rose and softly closed that door. What he was about to tell me evidently seemed to him a serious matter or a scandal.

It had never satisfied poor Sheldon, he said, to be well-known and successful along with the other accomplished comedy-writers and melodrama-writers of those days, such as Maugham himself, and Clyde Fitch and Henry Arthur Jones and Pinero and Barrie and Sardou. He wanted to be great, great like (let us say) Shakespeare; that is to say, in contemporary terms, like Rostand, like d'Annunzio, or at least like Stephen Phillips. Perhaps these assorted turn-of-the-century dramatists were not the ones Maugham mentioned; but their names will sufficiently suggest the point that he was making: Sheldon's dissatisfaction with his early career, and his perilous further aspiration.

He was a man of independent means. *Romance* especially, which was a perfect vehicle for Doris Keane, who was a perfectly beautiful actress—I saw her in it—had enriched him. He borrowed a theme and a plot from Hans Christian Andersen, the tale of the heartless and immortal mermaid: how she fell in love and then died of a broken heart. Adapting it to suit his own original imagination, he labored away at it for a long while, taking great pains, doing his level best, mustering up his every resource of talent and culture, endeavoring to bring out all the significance and emotion that, in his opinion, pervaded it.

His reputation in the theatre at that point was something to conjure with. A new play by him, especially a more poetical play than his previous contributions to the repertory, was eagerly looked forward to, as a great event in show business and possibly in American theatrical history. Nothing is so likely to succeed, theatre-going New Yorkers think, as the work of writers who have already been successful. Furthermore, they delight in any prospect of a more serious type of drama-writing than the usual box-office fodder, though as a rule, when the curtain goes up, they get bored suddenly.

At last Sheldon finished his work, and after the usual negotiations and intrigues and changes, turned it over to an agent and a producer and a director and a stage designer, and to various performing artists, and to the necessary numerous theatrical proletariat. In due course it was presented under good auspices in a fashionable new theatre, with éclat, painstakingly produced, not counting the cost, and with a cast of able and popular actors; and it flopped.

Not long after this, the dreadful series of Edward Sheldon's ailments began: mysterious arthritis, perhaps a mysterious virus infection, or a cerebral vascular accident, or two or three successive cerebral vascular accidents, and presently, either retinal detachments or an atrophy of the optic nerve in both eyes. Maugham could not remember exactly the various conflicting diagnoses that had been reported to him at the time.

Possibly Sheldon's doctors did not discover what the matter was, what the several successive matters were; if they did, it was never made clear or convincing to his friends and admirers. Perhaps a physiological syndrome and the crisis of talent and disillusionment just happened to coincide. In some cases, we are told, when the initial breakdown has been spiritual, hysterical, the poor body little by little actually and irremediably assumes the role assigned to it by the terrible psyche. Things that were not even noticeable in the first instance get to be undiagnosable. Body and soul intermingle; nothing is worse.

Maugham's talk about all this was prosaic and dry and a little violent, in his way; but obviously it touched him to the heart, and indeed agitated in him something that might be called the fear of God.

It probably was easier for Sheldon to become a genuine martyr than simply to go on as a lost or lapsed genius, a man of mere talent, a Broadway professional, a has-been or a hack. What might be called the finger of God having put his eyes out, twisted him, deadened him, he could forgive himself for the pretentiousness and the weakness of his Hans Christian Andersen play. With the excuse and the disguise of his half-dead body and the endless midnight in his eyes, he could go on believing in the other, better, and still more poetical plays that he might have written.

"Pride is the dangerous sin," Maugham said, "beyond all the other sins."

◆

Now reopen *The Ides of March* and consider what inspiration Wilder derived from these two twentieth-century men in the creation of his two corresponding Roman characters: in the bright light of his history lesson, the shadows cast by them; amid the immemorial passionate colloquy and philosophical discourse, the echoing of their recently departed voices. With his imagination moved by the heroism of the anti-Fascist Italian poet, especially his harassment of Mussolini with seditious texts, and by the helpless, vicarious, inspiring way of life of the New York playwright, he sea-changed them, ennobled them, and above all, simplified them, in the way of epic poetry and dramatic poetry; not in the usual fictitious way.

Indeed Wilder's character creation, in *The Bridge of San Luis Rey* and *The Woman of Andros* as well as in this Roman novel, is the furthest thing in the world from the principles and techniques of eighteenth- and nineteenth-century novel writing which so many of us still follow: imitation and transposition and combination and amplification; every matter of individual humanity and particular circumstance to be substantiated by a quantity of learned and observed fact, and quantitative hallucinating small talk also (vide Jane Austen); every conceivable protagonist to be situated in the midst of an almost scientific ecology, with a substratum of persons less fortunate than he, and a superstructure of persons more fortunate (vide Trollope), and powerful and voluble arguments to prove that he exists, or could have existed (vide Balzac), and a vast sampling of his ideas, and of the author's own ideas (vide George Eliot), sociology and theology and uplift and worldliness and, of course, snobbery.

Neither, for that matter, does the author of *The Ides of March* ever remind us of Walter Scott and his multitudinous progeny throughout the nineteenth century and flourishing still; nor does he conform to the standards of truthfulness and artistry of the more sophisticated present-day practitioners of the historical novel: their mountainous evidences of research, and reflections of and repercussions from the work of previous workers in their area and period, all in a sort of counterpoint of scholarliness, augmenting and inverting and counterstating and resolving things. Rather, he reminds us of Plutarch and Lucian, of the medieval fabulists, and of Voltaire.

Wilder's Catullus must be closer to the actual biographical, historical man than any of his other Romans (except perhaps Caesar). For one thing, he had the mighty, black, and fiery love lyrics, *Odi et ami* and *Nox est perpetua* and the rest, and some of the doggerel against the Dictator, to go by. (Caesar's *Commentarii de bello Gallico* is an oddly impersonal work, almost characterless.)

The perfectionism and puritanism of the Roman poet from Verona, his willingness to be fooled part of the time, and then violently disillusioned, and other fluctuations of the psyche, may be observed in a good many men of amorous disposition, especially those not so highly sexed physically as they would like to be. But if Catullus has feelings of inferiority as a man, they are soon swallowed up in the certainty of his power and glory as a poet. When Clodia deals with him cruelly, he rages back at her in perhaps a worse way: immortal versification worsens it.

To state the matter in its simplest, most obvious aspect: it is a sado-masochistic relationship, in which they both play both roles. Let me remind you that the rather ugly modern word has a wider reference than mere inflictions of pain, dances of death. For example, it may be said to be sadistic to try to compel one's beloved to be more virtuous (or, for that matter, more talented or more beautiful) than he or she is capable of being. Certainly in this sense, as well as in his occasional abusive verses, Catullus cruelly torments Clodia.

Love most ill-advised and incorrigible; love spellbound for a while, then infuriated for a while, drunk on its every satisfaction, and vomiting itself back up when frustrated! It is all a folie à deux, to borrow an old term of jurisprudence, perhaps no longer in use: a crime that might never have happened but for the chance meeting of two unique persons, thus a kind of accident.

However, Clodia is not to be thought of as a passive person, either in love or in her general morality. In a sense, all her life she has looked back in envy of that uncle who raped her, and somewhat imitated him. All her misbehavior is an aggression against people whom she somewhat admires, a violation of traditions and rules that she somewhat believes in. Her very reveling in her own wickedness is an indication of her moral, indeed moralistic feeling.

On the other hand, in a city the size of ancient Rome there are bound to be a good number of virtuous women, and it never occurs to Catullus to pay court to them. What interests him is the far-fetched, improbable, impossible potential of virtue in the mind and heart of just that one mature, post-mature great lady, although she takes pride in her viciousness, or *because* she takes pride in it.

Furthermore, if one thinks of oneself as a wronged lover, and makes a moral issue of it, as Catullus did, surely there must be some complacency in letting oneself be wronged over and over again. Even the murderee, with his last gasp, can be thankful pharisaically for not having been murderous, though perhaps he brought on his fate to some extent. To some extent the mouse seduces the cat.

This ambivalence of course appears in Catullus' lifework not only as subject matter but as style. The bluntness and nakedness of his language almost belie his amorous idealism. Righteous indignation gives him an excuse for passages of feverish and biased erotic writing, and he so exploits it, pretending to be shocked in order to be shocking. As Wilder points out also, he sometimes expresses his detestation of Caesar's politics in terms of a kind of inverted sensuality. Certainly a part of his political thinking was just his jealousy and competitiveness about Clodia.

The truth of the matter of poetry is this.—The important poet is one whose endowment of vocabulary and imagery and style happens to suit the kind of experience that he has had, and keeps on having; or is it the other way round? Does he set out in life to have the experiences that his talent or genius is meant for? Catullus as a poet would have been lost without a Clodia, without a Caesar. With all the energy and intellect that his mastery of expression indicates, he seems not to have experienced anything very intensely or profoundly, *except* subject matter.

What a poet wants, I guess, is to be an everyman in his life, a superman when he takes pen in hand; and as a rule, needless to say, he is neither. He is a combination of the abstract and the animal, of devotion and disgust, flame and flood, truth and delusion, knack and hazard; and it may be a good combination or a bad combination, humanly speaking, but either way the dualities are favorable to his lifework.

◈

Just as Wilder's Catullus personifies poetry, his Turrinus personifies friendship. Presumably his personal familiarity with Edward Sheldon provided the basic concept of the great incapacitated absentee friend, the man of broken body but unvanquished spirit, partaking of others' lives in lieu of a life of his own, worth living. Save for this essential, Turrinus is more imaginary, less historic than the other principal figures in *The Ides of March*.

Or is this another of the errors that, as an autodidact, I naturally fall into? My education in the matter amounts to only a few reference books, a few translations, and certain other works of historical fiction; none of the recondite source materials and off-beat prototypes. I am reminded of my blessed innocence about *The Cabala* years ago, Wilder's correction of which was the first interesting thing I ever heard him say.

At any rate, while counting on his readers' having some slight background about Caesar and Cicero and Cleopatra and even Clodia, he starts from scratch about Turrinus. In the very first notes of the supposed compiler and editor of the fictitious documents of which the book consists, we are given essential information: he is a man haplessly taken prisoner and terribly injured just at the end of the Gallic Wars, now resident on the Island of Capri, to whom, in the interval of five or six years, Caesar has written several letters a week. A little farther along, Caesar's Aunt Julia and another elderly aristocratic woman wonder about him, reminisce about him, and ask the Dictator questions that he does not see fit to answer. Toward the close of the work we are given two letters written to him by the Lady Julia, and two by the actress Cytheris, which add a little perspective to the shadowy portrait.

In the entire mass of imaginary documents there is not one page or paragraph written or dictated by Turrinus himself. For the most part we deduce his qualities from Caesar's correspondence, reflecting their intellectual interests in common.—Poetry and prosody and indeed etymology. The psychology and psychopathology of love, and the ethical issues that arise in this connection. The rites of the old Roman state religion (though neither of them is a believer). Political science, particularly the tremendous and insoluble problems of Caesar's rule, historic (and brand-new in history then). The great premonition of the fate awaiting the Dictator at the hands of the anti-Caesar faction, and all the issues of philosophy that the near prospect of death raises for the man under sentence of death and for those whom he loves and who love him. It is like looking at the mold of clay or wax appertaining to a distant or lost work of art, bronze or terra cotta; and indeed, in friendship, the mind of each one molds and cools and hardens the other.

He was Caesar's intimate, chum, pal, buddy, in their boyhood. They studied together, swam and hunted together, traveled to Greece and Crete together. Wilder says nothing about the nature and custom of the relationship in their prime of life; it must have been close and continuous, for in 51 B.C., when they were middle-aged, they went to war together in Gaul, that is to say, France and Belgium, pitching their tents side by side. There presently Turrinus was captured by the Belgians, and because he would not inform against Caesar, had his ears cropped and his eyes put out, and one arm and one leg cut off, and other unspecified parts of his body mutilated. Caesar counter-attacked and rescued him, almost annihilating one of his regiments in so doing. Since then, with no further capability for the public service, and no interest in any sociability or expectation of pleasure, he has been living secludedly in a walled villa on Capri, where Cytheris sometimes goes to read classical literature to him, and where Caesar spends a few days every spring.

We are given to understand that his sufferings and mutilations have not impaired his faculties of mind and spirit. Caesar speaks of him as the only man alive with an intelligence as important and vigorous as his own and Cleopatra's and Catullus'; and of these three peers, certainly the maimed man is the one he loves best. One-sided friendship is a painful and almost an ugly thing. It can't be helped: the Dictator's devotion to Catullus is rather dutiful and cold, a matter of almost ritual observance of the sacredness of great verse, the impunity of the poet. There is an excess of pride in it, even on Caesar's part, for he must keep reminding himself not to return Catullus' hostility, tit for tat.

Cleopatra delights him: a creature more royal than he, less civilized than he, incorrigibly foreign, and the most feminine of women. In his very last letter to Turrinus he speaks of her enchanting animality combined with rare human qualities. Of the great gulf between the two realms, he says, she has no inkling; and often he seems to think of her as on the far side of that gulf.

Perhaps in his youth and young manhood Turrinus had an animal side; all butchered away now, and the spirit distilled and strengthened. Is there anything more essentially human than self-sacrifice? Also, in the nature of his martyrdom, in the persistence of his cerebral and affective capacities in a body half-dead, there is an image of our absolutely human dream of immortality, which indeed distinguishes us from the other mammals in so far as we are able to believe in it.

Philosophizing at midnight, in the very first of the journal-letters, Caesar is reminded how he and Turrinus used to theorize and argue when they were teen-agers, and quotes Plato's saying that new-bearded boys are the best philosophers in the world. And he, Caesar, the weary and doomed principal chief of state of the known world at that time, writing to the maimed recluse, feels like a boy again.

In the philosophical way surely Turrinus set Caesar a good example, as to fidelity and fortitude and submissiveness to fate. As the ides approached, it was a lesson very applicable to his different ordeal and end. If he felt tempted to dicker with his murderers gradually grouping around him, the thought of the atrocity of the Belgians must have shamed him. His friend having endured so much for his sake, could he now jib at mere assassination?

Very great men as a rule seem incapable of any very satisfactory self-love. They tire themselves out incessantly, and a great part of their work is inward, another part is self-expression and acting out the role of self. Naturally they weary of themselves to the point of surfeit, of dangerous revulsion. The mind of the ideal friend provides a holiday from their drudgery, a shield against their self-criticism and self-bedevilment, a hidden pool in which to wash away whatever has put them to shame, a cool pillow for the hot cheek.

Is this a poor concept of friendship? Indeed I have stated it gloomily, in terms of the extraordinary understanding between the great statesman and that most miserable casualty of the most important of his wars; and certainly it is inequitable in a way. All the sacrificing in it is on Turrinus' part. There appears never to have been any question of Caesar's really devoting himself to his friend, except in thought and correspondence, or of his spending much time in Capri, or ever letting his worldly power and pleasure go.

It corresponds to a perhaps old-fashioned concept of the relations between men and women also, even marital relations, when the man's position or function or vocation or services to general humanity have seemed worth while to the woman concerned. Once in a while, for the sake of some female genius, a man has assumed the role of helpmate. I have in mind, for example, a widow in Germany and a widower in France, whom I need not designate by name to any reader of this volume, to whom everyone in the world who loves literature must be thankful. It is safe to say that they have never regretted their overshadowed way of life.

The oddest and most meaningful detail of the character of Caesar's friend as conceived and narrated by Wilder is his apparently not having any particular talent. Presumably when he had his health he was a political man, a civil servant, a soldier; something of that sort he would have had to be, or make a pretense of being, to keep close to his dear one. In any passage of narration having to do with someone's ability or lack of ability, ambition or lack of ambition, if one is not told what his exact status or undertaking or employment is or has been, I think one may detect a reference to the literary life. For writing is written by writers, and their creative temperament rushes into any little void in their work. And if you consider Turrinus in this light, you will see that he is the very type and ideal and exemplar of the man who happens not to possess, or who happens to have lost, the expressive gift and technical facility to do important creative work, but who greatly inspires and allures and challenges and assists others to do it.

Paul Valéry, the most penetrating aphorist of the century, said, "Talent without genius is nothing much. Genius without talent is nothing at all." It is not easy to differentiate between those two big words. Genius in the abstract, genius by itself, as Valéry refers to it, is the more obscure and dubious condition; it may be somewhat morbid. But obviously the man who has it, though he may be inarticulate, unskilled, perhaps sensually cold, or physically feeble —or in the case of Caesar's friend Turrinus and of Maugham and Wilder's friend Sheldon, prostrate with injury and illness—can give or lend to the man of mere talent, even great talent, something that is essential to a great lifework: vision! incentive! spark! drive!

Indeed, blind and disfigured and broken and vicarious Turrinus is nothing, in his own right. But Wilder suggests that, without him,

Caesar's intellect and skill and energy and physical and mental health might have gone for naught. The ideas that preoccupy them mutually must be mainly Caesar's ideas; all we know of them is what Caesar expresses; but save for Turrinus' ardent interest and valuation, they might not seem to the Dictator worth expressing. Despite blindness and distance and detachment, or because of these disadvantages, Turrinus' watchfulness from afar, his vicariousness, his secondhand participation in Caesar's daily life and innermost preoccupations and historic destiny, are the mirror before which the easy journalistic writer, the busy man of the world, the responsible and insecure chief of state, chiefly contemplates himself, judges what he has done, and decides what to do next. Caesar rescued him just when the Belgians had cropped his ears and were about to pierce his eardrums; and now he is the listener par excellence, to whom the lonely worldling confides his innermost processes of thought and sentiment, even his disbeliefs, and his weariness unto death, his readiness to die, and his dread of dying.

I have known one such man well, for half a lifetime; and perhaps this accounts for a certain irony, almost bitterness, about not having made friends with the author of *Romance* and *Salvation Nell* and of the Hans Christian Andersen play that failed.

◆

Note that Wilder's handling of these two character creations, Catullus (de Bosis) and Turrinus (Sheldon), is more closely comparable to what is called mythopoeism, the hero-making and saint-making and indeed god-making process, than it is to the usual artistry of the novel or the deductive and reconstructive techniques of historial scholarship.

In my résumé of the life and self-sacrifice of Lauro de Bosis and my slight reminiscence of lunching with Edward Sheldon I have emphasized everything that (I thought) might lend itself to fictitious re-creation in the ordinary way; in reconsidering Wilder's Catullus and Turrinus I have stretched every point that might be taken to indicate a biographical or autobiographical impulse. But obviously there is a great gap or gulf between the two men, as I understand them, and Wilder's two heroic figures. Likewise there is an essential difference between the aesthetic of the nineteenth-century novel and its derivatives in our present literature, and Wilder's more poetical and dramatic purpose. In a nutshell: he isn't a novelist in the ordinary way; he has scarcely tried to be one; even with an effort, he might not have been an especially good one.

Nevertheless, for a good while after the publication of *The Ides of March* I kept on wondering and worrying about his novel writing; with a kind of phantom creativity, loosely imagining what he might do, tyrannously deciding what he ought to be doing.

What hurry was there? None, except that the minutes and the hours and the years of Wilder's life, likewise the life expectancy of his eager readers, were passing. As the Stage Manager in his early one-act play, *Pullman Car Hiawatha,* oracularly remarks: the minutes are gossips, the hours are philosophers, all except noon and twelve midnight, which, like the years, are theologians. Gossip about creative matters always worsens them a little. Philosophy having to do with the arts is either an oversimplification or a complication. Every sort of teleological concept, even metaphor along that line, in literary criticism as in other connections, brings on hastiness and tyrannousness.

What more has he to tell, I would ask myself, in conjecture and daydream, with this or that familiar volume by him in hand; what else does he think? O unmapped buried treasure, oracle tongue-tied! O unheard notes of the language, grammar without effort, syntax without a patch or a seam! Thoughts about him, drifting back and forth—gratitude and frustration, selfishness and hope—made a kind of suspense in the mid-century literary life, pleasant in a way.

Indeed, in the case of a man like that—with energy to burn; with a mind of uncanny liveliness, an intellect both playful and helpful, and of course, as a man of the world in his fifties, any amount of pent-up experience, and a crystal-clear view of the facts of life in the Western world; with a better education than any of the rest of us, and a real command of the language, perfect English that is at the same time lifelike American, and a natural popular touch—is there any sort of literary work that one could not plausibly have expected him to be able to produce, if he but chose to do so? Three or four times, in *The Cabala* and *Heaven's My Destination* and *The Ides of March,* has he not opened doors into the future of fiction, then chosen not to go on through them? What held his foot back on those thresholds?

I was not alone in this vicariousness about him. There were occasional expressions of it in the literary supplements, hints of it in schoolbooks having to do with the appreciation of contemporary reading matter, harangues about it in the midst of intellectuals' convivialities. There have been, indeed, a number of deplorable developments in our civilization of late, in education, in journalism, in the economics of publishing and the theatre, shadows stealing across the cultural scene; and some people talked as though, by not writing more, more and more, more of same, Wilder personally was casting some of them. It may well have appeared to him also that there were shadows stealing across the cultural scene, but *toward* him, not from him, cast by his well-wishers and his critics. A number of us who were pretentious for him, confusing his true potential with just an imaginary cloud of maximum collected works, or with the optimum great American novel, or with other hypothetical literature of a never-never land, indulged in a very dubious humility about our own work. American modesty gives one an excuse for American lack of real ambition, and hedonism and softness.

Imaginative readers indulge in this kind of bear-baiting as well as fellow writers. So many of us in this country at present have a latent creativity. Furthermore, in our love of life and prevailing felicity, we sincerely feel that experiences which we have had are worth perpetuating; why should not the actual work of creation be done by a man we admire, a creative expert? Very often, when you reproach a writer for not writing, this is the significance of it, unbeknown to you: he has left unwritten something that, in fact, has never entered his mind, something that you yourself have wanted or half-wanted to write.

It is a bothering, troubling thing for a man of talent or genius to have others' imaginativeness visited upon him like this, delegated to him. If he is a responsive and outgoing person, it may prompt him or inspire him to be productive, perhaps to overproduce. If he is not, it will make a melancholy impression. He will take it to mean that you are not really interested in what he has to tell or to expound; all you want of him is to be a mouthpiece. In any case, if you wish him well, bear your disappointment patiently; don't scold.

Adverse criticism as to sins of commission will not trouble the creative man so much as to have his sins of omission roughly commented on. He knows that his wrongdoing, that is, wrong-writing, will not be held against him long; indeed some literary vocations consist of a lifelong revision and correction of previously expressed errors and evils. His bugaboo is impotence as a writer. Among the causes of impotence, in literature as in love and war and government, are the dread of it and the rumor of it.

One ought not to specify too much about the creative process. For surely it is a question of processes (plural): a good many separate little faculties and indeed peculiarities in simultaneous operation, intertangled and arcane. They change from time to time in any given working life; and what works for one creative man or woman will fail in another's case.

Generally speaking, the cycle of the creator's mind in which, with some regularity, first one of his memories, then another, metamorphoses itself into something tellable, something that he feels like telling—in which experiences of his own are transformed in such a way as to be applicable to the psychology and the circumstances and the weal and woe of other people—requires a rather relaxed, unspecific, optimistic atmosphere. On the whole it is best not to ask a sensitive or self-respecting author certain questions, i.e., why have your novels not been forthcoming as expected, as promised, as announced, and why couldn't you make a book of what you have just been telling us? Why do you not write as well as you talk? As you certainly need a Boswell, can't you Boswellize yourself? In general as in particular, why have you just generally failed to fulfill your promise? Whose fault was it, or is it? What has gone wrong?

In Wilder's case, as we now know, all this was a fantasy; nothing had gone wrong. Only his interest and energy had turned more and more in the direction of the stage, riskier perhaps but (I suppose) less difficult, and in any event (I conclude) better suited to his disposition, his ethics and aesthetics, and the greater part of the thematic material of which his mind is possessed, the subject matter that he has to work with.

In the *Paris Review* interview he said, "I regard the theatre as the greatest of all art forms, the most immediate way in which a human being can share with another the sense of what it is to be a human being." It would be hard to declare oneself more warmly and plainly than that.

Only recently he told an interviewer, "Our plays get happier the older we grow. That has been my experience."

The theatre probably is the art form best suited to the summing up of experience, the synthesis of character, the retelling of old myths, and the mythopoetizing of present and recent happenings. The novel is an imitation of people or a more or less total recall of things they have done and things they have said. The theatre is most apt to express the world memory and to reiterate and re-use inherited wisdom. By means of it, eternal metaphor and polymorphous love come winding down out of the distant past and ever onward into everyone's living mind, as it were the sacred river in *Kubla Khan*. The novel is the form for politics and finance and sex life and regional differences and class consciousness and race prejudice, and other such modes and issues and emergencies and revolutions of the present day (to be outmoded tomorrow, and to become entrancingly romantic day after tomorrow). The theatre is able to dispense with all that, or to make of it a game, or a high abstraction or a sorrowful rite. Nowadays it has emancipated itself from investiture, from scenery and setting and lighting, which it cannot afford in any case. Whereas the novel virtually consists of hallucinating furnishings and fashions and properties and atmospheres (literal and figurative). Its realm is immediacy. The theatre is, relatively speaking, timeless.

The wonder is that anyone who knew Wilder (even I) should ever have expected him to make novel writing his exclusive or even his principal lifework. From the start, various profundities and intricacies of his way of writing, corresponding surely to fine strands and textures of his inner being, predestined him to dramaturgy.

❖

If I remember rightly, when we first met in Villefranche I thought of Wilder as only a novelist; I was unaware of his having written and published a number of one-act plays; certainly I did not foresee his present eminence in the theatre. It is well known that a man's beginning is often prophetic of his end. I have never been much of a prophet, least of all in matters theatrical.

A friend of mine in those days was an actress who, having made a reputation in the art theatres in Greenwich Village, had bad luck, got bypassed, and fell ill; and she not only needed work but knew and loved dramatic literature and especially admired Wilder. In the goodness of his heart, and to please me, he got her a walk-on part in his play: one of the townswomen at the wedding in the second act and seated ghostly in the cemetery in the third act.

On the opening night I went backstage to see her. The stage door opened into a sort of alleyway, and as I came back out of it, whom did I encounter but the playwright, who had been too nervous to sit it out inside the theatre. He was wearing an old trench coat, and looked as though he had walked for miles in haste. As I learned afterward, the reaction of the press and the public in Boston had been disappointing. In fact, they had had to reduce the intended run of a fortnight to just one week.

Rapid-fire, the uneasy playwright questioned me about the performance I had just seen. "How did it go? Was it worth doing? You didn't feel, I hope, that I had disgraced myself? Did it make you laugh? Did you feel that the emotions in it were too outspoken and common?"

Characteristically, his nervousness expressed itself in a series of pseudo-questions, with exclamation points rather than question marks. We were somewhat blocking the alley, as one or two parties of friends of the cast were proceeding to the stage door. Drawing back out of their way, I took his arm and noticed that he was trembling slightly, all the way up from his knees.

Of course I intensely appreciated the originality and the courage and the subtlety and the importance of what he had done, and told him so. The wedding scene, when the bride and groom suddenly find themselves not mature enough to marry and bolt downstage on either side and, close to the footlights, cling to their respective parents in childish changeableness and dismay, had brought tears to my eyes.

"Fine! fine!" Wilder exclaimed, "if you don't mind shedding tears. Most men do mind, nowadays, I'm afraid. Even some women mind!"

I also ventured to praise the scene in the cemetery, perhaps suggested by a famous last act by Shaw, who conceived of immortality as a rebuttal, a chance to argue some more, and to have the last word, the word after the last. Wilder's wraiths seated around in their kitchen chairs with the imaginary rain falling during the burial of the daughter-in-law of one of them, are still loving and anxious, but they are peaceable. They are subject to vestiges of earthly suffering, but with no fuss, no false rhetoric. It is a glorious and tender image of the afterlife; a matter of memory diminishing into indifference, passing into insensibility.

I was all enthusiasm, but I felt—and told my tired, impatient friend there all atremble inside his trench coat, in that Broadway sidestreet which made me think of the corridors in slaughterhouses along which the livestock are driven to their appointed demise, and of the little runways in circuses between the wild animals' cages and the ring—that probably it would not be a great success at the box office. Too delicate, I said, too philosophical, too sad.

The instant I said it I was sorry, realizing how passionately he desired to have it succeed. But the next instant I felt excused or consoled by his obviously not having believed one word that I had said.

I often make a fool of myself, with a mind too energetic for its own good—little flash floods, little brush fires, and what you might call quickness on the trigger—but perhaps this was my masterpiece. As you know, *Our Town* has been one of the most successful plays of the day and age, everywhere in the world except in France and England; even in the Balkans; even on television.

My thought was that, when people are to be reconciled to fate and death—which in oversimplified terms is the theme of *Our Town* —they expect a somewhat fuller orchestra; at least a pipe organ. What Wilder concludes this play with is chamber music, as in one of Beethoven's late slow movements, opus 130 (I think it is): the string quartet playing softly, softly, the pianissimo and the retardando gradually building up tension, gradually reducing participation, until one begins to feel hard of hearing; whereupon suddenly there is nothing more to hear. Evidently this did not impress the ordinary theatregoer as an anticlimax; how come?

I have often wondered whether Edgar Lee Masters's *Spoon River Anthology* did not also inspire this last act to some extent:

> *Where are Ella, Kate, Mag, Lizzie and Edith,*
> *The tender heart, the simple soul, the loud, the*
> *proud, the happy one?—*
> *All, all, are sleeping on the hill.**

But I have been shy about putting this question to Wilder directly. People have pestered him so wearisomely about his bookish inspirations, borrowings and mirrorings and echoings, though all that was standard procedure in the literature of the past, especially dramatic literature, and though the neoclassicist poets and musicians of our time, notably Eliot and Stravinsky, have accustomed us to something of the sort.

It is an interesting issue in criticism, and one of the riddles of the creative process. Valéry stated it unforgettably, somewhat jokingly: "Nothing is more original, nothing truer to oneself, than to feed upon others' minds. Only be sure that you digest them. The lion consists of assimilated sheep."

Thomas Mann, who was also a great borrower (but not so thor-

* From "The Hill" in *Spoon River Anthology* by Edgar Lee Masters (Macmillan, 1914, 1915, 1942).

ough a digester), in his account of the writing of *Dr. Faustus,* spoke of his own "mental alacrity in appropriating what I felt to be my own." Over the page he states categorically: "An idea as such will never possess much personal and proprietary value in the eyes of an artist." I agree. If a thing clearly appertains to his subject, and will function within the framework that he has created, he may think of it as his. I approve.

◆

Sometimes in recent years Wilder has acted in his own plays in summer theatres. I wish he would do so again. In my theatregoing experience, not assiduous but lifelong and international, I have seen only about twenty ideal performances of leading roles in plays of great importance: Otis Skinner's Falstaff in *The Merry Wives,* Féraudy as Molière's miser, Werner Krauss's Lear, Chaliapin's Boris, Olivier's Coriolanus, Laurette Taylor in *The Glass Menagerie,* Uta Hagen in *The Cocktail Party*—I name the first that come to mind—and whenever I recall them or list them, I include Wilder's Mr. Antrobus in *The Skin of Our Teeth.*

That symbolic comedy was his contribution to our morale and our vision of the future during World War II. If I remember rightly he did not undertake the role himself until four or five years later. Of course world history had scarcely gone beyond it or superseded it; still has not. He played it with no effect of author's afflatus; on the other hand, with none of the vanity or the cajolery of the amateur actor. Even in passages of serious reference to the destructiveness then going forward in the world and to other ever-possible future holocausts, he was able to characterize his Antrobus with humor, temperamentally: a familiar type of tired but sturdy, more or less indomitable man in a raincoat or a trench coat, universal male raiment of our particular time of troubles. As he came on stage he immediately established the reality of the scene by glancing all around it, taking possession of it, flashing his eyes; then turned and faced the audience and immediately began his portrayal of himself, gesturing strongly, as though wielding a brush, painting great everyman's portrait on the canvas of air between him and the audience, up over our heads.

It occurs to me that it was the kind of playing that Ruth Draper might have done if she could ever have submitted her uncanny solo power to the restraints of ordinary theatre, in full-length three-dimensional drama not written by herself. It was rather vehement and exalted, and yet it had an ordinary aspect. It was curiously self-assured, with a soft and rapturous tone in certain passages; and the mimicry in it was broader and simpler than that of the present-day psychological school of acting. Never for a moment did he seem self-concerned, although one couldn't help thinking of his Antrobus as autobiographical.

It made the oddest evening's entertainment. Most plays in which the human race is personified in any way are weak in performance, though with virtuoso techniques and the best will in the world. Everyman as a rule turns out to be just anyone, and the audience couldn't care less. Wilder prevented this by the intensities that I have just mentioned, by humorous simplifications of his movements and facial expressions, and by his absorption and self-absorption, which is the opposite of self-concern. At every point he was able to infuse the simple text with strange temperament; it was his own temperament.

In the letter to the sixteen-year-old schoolboy about how to play Antrobus, he advised specifically: "Pick out a few places where you'll be real loud." That is his way, keeping all the intervening places clearly in mind the while, with constant earnestness.

Throughout his performance he kept contrasting the explicit and the implicit, as though for every scene, every speech, he had decided in advance what part of the meaning and the emotion he could best express, and let everything inexpressible in it go. And one felt that it was just this simple aspect of the play that he had re-hearsed, practiced, perfected, so that he could have rendered it in his sleep, if asked to. But then, wide awake, when the curtain went up, he apparently concentrated all of his intelligence and spirit on those things that he could not exactly express. In timbres and inflections one heard significances that he was reading between the lines. Thus something in the play seemed to be striving to express *itself*, through him. I do not suppose that any such impressions as these passed through the mind of his audience at the time—it has taken me a long while to figure them out, perhaps with some preciosity—but we felt the vital effect; an overflow, rather than an undertone or an undercurrent.

Clear as a bell, but with a haunted clarity; plain as day, but casting a shadow! In that emphatic voice, with its little barking tones now and then, earnestly projecting the lines, some humorous, some sententious, some oracular, there was an intensely urgent utopian spirit, almost a wild spirit, expressive of that desirousness which above all else characterizes the human race, which stops at nothing and which never ends; that anarchy inherent in our nature which necessitates our will power; that strange habit of forgiving or at least forgetting, which causes us to pull our punches to some extent every blessed time, for better or worse, preventing the entire victory of any one aspect of our humanity over any other aspect, even of good over evil, or evil over good.

As you may gather, I am a believer in style. Often, I think, a writer's handling of language, vocabulary and diction and syntax, irony and imitation and colloquialism and rhetorical effects and figures of speech, and some degree of courteousness and ceremony in his writing according to his love of literature, express his knowledge of the world and his feeling about his life and his responsiveness to the environing world more originally and fundamentally than what he thinks of as his subject matter, his learnedness or cogitation or experience, as the case may be.

You see, the manner of his acting bears a relation to the predominant, prevailing quality of his prose style, in dramatic prose and narrative prose alike, polished and purposeful but also somewhat plain and modest; not presuming to tell everything or to give proof of anything incontrovertibly; not particularly aiming at anything unknowable or occult, but never disavowing or turning away from things irrepressible and unruly, things chaotic, even things inchoate.

He is a man of singular temperament, often delighting in paradox, willing and able to challenge us and disturb us. But he likes things to seem traditional, that is, to be stated within the traditional frame of reference, though they may be somewhat new or idiosyncratic. He likes every present expression to hark back to the entirety of beloved accumulated literature, and constantly shows or suggests that every current thought is based on someone else's thinking, every day of our lives is rooted in olden time.

The moderation and correctness of Wilder's way of writing are so reposeful that at times one can imagine them lulling us too much, but they never do. His definiteness and dispatch and his natural popular touch, and the bravery of his sudden little assertions every so often—as though for percussiveness, for punctuation—animate his every page and every scene. Verily, as he himself tells us, what he offers a good deal of the time is only fantasy and spirituality, illusion and hypnosophy. But we dance in his dream, throughout; it is active and bright. It is an art on the side of Apollo, though ever respectful of Dionysus.

Acknowledgments

Of the six famous writers whom I have chiefly ventured to portray and praise in this volume, the first is a lifelong intimate friend; the second is a close friend of many years' standing; with the sixth also I have enjoyed lifelong friendship, though not particular intimacy; and with the other three I have had the honor of acquaintance based on my admiring them greatly and marked by kind attentiveness on their parts. I have tried to make these differing degrees of personal connection clear in my successive chapters, without either boasting of my good fortune or shrinking from the friendly responsibility. It has been a labor of love, or more specifically, of enjoyment and thanksgiving.

Doing unto others as I should like to be done unto, I did not ask any of them to read and approve my text. If this or that in it were to irk them, I thought, it might seem beneath their dignity to protest. On the other hand, their not protesting might be construed as approbation, or as a commitment not to protest at a later date; too much to ask. Therefore I decided to publish and let myself be damned. In due course they can speak their minds against me, or direct their friends to do so.

For almost two decades Mrs. W. Murray Crane has arranged for me to speak to the well-read ladies of the Monday Class, four or five times a year; and Professor Henry Leffert of City College has invited me annually to address his students of contemporary literature. Those happy occasions were greatly instrumental in interesting me in critical writing; and I thank the two sponsors.

It has impressed and pleased me to recall the particular starting points and first uses of important portions of this book, and a brief account of this may seem worth while to certain of my readers. I give it not in self-importance or in bibliographical zeal, but as a bird's-eye view—or rather, a series of bird's-eye glimpses—of the somewhat internationalized American literary life of the mid-twentieth century.—

A first version of Chapter One was commissioned by Mrs. Crane at Mr. Maugham's suggestion, and read aloud to guests of hers one evening in the spring of 1942. I note that, for better or worse, my convictions about fiction writing have changed very little in the intervening years.

The passages in Chapter Two having to do with Miss Porter's volume of three nouvelles, *Pale Horse, Pale Rider,* were written to Robert Penn Warren's order when he was editing the *Southern Review,* and published in that excellent magazine in the summer of 1939. About half of this chapter appeared in the *Book-of-the-Month Club News* and the *Atlantic Monthly* in March and April, 1962.

In 1947 Mr. Maugham suggested to Doubleday and Co. that I be engaged to edit and introduce an omnibus volume of his work entitled *The Maugham Reader.* That introduction reappears here as Chapter Three, with some additions and revisions according to the further passage of his lifetime and mine.

Most of Chapter Four is to be found in the Dial Press's *Short Novels of Colette* (1951). This, too, I have brought up to date. At that time *Vogue* asked me for a page or two about "Gigi," and later H. D. Vursell of the firm of Farrar, Straus and Cudahy commissioned a foreword for their edition of *Break of Day* (1961), which I have inserted where they belong in the sequence of Colette's life and work. Chapter Five was commissioned by *Town and Country* as a compliment to her upon her eightieth birthday (January, 1953).

When Isak Dinesen first came to this country in 1959, Mrs. Crane prevailed upon her to read two or three of her stories one evening, or to be precise, to *tell* two or three; and as many guests knew her only by reputation, I introduced her at some length. Jacques Barzun was there, and he suggested to Russell Lynes that I be asked to commit my remarks to writing for *Harper's Magazine* (March, 1960). Hence Chapter Six; my compliments to them both.

Miss Caroline Newton, who presented me to Thomas Mann when he was living in this country during World War II, years later arranged for me to deliver an address of commemoration at Haverford College, October 9, 1959. This led to further study of Mann's fiction and the subsequent composition of Chapter Seven. Two German-born friends, George Albert von Ihering and Mrs. Hedwig Leser, also encouraged me to write about Mann, despite my limited competence in German literature; and the latter kindly reviewed my pages and made certain corrections.

As for Chapter Eight, Miss Isabel Wilder, friendly to me always, gladly and authoritatively answered some questions about the circumstances and the chronology of her brother's life and lifework but she is not to be held responsible for any of my notions and judgments, or for matters of fact that I neglected to submit to her.